God's Gift

A PRAYERFUL CONTEMPLATION OF

The Gospel According to John

by

Ruth E. Dodge

Copyright © 1990
Ruth E. Dodge

Greenberg Publishing Company, Inc.
7566 Main Street
Sykesville, MD 21784

First Edition
First Printing

Manufactured in the United States of America

ISBN   0-89778-200-3

Library of Congress
Cataloging-in-Publication Date

Dodge, Ruth E.
God's gift: a prayerful contmplation of the Gospel-
according to John / by Ruth E. Dodge — 1st ed.

1. Bible. N. T. John —Devotional literature.
2. Bible. N. T. John—Commentaries. I. Title

BS2615.4.D63   1990

226.5'077—dc20   90-42439
                                                        CIP

Dedication

I dedicate this book

to my two grandmothers and my mother who, when I was three,

began to read to me from the King James Bible;

also to my dear husband who not only encouraged me

but provided me with necessary books as well as

the quiet time to pursue this study.

Above all I offer this book

in gratitude and thanksgiving

to God

for the outpouring inspiration that opened to me

the Gospel According to John.

I give a special benediction of love

to those many faithful friends who gave their time

and who contributed so much,

to bring this book into being.

Bibliography

Revised English Bible © 1989, Oxford and Cambridge University Presses.

King James Bible (Cambridge, England: Cambridge University Press, 1976).

Raymond E. Brown, S.S., *The Anchor Bible*, Volumes 29 and 29-A, The Gospel Acording to John (New York, New York: Doubleday & Company, Inc., 1970).

The Interpreter's Dictionary of the Bible (Nashville, Tennessee: Abingdon Press, 1976).

William Temple, *Readings in St. John's Gospel* (First and Second Series), (Wilton, Connecticut: Morehouse Publishing, 1959).

Merriam-Webster's Ninth New Collegiate Dictionary © 1990 (Springfield, Massachusetts: Merriam-Webster, Inc., publisher of the Merriam-Webster dictionaries®).

Archbishop J. H. Bernard, *A Critical and Exegetical Commentary on the Gospel According to St. John* (Edinburgh, Scotland: T. & T. Clark Ltd., 1928).

Brother Lawrence, *The Practice of the Presence of God*, translated by E. M. Blaiklock (Nashville, Tennessee: Thomas Nelson Publishers, 1981).

The Laymen's Parallel Bible (Grand Rapids, Michigan: Zondervan Bible Publishers, 1973).

Table of Contents

Introduction

For many years scholars have thought that The Gospel According to John was written some three hundred years after the crucifixion, by an unknown "John." But since World War II further research has brought the conclusion to some that the thoughts and views expressed therein could have been written down within John the Apostle's lifetime. Few can doubt that his students undertook to edit the work, or perhaps even undertook all the writing, although taking care to preserve the authorship of John the Apostle, the Beloved Disciple, the son of Zebedee.

The Gospel of John has appealed to me more than any book of the Bible. But before writing this book I had to come to terms with the many controversial facets of the Gospel, such as: Who is its author? When was it written? Are the Chapters out of their proper sequence? And, which Bible translation shall I use?

I chose the *New English Bible* because I particularly like the New Testament translation, having received much inspiration from the freshness of its wording. *God's Gift* has now been updated to conform to the *Revised English Bible* which brings clarity to the text, Oxford University Press, Cambridge University Press, 1989.

After deep consideration I chose to write from the standpoint that John, the disciple and Apostle of Jesus, is the author of ideas found therein. It is legend that he lived to be very old. The text is the thought of a mature Christian and was probably recorded by his students during his late years, when his understanding of Jesus' teachings had reached their fullness.

For chapter order I decided to retain the familiar sequence found in the *King James Bible.*

My main sources of information have been *The Interpreter's Dictionary of the Bible*, An Illustrated Encyclopedia, Abingdon Press; and *The Anchor Bible*, Volumes 29 and 29-A, The Gospel According to John, A New Translation with Introduction and Commentary by Raymond E. Brown, S.S., Doubleday & Company, Inc.

Both sources have been of great value. I was able to use them for stimulation, discipline, and encouragement in setting down my own conclusions. These volumes offered me the opinions of many scholars of our Bible, and against this respected source I bravely weighed the thoughts that came to me concerning the text of John. The commentary by Father Brown was always inspiring and profitable.

John the Apostle, son of Zebedee, appears to be a man who after his discipleship achieved great humility, and when his apprehension had grown to such greatness he was able to communicate the thoughts and views of the most humble of all men, Jesus Christ. He has given us an eyewitness account of many episodes in his Master's life.

It is my hope that this book can be used both in Bible Study and Prayer Groups, or by the individual studying alone. General discussion should be stimulated by the commentary, and the Study Pages will serve as an initial guide in the application of the message.

The years of my joyous preoccupation with John's Gospel, for truly it has been foremost in my thinking all this time, are years of great spiritual growth for me. After writing the final chapter I began again at the beginning and with increased enlightenment I was able to strengthen weaknesses in the early sections of the book.

This work is inspirational; it is my prayerful thought concerning this scripture. Although I have tried to be accurate where history and known facts are concerned, the interpretation of our Lord's words has come after prayer, meditation, and an attitude of listening – always listening – to that beautiful, clear voice that speaks to one's inner consciousness.

Looking back on this period of devotion, I feel I have had the opportunity to be present with Jesus Christ on his earthly pilgrimage with his disciples. We have walked and talked together, and I have feasted sumptuously on the meat of the Word. If the sharing of these private thoughts can bring new light and joy to the reader in like manner, I shall find the exposure of my faith worthwhile.

Ruth E. Dodge
Fairhaven
Sykesville, Maryland

August 1990

Foreword

It is impossible to grasp the greatness and importance of John's Gospel without at least a brief comparison with the opening passages of the other Gospels: Matthew, Mark, and Luke.

Matthew opens with a genealogy and follows with the lovely account of Mary and Joseph and the birth of the Child.

Mark does not begin his gospel with a birth but with the prophecy concerning John the Baptist and his work of heralding the coming Christ. He next writes of the baptism of Jesus and the beginning of his ministry.

Luke's narration is comprehensive in theme. It places the events of the Nativity in their historical context and adds much information concerning those times.

Presumably writing at the end of his long earthly career, John's spiritual understanding of his Master's message has fully developed.

John's church symbol is the Eagle. In his Gospel he soars above the earthly and begins his message in heaven's vastness. Before the beginning is his starting point. He has learned that Jesus' life does not begin with his human birth, but antedates creation. He wants us to know this. He takes us on eagle wings of faith and reveals to us our Source, God and His Word dwelling in infinite Spirit.

Note

Unless otherwise indicated all Bible references are from the *Revised English Bible,* Oxford University Press, Cambridge University Press, 1989.

All Bible quotations retain the English spelling.

For purposes of clarity, "He" and "His," when used for God the Father, will always be capitalized.

When speaking of Jesus, "he" and "his" will not be capitalized.

✞

John the Baptist — Born of Elizabeth and Zechariah. The one who announces the coming of Jesus. The cousin of Jesus (Luke 1:5-80).

John, the son of Zebedee — called the Evangelist, Apostle of Jesus, the presumed author of the Gospel According to John.

John the Revelator — legend says John the Apostle; scholars say some other "John."

I, II, III **John** — presumably all agree on John the Apostle as the author.

God's Gift

Chapter One

The Coming of Christ

John wants us to think back and then back even farther in time and eternity. He wants us to stretch our vision until we perceive the moments before creation.

John 1:1 *In the beginning the Word already was.*

John 1:1 *In the beginning was the Word, and the Word was with God, and the Word was God (King James Bible).*

Unlike Matthew and Luke, John does not write about the birth of the baby Jesus, nor does he start with prophecy, as does Mark. He wants us to start our consideration of this Gospel where it should start, with God and His Word. John does not lead us gradually to this spiritual platform which is the foundation of Jesus' teaching. His opening statement may be likened to trumpets blaring, "I AM THAT I AM!" The above text, and those that follow, are glorious chords opening his symphony of "Jesus, The Word made flesh."

Speaking of the Word-made-flesh, we read in the Epistle, 1 John 1: "It was there from the beginning; we have heard it; we have seen it with our own eyes; we looked upon it, and felt it with our own hands: our theme is the Word which gives life."

How do we define "Word"? Raymond E. Brown writes:[1] "...It was at Ephesus, the traditional site of John's Gospel, that Heraclitus in the 6th century B.C. first introduced logos into Greek philosophical thought. Striving to explain the continuity amid all the flux that is visible in the universe, Heraclitus resorted to logos as the eternal principle of the universe..."

The term *logos* for *word* is familiar to the early Christians, and they are no doubt aware of the overtones of law and order implied in the use of logos for Christ. Jesus teaches an orderly, harmonious spiritual universe governed by his benevolent Father, so this aspect of logos is valuable.

Hebrew teaching holds the "word of God" in high regard whether spoken by patriarch or prophet. Does not the Lord say: "So shall my word be that goeth forth out of my mouth: it shall not return unto me void, but it shall accomplish that which I please, and it shall prosper *in the thing* whereto I sent it" (*King James Bible*, Isaiah 55:11).

The Hebrew word "dabar" corresponds to logos. Father Brown continues: "We have mentioned the Hebrew dabar. This means more than 'spoken word'; it also means 'thing,' 'affair,' 'event,' 'action.' And because it covers both word and deed, in Hebrew thought dabar had a certain dynamic energy and power of its own."

He further states that when the "word of the Lord" came to a prophet it "challenged the prophet himself, and when he accepted it, the word impelled him to go forth and give it to others." [1]

John 1:1 *The Word was in God's presence, and what God was, the Word was.*

A passage from the Letter to the Hebrews 1:2-3 gives insight to the nature of the Word: "But in this final age he has spoken to us in his Son whom he has

---

[1] Raymond E. Brown, S. S., *The Anchor Bible*, Volume 29, page 520, Doubleday & Co., Inc.

appointed heir of all things; and through him he created the universe. He is the radiance of God's glory; the stamp of God's very being, and he sustains the universe by his word of power."

All these attributes — the Word that is creative life; the Word that brings law and order; this Word that is the enabler; the Word that is the radiance of God's glory; the Word that is the stamp (authorized and exact likeness) of God's very being; the Word that sustains the universe by his word of power — all these aspects give us a more complete picture of the Son of God, His Word.

Co-existent with God, the Word expresses God in every quality and attribute, in nature and power.

John 1:2-3 *He was with God at the beginning, and through him all things came to be; without him no created thing came into being.*

The oneness of the Word with God in the creative process is emphasized. Divine power operates and no single thing can be created without Him and His Word. Because we accept a God who is perfect we must not flaw our argument by reasoning He has a creation that includes evil. To consider man as evolved by God with an evil element in his being that can master him at some future time is incorrect. God's conception and creation are in the measure of His own perfection. We must learn to reach out for this concept of ourselves as we strive to live more godly lives.

John 1:4 *In him was life, and that life was the light of mankind.*

The Word gives life to creation. It is the light of intelligence and separates ignorance from understanding.

John 1:5 *The light shines in the darkness, and the darkness has never mastered it.*

The light of the Word is in each individual. It is there even if it is unrecognized and ignored. It is the seed of faith and spirituality in man. This light is the essential potential for a full and complete life for it is perpetually united with the forces of Spirit. This light is a holy presence within that sin, disease, wickedness, and even death cannot quench!

We should recognize the fact of a holy Presence in our being, and, in this inner sanctuary we should bow low before our Lord. "Do you not know that your body is a temple of the indwelling Holy Spirit, and the Spirit is God's gift to you?" (1 Corinthians 6:19).

John writes: "The darkness has never mastered it" (the Light). The evidence before men of the most outrageous cruelty and vileness has never dimmed his reliance on, and response to, a God who cares for all. God speaks to this pure desire within man. Of this Light, Paul writes:[2] "For the God who said, 'Out of darkness light shall shine,' has caused his light to shine in our hearts, the light which is knowledge of the glory of God in the face of Jesus Christ. But we have only earthenware jars to hold this treasure, and this proves that such transcendant power does not come from us; it is God's alone."

In orderly fashion John begins the Gospel with this manifesto of Christ. In irrefutable statements Christ's oneness with God is established and declared unchanging and everlasting.

A Man Named John

John 1:6-7 *There appeared a man named John. He was sent from God, and came as a witness to testify to the light, so that through him all might become believers.*

God, in love and wisdom, sends a most special witness to us to point out to a people of little vision His Chosen One who possesses and reveals the light and life of Divinity in his own person. John the Baptist is equipped by God with the ability to discern and appreciate the nature of Christ. This capacity of John the Baptist to recognize and witness to the Christ, seen as the man Jesus, is essential to the Messiah's mission.

John 1:8 *He was not himself the light; he came to bear witness to the light.*

---

[2] 2 Corinthians 4:6-7.

This emphasis is interesting, because it tells us that John the Baptist will be inspired by the Holy Spirit to recognize the light that is the Son of God. John the Baptist's role is that of verifier; one who is equipped by God with spiritual discernment to brush aside the false prophets and false messiahs and to proclaim the true Christ. His spiritual sensitivity and pure thought, as evidenced in his communion with God, attracts a following of disciples who are like-minded and who trust his vision. In this way God provides from this group the nucleus of Jesus' disciples. Their thoughts are prepared to accept, at the proper moment, God's presence in the flesh with men.

John 1:9   *The true light, which gives light to everyone was even then coming into the world.*

Here John lets history and time speak out and we learn that the appearing of God's Anointed coincides with the time of John the Baptist. Luke 1:36-45 tells us that John the Baptist was born six months before Jesus.

John begins his Gospel in the manner of Genesis 1, but he takes us farther than the orderly steps of creation; he leaps the centuries to the time when the Word itself assumes the prerogative of entering the realm that has been its own since the beginning.

John 1:10-13   *He was in the world; but the world, though it owed its being to him, did not recognize him. He came to his own, and his own people would not accept him. But to all who did accept him, to those who put their trust in him, he gave the right to become children of God, born not of human stock, by the physical desire of a human father, but of God.*

John is speaking of Jesus Christ as coming to his own; the Son of God who becomes the Son of Man is taking possession of his earthly realm; the ruler of the universe is taking possession in person; the Son of the Most High is establishing his authority in his realm, seeking and finding his loyal followers — whose dedication is unquestioned.

In Medieval times it was customary for a lord to put his foot on the neck of his serf when he bowed low to give his oath of fealty. By this gesture the serf yielded his all, even his life, to the lord's will, and in return the lord was expected to allot him food and protect him and his family. In this exchange both benefited.

There is an important moment in life, an instant when a decision is made and suddenly thought opens to Christ. This is the time when the individual's heart tells him, "Yes, this I believe!" and he is willing to sacrifice all for his Lord.

When human will is put aside, and God's grace floods one's heart, the opportunity to yield to Christ becomes a new birth. It is the opportunity to cease thinking in terms of mortal life exclusively; and to enter into an awareness of our oneness with our heavenly Father, to dwell in "the secret place of the Most High," protected in the bosom of the Father. It is the opportunity to enter the kingdom where God's will is done.

When Christ knocks at the door of men's minds the Christ-life hidden in each man that comes into the world is roused to respond. The mortal is then able to open the door of his thought. After accepting the Lord, growth begins for the Christian. Even as a human child is gradual in maturing, so the individual's spiritual apprehension is at first immature, then, empowered by Spirit, he grows in spiritual strength and understanding.

The Word Became Flesh

John 1:14   *So the Word became flesh; he made his home among us, and we saw his glory, such glory as befits the Father's only Son, full of grace and truth.*

"The Word became flesh..." God sends His Son to humanity in the flesh and blood of a man. His body is like our body — it feels cold, heat, and hunger; this man is emotionally equipped, as we are, to love, to be hurt, to have joy, and to be at peace. But as the Son of God he also possesses a glory that is visible to others, for John says, "We saw his glory" (John 1:14). An aspect of this glory must be the radiance of his assurance of God's presence with him; his authority of righteousness; a beauty of holiness that is visible and that touches the hearts and minds of those who seek the Messiah of God.

The glory that his disciples behold must seem to them a royal diadem; for it is significant that only those touched by the Holy Spirit perceive that here is the Prince of Peace!

There is only one Son, anointed by the Father as the Christ, only one Word of God, held in special relationship to the Father. This grace that fills him is the oil and unction of his Father's favor bestowed on him; the in-filling that perpetually renews his being. This grace is the wellspring of Life itself flooding his being and overflowing to humanity. It is graciousness, warmth, and forgiving love that reaches out to heal, cleanse, and redeem all whom it touches.

Christ's grace and truth continues to lift humanity from despair to joy, from illness to well-being, and from sin to righteousness.

Jesus comes to teach men to find their sonship with God and to assert his authority over all that hinders men from knowing God as Father; that hinders men from finding and obeying the will of God. He comes to be the "last Adam," the man in God's image and likeness.

St. Paul writes of Adam in his letter to the Corinthians (1 Corinthians 15:45-49), "It is in this sense that scripture says, 'The first man, Adam, became a living creature,' whereas the last Adam has become a life-giving spirit. Observe, the spiritual does not come first; the physical body comes first, and then the spiritual. The first man is from earth, made of dust: the second man is from heaven. The man made of dust is the pattern of all who are made of dust, and the heavenly man is the pattern of all the heavenly. As we have worn the likeness of the man made of dust, so we shall wear the likeness of the heavenly man."

Jesus gives us the right to become sons of God. Here action on our part is called for. We are given a right. If we pick up or accept this right, we may become children of God. What does this involve? That is what Jesus comes to tell us.

The legalism and ritual that has smothered the worship of the Jews is the veil rent forever by the love of his Passion. Those who seek him can freely go into the inner holy of holies through faith. No barrier keeps them out. The Gnostic notion prevalent in Jesus' time and later, [3] teaches an all powerful good counterbalanced by an all powerful evil, with man caught in the middle. This is a false theory. It is rejected by every recorded action of Jesus' career. The goodness of God is declared by Jesus to be supreme. God never shares His infinite and eternal power with another. The essence of his message emphasizes that now the goodness of God's provision is for man. Right now His loving outpouring is ready to supply every need.

John's Testimony — The Pre-Existent Christ

John 1:15 *John bore witness to him and proclaimed: 'This is the man of whom I said, "He comes after me, but ranks ahead of me"; before I was born, he already was.'*

John the Baptist shows clearly by this statement his grasp of Jesus' pre-existent identity and life; of his life pre-existing his physical appearance on earth. His statement reaffirms the eternalness of Christ as the Word of God, for he tells his disciples "Before I was born, he already was!" John the Baptist is vividly aware that here is the Son of the Most High, one who outranks all others, one who is born with the highest authority, prestige, power, and favor, "full of grace and truth" to represent the God of all creation to His people!

Grace Through Jesus Christ

John 1:16-17 *From his full store we have all received grace upon grace; for the law was given through Moses, but grace and truth came through Jesus Christ.*

John, the Apostle, tells us "From his full store we have all received grace upon grace..." We have bountifully received the same quality of grace — of favor with the Father empowering us to do the works that He demands. "From his full store..." can only mean unlimited abundance, all sufficiency for every need. Jeremiah recognizes this when he speaks of God's favor as a Father to a returned Israel: "They will be

[3] *The Interpreter's Dictionary of the Bible*, "The Gospel of John," page 938, Abingdon Press.

like a well-watered garden and never languish again" (Jeremiah 31:12). Out of His full store we have all received. We can accept this truth and draw from our wellspring of life and find God's constant provision for every detail.

At this point consider two clergymen's views. John Marsh, in his commentary on "The Gospel of John, speaking of the "fullness of grace," points out that the coming of the Christ, the Word-made-flesh, was not just for those of Jesus' time to see, but is a gift for all believers for all time; a gift that brings them into close relationship with God. He then compares the limitations of the law to the amplitude of divine grace revealed by Jesus Christ.

And in *Readings in St. John's Gospel*, Bishop Temple writes: "So we learnt the difference between the old dispensation and the new. That was law — commands and prohibitions enforced by rewards and punishments; in fact it was what St. Paul calls "the spirit of slavery" (Romans 8:15) for the slave has his orders and is rewarded if he obeys them faithfully, and is punished if he disobeys...or if our hearts are open to the love of God made known in Jesus Christ we no longer ask chiefly what has God commanded or what has he forbidden but rather what — apart from any known command or prohibition — will please our Father; and we do this not to gain reward or avoid punishment but because our desire and joy is to please our Father." [4]

John 1:18 *No one has ever seen God; God's only Son, he who is nearest to the Father's heart, has made him known.*

The definition of God's nature is beautifully but not completely set forth in the Old Testament. The descriptive names for God, such as "The Most High" or "Lord of Hosts," convey meanings beyond the actual words — even though no one has ever seen God. A burning bush that is not consumed first brings a message to Moses. Others hear God in the wind. Noah sees his promise in a rainbow. Now, records John, the time has come for a clearer understanding of God. He who is nearest to the Father's heart, "the only begotten of the Father" (*King James Bible*), will make Him known. God entering His world in the flesh means the extension of His visible dominion to mortal bodies and to all that is needed to support the life of men. The children of Israel have come to accept God's concern for them collectively. Now in this new covenant the Father's concern for the individual will be manifested by His own Son — a Son placed in the environment and situation of mortals — a Son who can walk through the dust of the earth and then mount to heaven.

The two phrases, "he who is nearest to the Father's heart" and "the only begotten of the Father," indicate the outpouring and self-giving nature of God, a love revealed in Jesus' statement, "O Jerusalem, Jerusalem, ... How often have I longed to gather your children, as a hen gathers her brood under her wings; but you would not let me" (Matthew 23:37). This love of God comes and dwells among men. It abides with us today, enfolding, comforting, and sustaining all who appeal to Him.

John 1:18 *(Jesus Christ) has made him known.*

In Jesus Christ God's nature is defined, the scope of His works revealed to be infinite, the depth and warmth of His love for each one shown unmistakably. The demands of His strict discipline guard us as well as guide us, and as a "mother" forgiving love washes away our tears from the trials of our learning process.

Now our symphony ends with as great an emphasis as its opening chords. We hear "The Son makes Him known!" Now we will see the Father in the Son. The rest of John's book will expound this glorious revelation.

Throughout the vivid presentation of the Gospel According to John we will walk with the Son of God, hear his words, see his works of faith and dominion, and follow his footsteps through degradation and death to triumphant resurrection.

In this way we shall come to know the Father. Thus we too shall be equipped to gain the victory.

---

[4] William Temple, *Readings in St. John's Gospel*, page 15.

The Deputation of Priests and Levites

John 1:19-28 *This is the testimony John gave when the Jews of Jerusalem sent a deputation of priests and Levites to ask him who he was. He readily acknowledged, 'I am not the Messiah.' 'What then? Are you Elijah?' 'I am not,' he replied. 'Are you the Prophet?' 'No,' he said. 'Then who are you?' they asked. 'We must give an answer to those who sent us. What account do you give of yourself?' He answered in the words of the prophet Isaiah: 'I am a voice crying in the wilderness, "Make straight the way for the Lord." '*
Some Pharisees who were in the deputation asked him, 'If you are not the Messiah, nor Elijah, nor the Prophet, then why are you baptizing?' 'I baptize in water,' John replied, 'but among you, though you do not know him, stands the one who is to come after me. I am not worthy to unfasten the strap of his sandal.' This took place at Bethany beyond Jordan, where John was baptizing.

"Make straight the way for the Lord!" Make plain to all the presence of the Messiah and prepare the thought of the people to receive him!

"Why are you baptizing?" the deputation asks. John replies "I baptize in water," the baptism that is the renunciation and cleansing of sin.

This cleansing is a first step. A willingness is a great necessity, to be followed by a desire to go forward and to know the Lord. This latter desire is manifest in the actual baptism, in this instance, probably immersion. The penitent is cleansed of his unwillingness to follow God's commands. Here, then, is a man made ready to receive the Messiah.

"But among you, though you do not know him, stands the one who is to come after me."

John the Baptist looks among the throngs converging at the site of his baptisms knowing that Jesus will come there.

To show the great disparity between them he says, "I am not worthy to unfasten the strap of his sandal." Here John the Baptist shows his humility. Even

before he sees the One for whom he has waited he is lowly and meek before him.

There is the Lamb of God

John 1:29 *The next day he saw Jesus coming towards him. 'There is the Lamb of God,' he said, 'who takes away the sin of the world.*[5]

Imagine the excitement in John the Baptist's voice when he speaks the above. It is he of whom I speak! He is right here, the very one I have been talking about!

The sacrificial lamb of Jewish rite is perfect and without blemish. As a sin offering the lamb symbolizes cleansing. What Christian follower of our Lord Jesus Christ can conceive of a more appropriate name than "Lamb of God." To his contemporaries John the Baptist's words, "Lamb of God," convey the whole story. God has provided His own Lamb for the ultimate sacrifice, and for the ultimate victory for the redemption of God's people.

John 1:30 *'He it is of whom I said, "After me there comes a man who ranks ahead of me"; before I was born, he already was.'*

John the Baptist continues: I am not the important man. This man takes rank before me — before I was born, he was! His emphasis to the deputation of priests and Levites is always that Jesus is greater, and to support this contention he points out Christ's prior existence, or pre-existent life. The Son of God does not just come into being — he already is!

John 1:31 *'I did not know who he was; but the reason why I came, baptizing in water, was that he might be revealed to Israel.'*

Here John the Baptist is saying that he has been sent to prepare the thought of Israel to receive the Messiah. If their minds are not turned from false gods, and from infidelity to the one God, they cannot know or recognize His Son. Their baptism in water (humility and willingness to be taught) is the neces-

---

[5] "Lamb of God" derives from Isaiah 53:7-12. See also 1 Corinthians 5:7 where Jesus is identified with the Paschal Lamb of Exodus 12:3-10.

sary preparation for this great coming. "And now he has come! He is here! I will tell you how I know him."

John 1:32-34   John testified again: 'I saw the Spirit come down from heaven like a dove and come to rest on him. I did not know him; but he who sent me to baptize in water had told me, "The man on whom you see the Spirit come down and rest is the one who is to baptize in Holy Spirit." I have seen it and have borne witness: this is God's Chosen One.'

John the Baptist obviously is instructed by the Holy Spirit. He grows up in the desert, spending long hours and days alone. Communion with God comes easily to one filled with the Spirit as he was at birth (Luke 1:15) and whose parents are also filled with the Spirit (Luke 1:41, 67). He baptizes in water, a precious liquid in an arid land that means life to those who have it.

Are we aware of the deep significance of water? Throughout religious history it has stood for life, and for physical and spiritual purity.

The purity of John the Baptist's thought cannot help but be noted. When called, he assumes the awesome responsibility of pointing out the Chosen of God. With unfaltering trust he waits for the sign of the "Spirit coming down upon someone and resting upon him."

The sign comes from heaven, a hovering splendor, a glory that rests on Jesus. Until this moment of illumination, although John probably knows his cousin, he has not known that Jesus is God's Chosen One. Of all men on earth only these two can appreciate the full meaning of this experience.

The baptismal water that washes the Son of God as John the Baptist baptizes him, transcends any earthly liquid — it becomes the outpouring of Spirit itself, a glimpse of the continuing Presence that will stay with Jesus throughout his earthly career. Jesus' baptism performs a necessary climax to his education. It is the "seal" of the Father's approval, his "graduation" after years of tutelage. For though the Christ of God needs no teaching, the humanity that is the man Jesus needs to become thoroughly awake to the infinite capacity of his own Christ nature. There is a great lesson in this fact for Christians, for

they too are equipped by the righteousness of grace! From this moment on the Son is seen in strength and power. And John the Baptist says, "I have seen it and I have borne witness: this is God's Chosen One."

Are we individually using the spiritual water of baptism? Are we treasuring the cleansing and purifying waters of Spirit that can make our being a fit temple of God? Each drop is precious to us in preparation to recognize and receive our Lord Jesus Christ.

Jesus Passes By

John 1:35-36   The next day again, John was standing with two of his disciples when Jesus passed by. John looked towards him and said, 'There is the Lamb of God!'

It is startling to think of Jesus just casually walking by the place where John the Baptist is standing with two of his disciples. Perhaps Jesus is walking with someone he knows. Look back over the centuries to that moment when he, an unknown, passes by. No crowds follow him. He is — just walking by.

John the Baptist has discussed the coming Messiah with his disciples, for it is a burning subject in Israel. They look for a God-sent king, like David, to free them and restore the glory of Israel.

But John the Baptist calls this man walking by not Messiah, but the Lamb of God. How different is this concept from the general desire for a warrior king!

John 1:37   When the two disciples heard what he said, they followed Jesus.

John the Baptist's remark stirs the disciples deeply; an explosion of inward illumination becomes an urgent necessity to follow Jesus.

When a heart is touched by the Holy Spirit there is such a surge of love and joy that forever after one seeks the source of that ineffable moment. Such must be the wonderful instant of "forever-change" that touches the two disciples.

What Are You Looking For?

John 1:38   He turned and saw them following; 'What are you looking for?' he asked.

These soul-searching words are our introduction to Jesus. Prior to this he has not been quoted in the Gospel of John. This same question is usually our introduction today. The "still small voice" of inner consciousness asks us, "What are you looking for?" Are you looking for material wealth, position, and power? Are you looking for accomplishment with which to satisfy self? Or are you searching to find a life that seeks not pride of performance but is expressive of the Father's love — a life that exchanges personal will for the will of God. To become an instrument of God there must be no resistance to His spiritual demands.

John 1:38   *They said, 'Rabbi,' (which means 'Teacher') 'where are you staying?'*

The radiant faces turned to Jesus must have revealed the thoughts of the two disciples. They ask the profound question that each of us must ask of our Lord Jesus. Where can we find him? Where is your dwelling place that I may come and sit at your feet and be taught of you?

John 1:39   *'Come and see,' he replied. So they went and saw where he was staying, and spent the rest of the day with him. It was about four in the afternoon.*

What a glorious, loving invitation, "Come and see!" The invitation to come is as pertinent to us today as it is to the two who first seek the Christ of God. Such warmth of love is breathed through those words that it wakens in the hearer the undeniable desire to abandon all in order to seek, and find, and dwell with Jesus, Son of God. Jesus calls us to come to him, to seek his presence and to dwell with him. He lifts us to see ourselves and others in our true nature and being. He opens heaven and invites us to walk with him there.

One cannot help but wonder what far horizons of thought are glimpsed during the two or three hours these men of God have together.

Jesus Calls His Disciples

John 1:40   *One of the two who followed Jesus after hearing what John said was Andrew, Simon Peter's brother.*

Who is the second disciple who follows Jesus? Possibly it is John, the writer of this Gospel.

John 1:41   *The first thing he did was to find his brother Simon and say to him, 'We have found the Messiah' (which is the Hebrew for Christ).*

Filled with joyous energy Andrew seeks his brother. He immediately has to share this great goodness he has found. His simple statement reveals that both of them must have been seeking the Messiah. God has prepared their hearts and minds for their faith flames instantly, like a torch.

John 1:42   *He brought Simon to Jesus, who looked at him and said, 'You are Simon son of John; you shall be called Cephas' (that is, Peter, 'the Rock').*

Jesus, foretelling the change that will be wrought by the Spirit in this disciple, renames him Cephas, or Peter, the Rock. Out of the weakness Peter will show in his denial of Jesus Christ at the time of the crucifixion will come a spiritual strength that will be rocklike.

John 1:43-44   *The next day Jesus decided to leave for Galilee. He met Philip, who, like Andrew and Peter, came from Bethsaida, and said to him, 'Follow me.'*

If these men have known Jesus prior to this moment we do not know, but Jesus' words "Follow me" produce such instant compliance in Philip that it shows that more than the spoken word is involved. The Christliness of Jesus touches Philip awakening his loyalty and love. The inward light given Philip in the beginning (John 1:4) begins to burn brightly and it illumines his path.

John 1:45-46   *Philip went to find Nathanael and told him, 'We have found the man of whom Moses wrote in the law, the man* *foretold by the prophets: it is Jesus son of Joseph, from Nazareth.' 'Nazareth!' Nathanael exclaimed. 'Can anything good come from Nazareth?' Philip said, 'Come and see.'*

In the above conversation we also have an example of the humor John shows throughout this Gospel.

The text indicates that Philip and Nathanael may know of him as Joseph's son from Nazareth. There is supposed to have been rivalry between Cana, Nathanael's town, and Nazareth. This may account for his exclamation. Philip quietly says, 'Come and see.'

John 1:47 *When Jesus saw Nathanael coming towards him, he said, 'Here is an Israelite worthy of the name; there is nothing false in him.'*

Jesus insight must have noted purity and straightforwardness in Nathanael. Devious ways and slyness are apparently no part of his character. Note the quality of thought of those who surround Jesus or have anything to do with his coming. Elizabeth and Zechariah both are filled with the Spirit. John the Baptist, their son, is filled with the Holy Spirit from birth. Jesus' mother, Mary, has ever symbolized purity and willingness to do God's will. Joseph follows God's directions and is a good, kind man. All the disciples have the potential to become remarkable, self-sacrificing men. The Spirit touches such as these.

John 1:48-50 *Nathanael asked him, 'How is it you know me?' Jesus replied, 'I saw you under the fig tree before Philip spoke to you.' 'Rabbi,' said Nathanael, 'you are the Son of*

God; you are king of Israel.' Jesus answered, 'Do you believe this because I told you I saw you under the fig tree?'

This passage emphasizes Jesus' ability not only to see into the minds of men, but to know what is transpiring at a distance from him. The fact of God's omnipresence makes this a natural act for Jesus. This ability increases Nathanael's conviction that he has found the Christ.

But Jesus notes that his faith, that will justify the bestowal of such titles as Nathanael has given him, is at present based on the slim evidence that Jesus "sees" him under the fig tree, rather than on the firm foundation of spiritual knowledge that Jesus will ultimately give his students. Jesus says, in effect, "You call me Son of God and King of Israel because of the vision I had of you?"

John 1:50-51 *'You will see greater things than that.' Then he added, 'In very truth I tell you all: you will see heaven wide open and God's angels ascending and descending upon the Son of Man.'*

Jesus blesses Nathanael with the words, "You will see greater things than that." Then, turning to his little band, he gives them a glimpse of things to come. "You will see heaven wide open..." No longer will the God men worship be a mystery and unknown. His teaching (the revelation of the Word made flesh) will open this great reality. There will not be just an occasional glimpse, or intimation of things heavenly — the heavens will be wide open, reality will be understood. The whole area of Spirit will be revealed and explained by the Son of Man, and the angels of God, His messengers, will ascend and descend giving communication between God and man.

Chapter Two

The Commitment

John 2:1-10   Two days later there was a wedding at Cana-in-Galilee. The mother of Jesus was there, and Jesus and his disciples were also among the guests. The wine gave out, so Jesus's mother said to him, 'They have no wine left.' He answered, 'That is no concern of mine. My hour has not yet come.' His mother said to the servants, 'Do whatever he tells you.' There were six stone water-jars standing near, of the kind used for Jewish rites of purification; each held from twenty to thirty gallons. Jesus said to the servants, 'Fill the jars with water,' and they filled them to the brim. 'Now draw some off,' he ordered, 'and take it to the master of the feast'; and they did so. The master tasted the water now turned into wine, not knowing its source, though the servants who had drawn the water knew. He hailed the bridegroom and said, 'Everyone else serves the best wine first, and the poorer only when the guests have drunk freely; but you have kept the best wine till now.'

We learn from these verses that his disciples have accompanied Jesus and his mother to the wedding feast. He is now a recognized and acknowledged Teacher.

A wedding feast in those days usually lasted at least a week and food and drink for the assembled well-wishers must have severely taxed the family! Before it is over, Mary, Jesus' mother, brings him the news, "They have no wine left." He answers, "That is no concern of mine. My hour has not yet come."

To the modern reader this statement is startling in its abruptness. *The Revised Standard Bible* translates it; "Oh woman, what have you to do with me? My hour has not yet come."

Jesus' answer is probably intended to have a double meaning to Mary. "Your concern (about the wine) is not my concern (which is about my life work). The hour (to start my public ministry) has not yet come!"

John must feel that instruction will come to the reader of the dialogue between Jesus and his mother or he would not include it. Immediately it tells us several things.

1. Jesus' mother is perhaps one of his followers at that time.
2. She apparently knows he has a proven capacity to perform what are generally called miracles.
3. When he says "My hour has not yet come," we realize that mother and son share the knowledge that he is the Man of Destiny.
4. We recognize that both Mary and Jesus respond with compassion and understanding to the embarrassing situation of their hosts.
5. In matters of her own household, Mary has, by custom, the full management of her affairs. Therefore it is easy to assume the prerogative now to help her friends; she orders the servants and asks her Son's help.
6. Mary's instruction to the servants, "Do whatever he tells you" is based on her prior knowledge that Jesus can provide whatever is necessary.

It should not seem unnatural to us that Jesus, when a boy and a young man, should practice his divine power. We first learn of him at twelve wistfully asking his parents, when they find him in the temple, "Why did you search for me?" he says, "Did you not know that I was bound to be in my Father's house?" (Luke 2:41-51).

"Do you not know, you who should know!" Jesus is very conscious of who he is and what he has to do. But he is also Mary's son. As he becomes more and more aware of his Christ dominion his human nature demands proof. It is probable that in his home, under appropriate circumstances, he has provided some necessary proof of his spiritual power. Such occasions are a part of his spiritual education by the Holy Spirit. The immeasurable grace bestowed upon him by his Father anticipates and makes provision for every demand and situation. For him to carry out his Father's foreordained assignment he must be tested at all points. By the time of his ministry there will not remain an iota of self doubt nor fear to creep into his consciousness; he will have overcome every sense of inadequacy; and at all times he will know not only what he is to do, but how to bring it about. This is the necessary education of Mary's son, and this also illustrates the process of salvation for humanity.

Have you not wondered why Jesus waits until he is about thirty years old to start a ministry? We hear he probably is a carpenter like Joseph. During those busy years Mary knows that preparation for his ministry is going on, but this is probably unknown to the rest of his family for his brothers seem unaware of his abilities. In his ministry Jesus speaks with authority. This can only be the case when the son of Mary yields to the Son of God.

When Jesus tells his mother "That is no concern of mine," he stands at the brink of his ministry. He must appreciate fully the awesome demands that will be made upon him in the coming two or three years. Jesus is human "as we are" and his humanity must yearn to linger just a little while longer in his haven of anonymity. He knows the great tide of feeling that will be stirred against him by his preaching and healing. His "hour has not yet come," he says. His mother has faint glimmerings of his stupendous task. Have not angels and prophets foretold his career? And has it not also been foretold that her own heart will be pierced by the sword of sorrow? Her human enthusiasm based on her son's "talent" and her desire to rescue her friends from their terrible situation makes her go forward; abruptly she tells the servants to "Do whatever he tells you." It is this that begins Jesus' public works. She literally has pushed the nestling out of the nest.

Glory

John 2:11 *So Jesus performed at Cana-in-Galilee the first of the signs which revealed his glory and led his disciples to believe in him.*

John sees the provision made at Cana as a revelation of glory. This glory is not the water turned to wine. The glory is his "talent" or ability to reveal that God provides for our necessities; that in His love for us He provides us with evidence of that love. John must see great significance in this first of many mighty works, for he presents it to us through the dialogue of two, both of whom are chosen of God.

Cleansing The Temple

John 2:12-16 *After this he went down to Capernaum with his mother, his brothers, and his disciples, and they stayed there a few days. As it was near the time for the Jewish Passover, Jesus went up to Jerusalem. In the temple precincts he found the dealers in cattle, sheep, and pigeons, and the money-changers seated at their tables. He made a whip of cords and drove them out of the temple, sheep, cattle, and all. He upset the tables of the money-changers, scattering their coins. Then he turned on the dealers in pigeons: 'Take them out of here' he said; 'do not turn my Father's house into a market.'*

John places the account of Jesus' visit to Jerusalem at Passover next in the events he records, for he understands Jesus' ministry to have spanned three Passovers, of which this is the first (John 6:4, 11:55). Contrast the Synoptics[1] where only a single Passover is involved.

Having just said his "hour" has not yet come, we find Jesus going to the temple at Jerusalem. He finds the court of the temple a veritable marketplace. In it dealers are selling cattle, sheep, and pigeons to the worshipers, and to facilitate the whole proceeding, money changers also sit there. A tremendous rage wells up in Jesus. He worships his God in such purity and here he finds a commercialism that disgusts him — bargaining is going on over offerings to his Father. Making a whip of small cords he drives them all out, including the money changers. What tremendous force and determination must be sensed by all as they scurry to get away from this man flailing his whip at the vendors and their animals. "He must be mad," some think. What else can they think in their dumbfounded surprise!

John 2:17-18 *His disciples recalled the words of scripture: 'Zeal for your house will consume me.'*

The disciples who accompany him must be horrified and amazed at his actions. They recall a verse

---

[1] The Synoptics: The Gospels of Matthew, Mark, and Luke.

from Psalm 69:9. This, they think, at least substantiates by prophecy what he is doing; but one can imagine them standing to one side, trying to be separate from the whole awful proceeding!

Jesus is acting in a way that causes all present to become aware of him. His accusation to the priests is derogatory, and includes not only the priests but the doctors of the law and worshipers.

All have condoned the practice.

John 2:18 *The Jews challenged Jesus: 'What sign can you show to justify your action?'*

Jesus has attacked their sense of propriety and they throw the challenge back to him! What authority have you to show us? What right have you to disrupt our ways and accuse us?

John 2:19 *'Destroy this temple,' Jesus replied, 'and in three days I will raise it up again.'*

By giving this mystical answer, Jesus draws even more attention to himself. His hour has come! His words, in effect, say, "I AM HERE!"

John 2:20-21 *The Jews said, 'It has taken forty-six years to build this temple. Are you going to raise it up again in three days?' But the temple he was speaking of was his body.*

The use of the word "temple" for his body is of great importance. A temple is a place of worship or a place set apart that is holy to God. Paul asks us: "Do you not know that your body is a temple of the indwelling Holy Spirit, and the Spirit is God's gift to you?" (1 Corinthians 6:19).

In John 15, Jesus speaks of dwelling with the Father, and the Father in him. He knows the indestructible nature of his Father, and he also knows that all that expresses the Father will thereby be preserved — will partake of the immortality of his Father. He does not fear to trust the divine Presence with him to lift his humanity to life. It is this inward divine life to which he turns and on which he depends. This Christ of Jesus is the fullness of the Father's being, His grace and love with him always.

John 2:22 *After his resurrection his disciples had recalled what he had said, and they believed the scripture and the words that Jesus had spoken.*

From the standpoint of one who is there, John tells us the disciples believe the scripture following the resurrection. It is of utmost importance that the prophecies of God concerning the Christ, which are found in the Old Testament, be vindicated. The pattern of worship of the true God woven in the history of the Jewish tribes is clear and strong.

John 2:23-25 *While he was in Jerusalem for Passover many put their trust in him when they saw the signs that he performed. But Jesus for his part would not trust himself to them. He knew them all, and had no need of evidence from others about anyone, for he himself could tell what was in people.*

Jesus' capacity to know the hearts of men shows his penetrating insight that enables him to go right to the core of the problem he confronts, whether of sin or disease. Perceiving the cause of their dis-ease, or sin, he can quickly loose them from their bondage. We are told in this instance he does not entrust his person to those who give him allegiance because of the wonders he performs; instead we are told of his spiritual insight and the fact that he does not go among them to teach. For us, it is important to know what Jesus does not do. Insight preserves him from harm in this case.

Chapter Three

The New Birth

John 3:1-2 *One of the Pharisees, called Nicodemus, a member of the Jewish Council, came to Jesus by night. 'Rabbi,' he said, 'we know that you are a teacher sent by God; no one could perform these signs of yours unless God were with him.'*

Nicodemus acknowledges Jesus to be a man come from God because of the proofs he has given, the signs of divine power. Therefore he accepts the fact that God is with him. Though he highly regards Jesus as a teacher, he comes by night to confer with him so that he will not be noticed.

John 3:3-5 *Jesus answered, 'In very truth I tell you, no one can see the kingdom of God unless he has been born again.' 'But how can someone be born when he is old?' asked Nicodemus. 'Can he enter his mother's womb a second time and be born?' Jesus answered, 'In very truth I tell you, no one can enter the kingdom of God without being born from water and spirit.'*

To be born again in the way Jesus means is a spiritual experience. A spiritual experience does not mean a mental experience, but rather thought involving divine influence. The bewildered Nicodemus, who thinks only in terms of physical birth, has difficulty lifting his thought to think along spiritual lines. Jesus has only the language of earth with which to tell his hearers of things heretofore beyond their comprehension. In the effort to lift Nicodemus' thought to a more spiritual level Jesus says, "No one can enter the kingdom of God without being born from water and spirit."

Water is well known as a purifying element in Temple rites. Spirit (the same word in Greek also means wind) stands for freedom as well as spiritual life itself. So Nicodemus is being told that only

through the cleansing baptism of repentance and humility (the willingness to accept new concepts) can this new birth take place. This new man, when filled with the Spirit, is free from old beliefs, is literally born again, now partaking in his being of the substance and life of God, and is able to grasp new ideas.

Jesus continues: John 3:6-8 *'Flesh can give birth only to flesh; it is spirit that gives birth to spirit. You ought not to be astonished when I say, "You must all be born again." The wind blows where it wills; you hear the sound of it, but you do not know where it comes from or where it is going. So it is with everyone who is born from the Spirit.'*

"It is spirit that gives birth to spirit." Only elements divine can bring to light the man made in God's image and likeness. The individual who has yielded his being and identity to the transforming power of the Holy Spirit opens the door of a new life. Freedom of movement "like the wind that bloweth" belongs, both mentally and physically, to those new-born of Spirit.

John 3:9-12 *'How is this possible?' asked Nicodemus. 'You a teacher of Israel and ignorant of such things!' said Jesus. 'In very truth I tell you, we speak of what we know, and testify to what we have seen, and yet you all reject our testimony. If you do not believe me when I talk to you about earthly things, how are you to believe if I should talk about the things of heaven?'*

Nicodemus, steeped in restrictive, narrow views, asks, "How is this possible?" — and Jesus chides the famous teacher for his ignorance.

Jesus gets to the crux of the matter. He is not believed! His testimony is rejected. He has spoken plainly and roused disbelief. If men will not understand this plain speaking, how can they comprehend when he tells them of the wholly spiritual — of heaven itself?

The following verses may also have been included in the conversation with Nicodemus. In any event, John gives them value at this point.

Jesus continues: John 3:13   *'No one has gone up into heaven except the one who came down from heaven, the Son of Man who is in heaven.'*

Here Jesus speaks of his divine origin and of his humanity through which he reveals the incarnate God, the Son of Man whose home is in heaven.

Home is an abiding place, a point of origin, a shelter, a secure dwelling. Jesus, the Son of Man, maintains this viewpoint of heaven. He considers it at hand, and not afar. As one whose home is in heaven he looks out upon all men and all situations from this spiritual elevation; he knows that as in heaven, so on earth, Spirit is the only causative power to be considered.

These phrases speak of heaven as home for him who came down from heaven, for he speaks of himself as Mary's child — the Son of Man.

Lift Up the Son of Man

John 3:14-15   *Just as Moses lifted up the serpent in the wilderness, so the Son of Man must be lifted up, in order that everyone who has faith may in him have eternal life.*

In the Book of Numbers 21:4-9, we read of the grumbling and complaining of the Israelites and their impatience and resentment against Moses and God. "Then the Lord sent venomous snakes among them, and they bit the Israelites so that many of them died." This scourge, which is attributed to the Lord, apparently opens their eyes and they come to Moses in contrition, saying, "We sinned when we spoke against the Lord and you. Plead with the Lord to rid us of the snakes." Moses then pleads with the Lord, and according to the Lord's instruction makes a bronze serpent which he puts on a standard so that anyone who has been bitten may look upon it and be healed. Under God's direction the serpent of death becomes the instrument of healing, but only when the power of the Lord is sought. Repentance opens the

minds of the Israelites; they realize their unjust accusations and turn away from the sinuous arguments of self-pity, impatience, ingratitude, and whining. The bronze serpent reminds them of God's care for them and heals them of the bite of resentment that kills all spirituality.

St. Paul tells us: "Let us not put the Lord to the test as some of them did; they were destroyed by the snakes. Do not grumble as some of them did; they were destroyed by the Destroyer. All these things that happened to them were symbolic, and were recorded as a warning for us..." (1 Corinthians 10:9-11).

Considering the way Jesus refers to this episode it must have been well known in his time. Now he says the Son of Man must be lifted up "in order that everyone who has faith in him may not perish but have eternal life." Each one, says Jesus, when they see the Son of Man, must be reminded that God created not only his humanity but theirs too, for Jesus appears as a man just as we do; his home is heaven and ours is too. By accepting Jesus in full faith, and recognizing the Father's care for him, we shall perceive that as children of God this everlasting care and concern is for us as well. Our Lord Jesus tells us that in lifting up the Son of Man we are acknowledging, and in faith accepting, the fact that the human Jesus is given eternal life. In so accepting we are accepting for ourselves this divine redemption and resurrection.

Jesus is speaking: John 3:16-17   *'God so loved the world that he gave his only Son, that everyone who has faith in him may not perish but have eternal life. It was not to judge the world that God sent his Son into the world, but that through him the world might be saved.'*

In love God sends His Son as a man, human — liable to our restrictions, fears, and dangers — so that we, seeing him start from our level of thought, from our standpoint of physicality, can be shown how to overcome these difficulties; "...that everyone who has faith in him (in his attitude, his viewpoint, his love) may not perish but have eternal life." That means life for everyone who has trust in his teachings; in his many proofs of the Father's continuing provision; in his dominion over wind and wave, disease, sin, and death itself. He teaches we shall never come to the end of God's care; we shall never exhaust God's love; we shall never be less than precious to God; because for us He gives His only Son for the purpose of our continuing life, our continuing well-being, and the continuing provision of all our needs. This is our "eternal life." "It was not to judge the world (to condemn it or chastise it) that God sent His Son into the world, but that through him the world might be saved." Through the Son we are to be assisted, helped, provided for, healed, and loved — loved by a most loving Father.

We must in faith turn to the Source that Jesus turns to, his Father, his Christ and the Holy Spirit, and trust his teachings for healing and provision. This is why Jesus came to us and why he comes to us today, to lead us to reject evil, to heal us, and to make us whole, because we are loved. Salvation is the overcoming of evil and deliverance from it.

Jesus continues speaking: John 3:18-21
'No one who puts his faith in him comes under judgement; but the unbeliever has already been judged because he has not put his trust in God's only Son. This is the judgment: the light has come into the world, but people preferred darkness to light because their deeds were evil. Wrongdoers hate the light and avoid it, for fear their misdeeds should be exposed. Those who live by the truth come to the light so that it may be clearly seen that God is in all they do.'

Jesus emphasizes the necessity for allegiance to God's only Son. On his firm foundation of the recognition of God as his and our Father we place our faith in him and do not come under judgment. Men make their own judgment when they either reject or follow Jesus Christ. Unspiritual men are afraid of the demands of God; the man born again, as Jesus tells Nicodemus, glories in the demands God makes of him. Those who trust the Holy Spirit find joy that the power and presence of God is with them in all they do and is found to be the central factor of their lives.

John 3:22-28   *After this Jesus went with his disciples into Judaea; he remained there with them and baptized. John too was baptizing at Aenon, near Salim, because water was plentiful in that region; and all the time people were coming for baptism. This was before John's imprisonment.*
John's disciples were engaged in a debate with some Jews about purification; so they came to John and said, 'Rabbi, there was a man with you on the other side of the Jordan, to whom you bore your witness. Now he is baptizing, and everyone is flocking to him.' John replied: 'One can have only what is given one from Heaven. You yourselves can testify that I said, "I am not the Messiah; I have been sent as his forerunner." '

Jesus and his disciples, and John the Baptist and his followers are in Judaea baptizing "for there was water there." Word has circulated that Jesus is baptizing. The first verses of Chapter Four (John 4:1-3) make it clear that it is his disciples baptizing with water, not Jesus. Jesus will baptize in the Holy Spirit.[1]

John the Baptist's disciples dispute with the Jews about purification, but their jealousy of Jesus and his followers is noted in John's gospel — "...a man to whom you bore your witness...is baptizing, and everyone is flocking to him." John the Baptist's answer is reaffirmation of his position. "One can only have what is given one from Heaven. You yourselves can testify that I said, 'I am not the Messiah; I have been sent as his forerunner.' " In beautiful language John the Baptist next describes their relative positions.

I Must Grow Less

John the Baptist continues: John 3:29-30
'It is the bridegroom who marries the bride. The bridegroom's friend, who stands by and listens to him, is overjoyed at hearing the bridegroom's voice. This is my joy and now it is complete. He must grow greater; I must become less.'

---

[1] John 1:33 "...The man on whom you see the Spirit come down and rest is the one who is to baptize in Holy Spirit."

Jesus is the bridegroom, John the Baptist the friend of the bridegroom. He pictures himself as standing by, listening to the voice of the bridegroom. In these times chosen friends bear witness to the consummation of a marriage. In picture language John the Baptist tells of his rapturous joy as he hears the bridegroom's voice: i.e., as he sees the consummation of the marriage between Christ and God's people. "This is my joy and now it is complete." And then he makes a most profound statement, "He must grow greater; I must become less." As Christ Jesus grows greater in my life, my ego must grow less. In the presence of divinity — of the Spirit within me — my will must grow less, until "not my will but Thine be done" is complete.

John the Apostle now speaks: John 3:31
He who comes from above is above all others;...

Jesus, whose origin is in God, outranks and possesses talents and attributes above all others. To him belongs dominion, power, and glory.

John 3:31   *...he who is from the earth belongs to the earth and uses earthly speech.*

John is now speaking of those whose mental level is never lifted from the earthly and worldly. All their thinking is predicated on finiteness and limitation. Spirit and its infinite wonders are unknown.

John 3:31-32   *He who comes from heaven bears witness to what he has seen and heard, even though no one accepts his witness.*

Jesus who comes from heaven, not earth, tells of things we have neither seen nor heard — and though we accept him as the Son of God, we do not believe him! Explaining further the great implications involved in accepting or rejecting Jesus as Messiah (Savior), John says:

John 3:33-34   *To accept his witness is to affirm that God speaks the truth; for he whom God sent utters the words of God, so measureless is God's gift of the Spirit.*

John has beautiful recognition of the Spirit-filled Jesus, as the Anointed of God, as the Son of God, as the reliable bearer of God's message uttering the very words of God — all because of the measureless (unlimited) gift of the Spirit, God-with-him.

John 3:35   *The Father loves the Son and has entrusted him with complete authority.*

John defines the love of God for Jesus as a Father-Son relationship with all the implications of inheritance. The Son has the same authority as the Father. What perception by John! Only the Spirit can reveal this to him. And what is the consequence of this?

John 3:36   *Whoever puts his faith in the Son has eternal life. Whoever disobeys the Son will not see that life; God's wrath rests upon him.*

To have hold of eternal life is to be eternally held in unity with God, to be beyond any possible hurt or destruction, to know only the warm love of our Lord and Father. "Whoever disobeys the Son will not see that life." To be outside the Father's love is truly to be deprived of all good and can be counted as being in "God's wrath." How bleak the existence where there is no love, no divine provision, no continuing support — only aloneness.

The Bible speaks of "God's wrath" in more violent terms in both the Old and New Testaments. Examples are the Flood (Genesis 6-9); the fire and brimstone that rains on Sodom and Gomorrah and obliterates them (Genesis 19:1-29); and the lake of fire and sulfur into which the devil is flung (Revelation 20:10). These three events depict "God's wrath" as cataclysmic finality.

Chapter Four

Jacob's Well

John 4:1-2   *News now reached the Pharisees that Jesus was winning and baptizing more disciples than John; although, in fact, it was his disciples who were baptizing, not Jesus himself.*

When their informers report to the Pharisees that Jesus is gaining followers in greater numbers than John the Baptist, we learn that the activity of these two leaders is under scrutiny. John, however, feels it necessary to emphasize that Jesus is not performing the water baptisms — Jesus has come to baptize with the Holy Spirit (John 1:33-34).

John 4:2-6   *When Jesus heard this, he left Judaea and set out once more for Galilee. He had to pass through Samaria, and on his way he came to a Samaritan town called Sychar, near the plot of ground which Jacob gave to his son Joseph; Jacob's well was there. It was about noon, and Jesus, tired after his journey, was sitting by the well.*

Geographically the setting of this conversation is accurate. It is thought that the rendering "Sychar" came about through the copyists corruption of the town named "Sychem" (Shechem). Father Brown writes:" If the real reading is Shechem, everything fits, for Jacob's well is only 250 feet from Shechem. Probably Shechem was only a very small settlement at that time... The site presently identified as Jacob's well at the foot of Mt. Gerizim can be accepted with confidence."[1]

The Samaritans are the descendants of a small group of Israelites who were not deported by their conquerors at the time of the fall of the Northern Kingdom in 722 B.C.; they also include colonists brought in by their Assyrian conquerors from Babylonia and Media. Their offense to the Jews of Jesus' time comes from their intermarriage with these colonists as well as their continued worship at hillside shrines dedicated to ancestral gods, while they at the same time acknowledge the God of Israel. (See 2 Kings 17:24-41 for further information.)

The setting of this episode at the well is dramatic. Some authorities consider the whole story the invention of John as a medium to convey Jesus' teachings.

Before writing of the significance of the meeting of Jesus and the woman of Samaria, let us examine the symbolism of Jacob's well, a spring that has supplied good water for centuries. John could say, "Jesus sat down by a well." Why is he telling us the name of this well?

In Genesis 28:10-22 we have the account of Jacob's first great spiritual experience. This is the turning point in his life.

Jacob is not a nice character. From birth he has practiced cunning, slyness, and duplicity in his dealings with his father and brother, and probably others. Yet God chooses him from among all to be the example of a life touched by divine grace, and to be part of the continuing cord of spiritual evidence woven in history.

In Jacob's first vision he sees a ladder that reaches to heaven and the angels of God going up and down upon it. In the dream the Lord stands beside him, the God of Abraham. God announces his gift to him of the land on which he lies, and gives him as well descendants countless as the dust. He also blesses Jacob with the promise, "I shall be with you to protect you wherever you go,... I shall not leave you until I have done what I promised." When he awakes Jacob's outlook is changed. He begins to see that God is with him and will take care of him. He no longer

---

[1] Raymond E. Brown, S. S., *The Anchor Bible*, Volume 29, "The Gospel According to John," I-XII, page 169, Doubleday & Co., Inc.

needs to live by his wits and practice deceit for God will prosper him.

In Genesis 32:24-32 we read of another of his great encounters with God. At this time he is in grave danger from his brother Esau from whom he has stolen the inheritance. Seeking his forgiveness he divides his great wealth in half sending Esau the portion, thus making an effort to appease his brother with this gift. Special instructions are given to his servants to guide them in presenting these gifts to Esau.

During the night before his encounter with his brother, Jacob arises and takes his wives, slave girls, and sons to a place of safety across a gorge. "So Jacob was left alone and a man wrestled with him there till daybreak" (Genesis 32:24). During this night of deep soul-searching the Lord probes deeply, and Jacob wrestles. It is not easy for him to give up old ways of thinking and acting! His concepts and views of life, of relationships, and even of God are dredged out of his innermost being and held before him to retain or discard during this night of tribulation; and finally when "daybreak" comes he has conquered self and won the victory. Now he asks the angel for a blessing. The great blessing comes in the new name — Israel, for he has wrestled and prevailed. He has changed. His whole being and his viewpoint are different. He is a new man. He is born again. As a new man he is given a new name.

Jacob's well thus symbolizes the action of God's grace and truth as an innerspring welling up in man's being to cleanse and spiritualize. It also is proof of God's love and concern for His creation.

John 4:7-9 *His disciples had gone into the town to buy food. Meanwhile a Samaritan woman came to draw water, and Jesus said to her, 'Give me a drink.' The woman said, 'What! You, a Jew, ask for a drink from a Samaritan woman?' (Jews do not share drinking vessels with Samaritans.)*

As a symbol in teaching, the Samaritan woman stands for a very material concept of life, and Jesus for the highest spiritual concept. Gently the Master Teacher lifts her thought from the narrow beliefs of her ancestry to behold God's limitless love.

In the opening sentences of their dialogue Jesus crosses the barriers of both cultural and religious intolerance — he speaks to a woman, and a Samaritan at that! Not only are their social and religious positions far different, but as the conversation progresses it is noted that the Samaritan woman reasons from the level of her own familiar environment, and that Jesus reasons from the standpoint of spiritual reality. Statement by statement Jesus lifts her thought from the material level to the spiritual level.

John 4:10 *Jesus replied, 'If only you knew what God gives, and who it is that is asking you for a drink, you would have asked him and he would have given you living water.'*

At once Jesus catches her attention: "If only you knew what God gives, and who it is that is asking...." He dangles a mystery before her. What is God giving and who is he that asks for a drink? A change is demanded in the routine of her thinking. God is brought into consideration as the giver of a gift — and if she but asks she will receive some living water.

John 4:11-12 *'Sir,' the woman said, 'You have no bucket and the well is deep, so where can you get "living water"? Are you greater than Jacob our ancestor who gave us the well and drank from it himself, he and his sons and his cattle too?'*

They are beside a spring of "living water" as opposed to a cistern whose waters are still and often stagnant. It is difficult for her to conceive of "living water" other than this bubbling well. "Are you greater than Jacob?" is her question. How close she comes to the truth! Her perceptive thought must have attracted Jesus in the first place.

Couching his message in terms that she can understand he patiently continues.

John 4:13-15 *Jesus answered, 'Everyone who drinks this water will be thirsty again; but whoever drinks the water I shall give will never again be thirsty. The water that I shall give will be a spring of water within him, welling up and bringing eternal life.' 'Sir,' said the woman, 'give me this water, and then I shall* not be thirsty, nor have to come all this way to draw water.'

The water that Jesus offers is deeply satisfying, the outpouring of all that is Life. Drinking his "living water" will bring the measureless grace of God that he himself enjoys. This innerspring of grace will be a surging, unfailing source of Spirit that will infuse the humanity of him who drinks it, satisfying all spiritually hungry and thirsty yearnings. In its purest essence it is the body and blood of Christ, God's Gift. He later says "....because I live you too will live: when that day comes you will know that I am in my Father, and you in me and I in you" (John 14:19-20). This is the innerspring of living water.

The woman is incapable at that time of following Jesus' reasoning, but in spite of all her limitations she knows she wants what Jesus Christ alone can give her. Her hunger and thirst for the things of Spirit will now be satisfied.

John 4:16-18 *'Go and call your husband,' said Jesus, 'and come back here.' She answered, 'I have no husband.' Jesus said, 'You are right in saying that you have no husband, for though you have had five husbands, the man you are living with now is not your husband. You have spoken the truth!'*

Jesus' penetrating insight not only discerns this woman's marital status, but he also sees teachableness and receptivity — a mind open to spiritual views.

John 4:19-24 *'Sir,' replied the woman, 'I can see you are a prophet. Our fathers worshipped on this mountain, but you Jews say that the place where God must be worshipped is in Jerusalem.' 'Believe me,' said Jesus, 'the time is coming when you will worship the Father neither on this mountain nor in Jerusalem. You Samaritans worship you know not what; we worship what we know. It is from the Jews that salvation comes. But the time is coming, indeed it is already here, when true worshippers will worship the Father in spirit and in truth. These are the worshippers the Father wants. God is spirit, and those who*

worship him must worship in spirit and in truth.'

Now the Samaritan acknowledges Jesus as a prophet and addresses him with more respect. Then seizing the opportunity (for how often does one have the occasion to speak with a prophet?) she asks a question that must have been troubling her; "where should we worship?"

There is Biblical evidence (Deuteronomy 27:4) that Joshua has made a shrine on Mt. Gerizem (Ebal), but it is possible that "hillside shrines to other gods" may also have been upon the sacred mountain. Jerusalem as the place of chosen worship is described in 2 Chronicles, Chapter 6.

Answering her question Jesus states that the time is coming when neither the sacred mountain nor Jerusalem will be the place of worship. He goes on to explain that the Samaritans have no real concept of God, but that the Jews do know whom they worship. The Jews as well as the Samaritans claim descent from Jacob-Israel, and the Jews claim to be the chosen of God to bear the message given the children of Israel. Their development illustrates an ever-watchful, concerned God, shepherding His people, recalcitrant though they are. Jesus considers himself to be the well spring for the message of salvation. The time is here, he says, for real worshipers to worship the Father in Spirit and in Truth. Here he introduces a new standard of worship: Such are the worshipers the Father wants — men and women who totally commit themselves to God. These are worshipers of vision and discernment who, like Jacob, will wrestle to overcome evil until they prevail, and who will receive a blessing at the dawn of their new spiritual perception.

When our Lord says, "God is spirit and those who worship him must worship him in spirit and in truth" he is telling us that we must worship him "in kind." Materiality cannot convey the spiritual. Worship must be spiritual in essence and substance. Our gifts to God must speak of the highest type of love and self-offering. Today the same total commitment, laid upon the alter, will carry the message of true worship. Lives consecrated to overcoming false traits of character; to yielding self will that one may do God's will; to the sacrifice of doubt and distrust that there may be faith in the shepherd who cares; to practice honesty in place of duplicity: all such efforts worship the Father in Spirit and in Truth!

John 4:25-26 *The woman answered, 'I know that Messiah' (that is, Christ) 'is coming. When he comes he will make everything clear to us.' Jesus said to her, 'I am he, I who am speaking to you.'*

It is greatly to the Samaritan's credit that she answers that she knows Christ is coming! He will explain all! Then, something that she has never expected to hear is said to her: "I am he, I who am speaking to you."

As the reader can you hear this glorious message? "I am he...speaking to you..."

Will you accept the truth of that admission? Will you let the glory of the Lord Jesus Christ blot out all doubt and misgiving as to his identity? What a wondrous moment of revelation! He has come! The One for whom the ages have waited!

The beauty of this incident is harshly broken by the return of the disciples from the village. The tension produced by Jesus' identification of himself must have been felt by the disciples.

John 4:27-30 *At that moment his disciples returned, and were astonished to find him talking with a woman; but none of them said, 'What do you want?' or, 'Why are you talking with her?' The woman left her water-jar and went away to the town, where she said to the people, 'Come and see a man who has told me everything I ever did. Could this be the Messiah?' They left the town and made their way towards him.*

When the woman ends her conversation with Jesus she puts down her water jar; therefore she must have been holding it during their talk. As a symbol of a material, earthy type of life, one can say that in setting down her water jar she is relinquishing her former ways, because in her brief encounter her hope has found a new height. Returning to the village she timidly shares this new hope, "Could this be the Messiah?" Just the mention of such a possibility brings her friends to sit and learn from Jesus, Son of God.

The Harvest

John 4:31-34 *Meanwhile the disciples were urging him, 'Rabbi, have something to eat.' But he said, 'I have food to eat of which you know nothing.' At this the disciples said to one another, 'Can someone have brought him food?' But Jesus said, 'For me it is meat and drink to do the will of him who sent me until I have finished his work.'*

On their return to Jesus, after having entered the town, the disciples are solicitous for his well-being and they offer him food; they are amazed that he accepts none. It is interesting that in this account, in the conversation with the Samaritan and with the disciples, Jesus speaks on a spiritual level as opposed to their material viewpoint. His outlook is wholly spiritual. He reassures them: ..."it is meat and drink to do the will of him who sent me until I have finished his work." Drawing upon the innerspring of his spiritual resources he finds at hand all that he needs. Truly these are the waters of eternal life. He knows God, his Father, will sustain him in every way until he has completed his work.

John 4:35-38 *'Do you not say, "Four months more and then comes the harvest?" But look, I tell you, look around at the fields: they are already white, ripe for harvesting. The reaper is drawing his pay and harvesting a crop for eternal life, so that the sower and reaper may rejoice together. That is how the saying comes true: "One sows, another reaps!" I sent you to reap a crop for which you have not laboured. Others laboured and you have come in for the harvest of their labour.'*

The people of the Samaritan's town poured across the intervening space to come to him.

Looking at them Jesus declares the "fields" ready for harvest. The sowing has been done by prophets and his forerunner, John the Baptist. They have done their work well; now he and his disciples will gather for his Father the ready minds and hearts awaiting their Savior. Time is not a factor in the divine harvest. Not years, but rather the grace of God, matures the Christian.

John 4:39-42   Many Samaritans of that town came to believe in him because of the woman's testimony: 'He told me everything I ever did.' So when these Samaritans came to him they pressed him to stay with them; and he stayed there two days. Many more became believers because of what they heard from his own lips. They told the woman, 'It is no longer because of what you said that we believe, for we have heard him ourselves; and we are convinced that he is the Saviour of the world.'

"When these Samaritans came to him..." Today we are invited to "come to Jesus." Here on an ancient hillside, the loathed Samaritans yield their allegiance to one who only a short time before had been a total stranger. God's grace has touched their hearts and opened their eyes and ears to their present Savior. He stays with them two days. No doubt there is preaching, and much talk — and surely much love is shown and felt by each one. Only great warmth of love can assure them of a Savior who is capable of reaching the whole world with salvation.

Jesus the Giver of Life

John 4:43-45   When the two days were over Jesus left for Galilee; for he himself had declared that a prophet is without honour in his own country. On his arrival the Galileans made him welcome, because they had seen all he did at the festival in Jerusalem; they had been at the festival themselves.

Jerusalem, in the land of Judaea, is not a happy place for our Lord. In the account given in John 2:12-25 we find Jesus does not trust the people there, and he does not tarry to struggle with those who do not accept him. It is of this period that Jesus declares of himself "that a prophet is without honor in his own country."

Cana-in-Galilee is a different story. Here he is welcomed.

The Officer's Son

John 4:46-54   Once again he visited Cana-in-Galilee, where he had turned the water into wine. An officer in the royal service was there, whose son was lying ill at Capernaum. When he heard that Jesus had come from Judaea into Galilee, he went to him and begged him to go down and cure his son, who was at the point of death. Jesus said to him, 'Will none of you ever believe without seeing signs and portents?' The officer pleaded with him, 'Sir, come down before my boy dies.' 'Return home,' said Jesus; 'your son will live.' The man believed what Jesus said and started for home. While he was on his way down his servants met him with the news that his child was going to live. So he asked them at what time he had begun to recover, and they told him, 'It was at one o'clock yesterday afternoon that the fever left him. The father realized that this was the time at which Jesus had said to him, 'Your son will live,' and he and all his household became believers.
This was the second sign which Jesus performed after coming from Judaea into Galilee.

This episode presents the story of a frantic father whose son is near death. In his extremity he turns to Jesus as his last resort. The episode presents two different viewpoints, the father's as almost hopeless, and Jesus' viewpoint of assurance that the boy will live. Jesus' question addressed to the father and others present seems almost angry, and perhaps it is designed to be a "slap in the face" to rouse them all to lift their viewpoints to higher ground.

Jesus does not judge a situation from the human standpoint. He always starts his assessment with the recognition of his Father's sovereignty in the matter, and with the certainty that the difficulty in question must yield to God's power. In spiritual healing one must never lose sight of God's presence, power, and control in the situation. He is so willing to heal!

This healing further illustrates the original theme of this chapter. When Jesus undertakes to heal the boy the innersprings of Life within the boy well up in living energies. Response is immediate.

The chapter closes with "This was the second sign..." of his Christliness that Jesus gives after he leaves those that do not accept him. Can the first sign be the conversion of the Samaritans?

Chapter Five

The Paralysed Man

John 5:1-9   *Some time later, Jesus went up to Jerusalem for one of the Jewish festivals. Now at the Sheep Gate in Jerusalem there is a pool whose Hebrew name is Bethesda.*[1] *It has five colonnades and in them lay a great number of sick people, blind, lame, and paralysed. Among them was a man who had been crippled for thirty-eight years. Jesus saw him lying there, and knowing that he had been ill a long time he asked him, 'Do you want to get well?' 'Sir,' he replied, 'I have no one to put me in the pool when the water is disturbed; while I am getting there, someone else steps into the pool before me.' Jesus answered, 'Stand up, take your bed and walk.' The man recovered instantly; he took up his bed, and began to walk.*

The account of the man who has been crippled for thirty-eight years shows Jesus initiating a healing. Why does he do this? What calls to him from the man's consciousness to rouse his compassion to go to him, rather than wait for him to ask? Is not it the hopelessness of the man's case? Hopelessness is making the man a cripple. He cannot ask because he believes his case is hopeless, and because he believes there is no one willing to help him. All this comes out in his conversation with Jesus. Our Lord reveals his Father's nature in that he comes to the man and does not hold himself aloof until called upon.

What a command, and what loving encouragement penetrates the closed mind and heart of the paralyzed man when he hears the authority of Jesus' voice: "Stand up, take your bed and walk." Instantly he obeys. He rises, takes up his bed and walks — a man free!

John 5:10-15   *That day was a sabbath. So the Jews said to the man who had been cured, 'It is the sabbath. It is against the law for you to carry your bed.' He answered, 'The man who cured me, he told me, "Take up your bed and walk."' They asked him, 'Who is this man who told you to take it up and walk?' But the man who had been cured did not know who it was; for the place was crowded and Jesus had slipped away. A little later Jesus found him in the temple and said to him, 'Now that you are well, give up your sinful ways, or something worse may happen to you.' The man went off and told the Jews that it was Jesus who had cured him.*

Because Jesus slips away into the crowds the man has no opportunity to learn the identity of his liberator until Jesus finds him later to give him some good advice. "Give up your sinful ways, or something worse may happen to you," he says. Jesus equates hopelessness as sin, and indicates that something worse than being crippled for thirty-eight years can befall him if he returns to this way of thinking about himself. Here again we find Jesus emphasizing a correct and spiritual viewpoint. The contrast between the material level and the spiritual level of thought is given repeatedly in John's writings.

John 5:16-18   *It was for doing such things on the sabbath that the Jews began to take action against Jesus. He defended himself by saying, 'My Father continues to work, and I must work too.' This made the Jews all the more determined to kill him, because not only was he breaking the sabbath but, by calling God his own Father, he was claiming equality with God.*

---

[1] "In this century the pool described in John has been discovered and excavated in Jerusalem on the property of the White Fathers near St. Anne's Church. The pool is trapezoidal in form, one hundred sixty-five to two hundred twenty feet wide by three hundred fifteen feet long, divided by a central partition. There are colonnades on the four sides and on the partition — thus, John's "five porticos." Stairways in the corners permit descent into the pools. In this hilly area the water may have come from underground drainage; some of it, perhaps, from intermittent springs." (From *The Anchor Bible*, Volume 29, I-XIII, page 207, by Raymond E. Brown, S.S., Doubleday & Co., Inc.)

Though John has given us only the healing of the paralytic by the pool as an example, he states plainly in verse 16 that "it was for doing such things on the sabbath," that upset the Jews. By this he means not only the Jewish authorities but the people as well.

Jesus defends himself by saying, "My Father continues to work, and I must work too." As the Son of God he considers himself the "extension" of God. He understands himself to be performing the works of his Father. The continuous work of the Father is the unceasing outpouring of His love and, as the Son of such a Father, it is unthinkable to Jesus that the outpouring of His Father's care for His own should ever stop.

His claim to God as his Father is an assault on the Jewish sense of propriety. They worship a God so sacred that they dare not pronounce His name! And here is a man claiming God as Father! This is outrageous and a great evil, a blasphemy, for he is thus claiming equality with God!

John 5:19-20   *To this charge Jesus replied, 'In very truth I tell you, the Son can do nothing by himself; he does only what he sees the Father doing: whatever the Father does, the Son does.'*

Jesus now speaks more profoundly. He expounds the nature of his relationship with his Father. By using the term "Father" we are given all the implications of an inherited likeness to the Father. His cognizance of God as Father includes his perception of the nature and scope of the divine Cause. Jesus means all this when he says the Son "does only what he sees the Father doing."

One of the most remarkable aspects of Jesus' life is his complete obedience to God. His Christ nature is in absolute accord with God, but his humanity, Mary's son (even though God's son, too), sometimes has to wrestle with the feelings and emotions that are natural to men: Witness his temptation in the wilderness (Luke 4:1-13) and his night of agony in the garden of Gethsemane (Matthew 26:36-46). His divine nature tells him, "...it was for this that I came to this hour" (John 12:27). Yet the human emotions that surface have to be overcome. He is human in shrinking before the crucifixion experience. He asks that "this cup" might be taken from him — but adds, "Yet not my will but yours be done" (Luke 22:42).

From this we learn that Jesus looks to his Source for guidance and direction. The attitude of his Father towards creation is always Jesus' attitude or viewpoint of creation. He always looks out from the heights of heaven. He stays there mentally. He does not see heaven above and far off, but surrounding him and his neighbor, and he sees it as a close and beautiful haven of righteousness and assurance and calm, the peace that he leaves with us as a legacy. If we will look out from his spiritual height upon the universe we also will abide in this serenity for we will know that God and His Christ prevail through the Spirit everywhere.

The Divine Capacity

John 5:20   *'For the Father loves the Son and shows him all that he himself is doing, and will show him even greater deeds, to fill you with wonder.'*

Here Jesus tells his antagonists that the power of God touches all life — no aspect is left out — and it is the Father's love that opens this great vista of the divine cosmos to the Son. And greater works, or the wider applications of spiritual power, will also be shown to men and will cause them to wonder — to be roused and stirred!

John 5:21   *'As the Father raises the dead and gives them life, so the Son gives life as he chooses.'*

It is accepted by the Jews that "at the last day of judgment the dead would rise up" — so on the basis of his statement, "whatever the Father does, the Son does," Jesus is saying that in his revelation of his Father to men he duplicates, or reproduces, the God-action in the action of the Son, and thus he also gives life to men as he, as God's ambassador, determines.

John 5:22   *'Again, the Father does not judge anyone, but has given full jurisdiction to the Son;'*...

Accepting the full jurisdiction given him, Jesus acts on his prerogative to judge: i.e., to separate fact from fiction, truth from falsehood. And he does this in the case of the man crippled for thirty-eight years. For example, his Christ power forgives (takes away or separates) from the man's consciousness the sins of helplessness, hopelessness, and self-pity, and with divine authority infuses the man's being with strength that brings the man to his feet. He is no longer helpless; he has Jesus' help and he can help himself. He is no longer hopeless; opportunities never before his stretch before him. Self pity no longer beguiles him. Now he can rejoice in well being.

John 5:23 ...'*it is his will that all should pay the same honour to the Son as to the Father. To deny honour to the Son is to deny it to the Father who sent him.*'

To Jesus his statement is perfectly logical. He knows himself to be the revelator of God, of His nature, character, and power. He knows that those who see him will, in effect, see the Father. Honor, praise, support, acceptance — all these are due to Divinity. If withheld from the Son, they are denied to God as well, for he is the One chosen by God to reveal Himself.

On the other hand, how absolutely appalling this line of reasoning must be to the Jews. He not only makes himself equal to God but also asks for like honor.

Trust, Faith, and Obedience Required

John 5:24 '*In very truth I tell you, whoever heeds what I say and puts his trust in him who sent me has eternal life; he does not come to judgement, but has already passed from death to life.*'

Anyone who listens to me, who grasps what I am saying and determines his thinking and action by it, and who trusts the Father who sends me, thereby acknowledging that I am sent of God — anyone who does this has hold of eternal life, "does not come to judgement, but has already passed from death to life."

So the final judgment day is unnecessary for those who perceive the Son, yield to his teaching, and follow him. Why? Because they have already made the separation from false viewpoints, negative thinking, and self-interests, and are now God-oriented and ready to assimilate in their lives the guidance of Jesus Christ. In so doing they mentally leave a poverty-stricken existence to enter into the abundant life of God's spiritual provision, and through this gift of God they come into newness of being — they are born anew.

John 5:25 '*In very truth I tell you, the time is coming, indeed it is already here, when the dead shall hear the voice of the Son of God, and those who hear shall come to life.*'

This statement can be understood as applying to those mentally "dead" — immersed in self and selfish pursuits; and to those dead for centuries who, because they predecease Jesus, apparently have no opportunity to hear his voice. "All who hear shall come to life" — and he tells how this shall be. The key to these statements is the response of the individual, for man is a free agent; he may choose the way he will go. In all ages the voice of Jesus Christ shall sound loud and clear, and those who not only listen, but who hear (accept) shall live. They shall know God and receive His gift.

John 5:26 '*For as the Father has life in himself, so by his gift the Son also has life in himself.*'

Each statement of Jesus' relationship to the Father emphasizes that there is one begotten by choice of God, disciplined by Him, endowed with divine qualities and attributes through Him, and empowered by Him with the God-prerogatives of Life itself. This "life-giving power in himself" is truly the Father's gift.

John 5:27-29 '*As Son of Man, he has also been given authority to pass judgement. Do not be surprised at this, because the time is coming when all who are in the grave shall hear his voice and come out: those who have done right will rise to life; those who have done wrong will rise to judgement.*'

In this statement Jesus calls himself "Son of Man," though previously (verse 25) he has spoken of himself as "Son of God." Is it not likely that in the statement using Son of God he is referring to his Christ-nature, and when using "Son of Man" he speaks of his incarnate-nature as the son of Mary?

To paraphrase the quotation: not only is his Christ-nature given the power of judgment, but his humanity, because imbued with his Christliness, is also given the right to pass judgement. Do not be surprised or bewildered by this, he says, because the time is coming when all who are in the grave shall hear my voice and come out. (At the time of Jesus' death and resurrection the power that raises him up also lifts up many that are dead and they are seen by the townspeople (Matthew 27:50-53).) "Those who have done right" — those whose thoughts and lives are in accord with Jesus Christ shall have continuing life and will benefit from the outpouring of God's blessing; "those who have done wrong" — those who have not obeyed His will, who have not loved selflessly, who do not follow righteousness and truth, will not know how to respond to our Lord's voice, and shall remain unaware of heaven.

John 5:30   *'I cannot act by myself; I judge as I am bidden, and my sentence is just, because I seek to do not my own will, but the will of him who sent me.'*

The "key" to this whole passage on judgment is voiced here: "I seek not to do my own will, but the will of him who sent me." Jesus speaks now of the sentence, or punishment. Its severity is not decided by him but by his Father. The judgment is made between the tares and wheat, the good and evil; all that do not meet with God's conditions are separated out from God's presence.

Jesus says: 'I cannot act by myself; I judge as I am bidden.'

It is most impressive that our Master illustrates such complete humility, such complete attention to the will of his Father, that he claims neither the desire to originate, or carry through, an idea or action that may not correspond to his Father's will.

My Witness

John 5:31-32   *'If I testify on my own behalf, that testimony is not valid. There is another who bears witness for me, and I know that his testimony about me is valid.'*

Jesus tells us that when he says that he is the Son of God we do not believe him. He looks human, he is human, so how can we accept him as the Son of God? But, he also says there is another who can speak about him.

John the Baptist, the forerunner of Jesus, has come before him.

John 5:33-35   *'You sent messengers to John and he has testified to the truth. Not that I rely on human testimony, but I remind you of it for your own salvation. John was a brightly burning lamp, and for a time you were ready to exult in his light.'*

Jesus does not rely on human testimony, not even John the Baptist's testimony, though he calls him a lamp burning brightly. Jesus reminds them that for a time they were ready to exult because they thought they had found the Messiah — but rather they find John the Baptist pointing to him, Jesus.

John 5:36-37   *'But I rely on a testimony higher than John's: the work my Father has given me to do and to finish, the very work I have in hand, testifies that the Father has sent me. And the Father who has sent me has borne witness on my behalf. His voice you have never heard, his form you have never seen;'...*

The "signs following,' the proofs of divine power active in the lives of men, this is the God-provided witness testifying to the Christ nature of Jesus. This is a testimony higher than John's. No argument to the contrary could have convinced the man who says, "...I was blind and now I can see" (John 9:25).

In speaking of his Father's testimony concerning him, "His voice you have never heard, his form you have never seen," Jesus could have been speaking of the Voice from heaven at his baptism or on the mount of Transfiguration. This Voice declares each time "This is my Son in whom I am pleased — hear him" Two of his disciples hear this Voice, but this Voice also speaks to Jesus. It is a confirmation from his Father assuring his human selfhood, the Son of Man, of their perfect and permanent relationship. The Holy Spirit as well as the Christ of God are inseparably within him. This measureless power that is the essence of his being brings about the awakening of each individual that his Christliness touches, and heals them.

In our own lives we should eagerly look for signs of the Christ-presence and the power of Jesus Christ acting for us and in us. Healings, changes in character that show the redemptive power of God, deliverance from evil and danger — all these and more speak to us as God-given proofs of divine power active in our lives.

John 5:38-40 *'...his word has found no home in you, because you do not believe the one whom he sent. You study the scriptures diligently, supposing that in having them you have eternal life; their testimony points to me, yet you refuse to come to me to receive that life.'*

As Jesus continues to defend himself before the Jews he reaches, in the above statement, the very crux of the matter.

The Jews have not accepted him, have not received the teaching as he presents it to them, because they do not believe that Jesus is sent by God. They study the scriptures to find eternal life, then do not follow them when they point to Jesus.

The faithful Jews are inconsistent in their study, for at the time of Jesus the practices of a man in carrying out his religious worship is so important that the evidence of divine power in their midst is scarcely noticed. They are completely preoccupied.

Accredited by God

John 5:41-42 *'I do not look to men for honour. But I know that with you it is different, for you have no love of God in you. I have come accredited by my Father, and you have no welcome for me;...'*

"Accredited" means furnished with credentials; vouched for; standing in the stead of.

God provides at the birth of our Savior herald angels and a magnificent star illuming the darkness, with a message for wise men. This is one of his credentials.

Thus Jesus comes, authoritatively sanctioned to stand in the stead of his Father as an ambassador — and they have no welcome for him. He comes vouched for by John the Baptist. This mighty "voice in the wilderness" beholds the Christ in preexistence as well as in the present, and sees Jesus Christ to be Lord, the Son of God. Though John the Baptist himself has many followers he knows that his place is as a witness to the Light, he himself is not the Light. When he sees Jesus he suddenly knows, "This is God's chosen One." At Jesus' baptism (purification before entering his priesthood) John sees the Holy Spirit descending and resting on Jesus, and hears a voice from heaven saying, "This is my beloved, my Chosen One. Hear him!" This, as well as the mighty works, is his Father's accreditation.

John 5:43-44 *'...but let someone self-accredited come, and you will give him a welcome. How can you believe when you accept honour from one another, and care nothing for the honour that comes from him who alone is God?'*

Jesus tries patiently to lead the rabbis to his viewpoint — but their teaching is so firmly planted that an "improvement" to their way of thinking seems illogical and sacrilegious. Their personal intellectualism hides from their view the significance of self-relinquishment. To them, to yield themselves to God will be to lose their identity. Yet for all their diligence and obedience in observing outwardly the Word of God, they cannot bring themselves to come to Him inwardly, or fully accept him as part of their present experience. God to them is the God of their Fathers and they worship Him in the manner of former generations.

John 5:45-47 *'Do not imagine that I shall be your accuser at the Father's tribunal. Your accuser is Moses, the very Moses on whom you have set your hope. If you believed him you would believe me, for it was of me that he wrote.[2] But if you do not believe what he wrote, how are you to believe what I say?'*

Moses, in faith, accepts from God the ideas of discipline that guide the Israelites. When his death nears he is inspired to record God's words to him: "Now write down this song and teach it to the Israelites; make them repeat it, so that it may be a witness for me against them. When I have brought them into the land which I swore to give their forefathers, a land flowing with milk and honey, and they have plenty to eat and are thriving, then they will turn to other gods and serve them, spurning me and breaking my covenant; and many terrible disasters will follow. Then this song will confront them as a witness, for it will not be forgotten by their descendants." (Deuteronomy 31:19-22).

---

[2] Moses writes: "Then the Lord said to me, ...'I shall raise up for them a prophet like you, one of their own people, and I shall put my words into his mouth.' " (Deuteronomy 18:17-18).

It is true that not Jesus, but Moses, will be their accuser at the Father's tribunal. In their case, they will be convicted by their own conscience.

Jesus meets many with closed minds. These are people self-assured and righteous in their own sight. They are sincere and pious, devoted to their concept of God, yet their thought is closed to the possibility that God can come to be with them. Matthew writes: "...the Lord declared through the prophet: 'A virgin will conceive and bear a son, and he shall be called Emmanuel, a name which means 'God is with us' " (Matthew 1:23).

Chapter Six

Feeding the Five Thousand

John 6:1-2 *Some time later Jesus withdrew to the farther shore of the Sea of Galilee (or Tiberias), and a large crowd of people followed him because they had seen the signs he performed in healing the sick.*

By now Jesus has become well known. Large crowds flock to see his works and follow after him as he journeys, for they have witnessed him healing the sick.

One can imagine the hope Jesus offers to this nation sorely oppressed by a foreign conqueror. Appearing on the scene among a people with a tradition of a coming Messiah — a people who live in such severe times that it causes them to cry to God for a deliverer — there comes a man who claims to be sent of God, and who does mighty works in support of this claim. He causes great waves of hope and consternation. To the Romans he is a disrupter of the peace. He stirs up the people and makes the policing of the country more difficult. To the oppressed he is seen as a possible soldier-king, one who can gather their forces and overthrow their enemy. Many have for years pinned their hopes on magicians whose "works" have falsely led them to believe that perhaps "here was the Messiah"; so by now suspicion is rife — but trust is eager. Of the vast number who turn in Jesus' direction, how many truly perceive his greatness as the Christ? Even some of the chosen twelve are preoccupied with thoughts of a political deliverer.

John 6:3-4 *Jesus went up the hillside and sat down with his disciples. It was near the time of Passover, the great Jewish festival.*

We find Jesus and his followers on a hill, resting amid the beauty of a lush rolling landscape, for it is spring. Maybe he fingers a blade of grass as they sit silently contemplating the view. As it is near Pass-over, in coming to this quiet spot Jesus seeks an interlude of rest and a time for privately instructing his closer students.

John 6:5-6 *Looking up and seeing a large crowd coming towards him, Jesus said to Philip, 'Where are we to buy bread to feed these people?' He said this to test him; Jesus himself knew what he meant to do.*

The great crowd comes. In a way they are uninvited and unexpected, yet as a perfect host Jesus assumes the responsibility of feeding them.

At this point John reveals another aspect of Jesus' teaching method — the test. This question would not have been asked as a test had it not been discussed previously. But learning something as theory can be easier than the application of that theory practically. Jesus is well aware that his students need practice in what he is teaching them, for the evidence of the problem before them can be overwhelming at times.

John 6:7 *Philip replied, 'We would need two hundred denarii to buy enough bread for each of them to have a little.'*

Dismayed by the sight, all Philip sees is a huge assembly, not enough money, no nearby stores, and no food for them. Philip sees the problem but does not see the answer.

John 6:8-9 *One of his disciples, Andrew, the brother of Simon Peter, said to him, 'There is a boy here who has five barley loaves and two fish; but what is that among so many?'*

Andrew, Peter's brother, tries to answer the test by offering the provisions of a boy who is with them. Has this boy plucked at Andrew's sleeve and asked him to offer Jesus his barley loaves and fish? It is perhaps significant that a boy comes forward offering food. Can he have been a rapt listener on the fringe of the group of disciples? He is young enough so that the disbelief that adults feel has not yet become real to him — with youth all things are possible, and his eager thought may have responded to Jesus' question to Philip.

Five barley loaves and two fish — here is something; but Andrew's faith and understanding fail as he lamely adds, "...what is that among so many?"

This particular test is difficult, but the disciples are being guided by their Teacher along new paths of thought. At the wedding feast in Cana the water is turned into wine. Step by step Jesus is opening the thoughts of his students to the actuality of God's constant provision for His creation through divine power. Jesus is very familiar with the scriptures. No doubt he points out to them that God's love for Israel is a history of His continuous provision for them.

Surely Andrew and Philip must know the account of Elijah and the widow of Zarephath (1 Kings 17:8-16). In that instance God extends the meal and oil so that the prophet Elijah, the widow, and her son may eat and live in a time of famine.

And do these students on a hillside remember how the Lord fed their ancestors for forty years, giving them quail in the evening and manna in the morning to sustain them? (Exodus 17:7). Even after all this providence they challenge Moses, "Is the Lord in our midst or not?" When they come to the land of Canaan and need water, Moses, at the Lord's instruction, strikes a stone and out gushes water. This question of monumental importance "Is the Lord in our midst or not?" is thus answered by Moses.

In every instance provision is made because the Lord is in the midst of His people.

John 6:10-11 *Jesus said, 'Make the people sit down.' There was plenty of grass there, so the men sat down, about five thousand of them. Then Jesus took the loaves, gave thanks, and distributed them to the people as they sat there. He did the same with the fish, and they had as much as they wanted.*

With a mind free of despair and worry Jesus gives thanks to his Father for he expects Him to adequately feed and bless those who have sought Him. Jesus' spiritual logic recognizes that God can increase, to the point of amplitude, even the smallest evidence of substance. In Hebrews 11:1, we read, "Faith gives substance to our hopes and convinces us of realities we do not see."

It is Jesus' rejoicing in his acknowledgment that brings into operation this beneficent law and its fulfillment. The love of God that Jesus so adequately expresses to all becomes a benediction of provision for each one as the seemingly meager supplies are shared. Jesus is teaching his disciples to expect to find his Father's help at hand always "All things come of Thee, Oh Lord, and of Thine own have we given Thee" (Anonymous).

John 6:12-13 *When everyone had had enough, he said to his disciples, 'Gather up the pieces left over, so that nothing is wasted.' They gathered them up, and filled twelve baskets with the pieces of the barley loaves that were left uneaten.*

The bread consecrated by Jesus Christ is increased to feed and sustain those who seek him. It prefigures that holy bread of the last supper. There is no waste in the kingdom of God. Thrift is a characteristic of His household. Like talents, the gifts of God should never be carelessly treated or wasted.

John 6:14-15 *When the people saw the sign Jesus had performed, the word went round, 'Surely this must be the Prophet who was to come into the world.' Jesus, realizing that they meant to come and seize him to proclaim him king, withdrew again to the hills by himself.*

In the great surge of amazement that follows this incredible work of feeding five thousand, the prophecy of Moses comes to the mind of the people. Murmurs of recognition, "Here is the man we have waited for!" ripple through the crowd. Becoming aware of this danger Jesus seeks safety in the nearby hills.

The hills Jesus seek are not only a sanctuary for security, but a spiritual height for his refreshment. His human selfhood is in as great a need of sustenance as the hungering crowd. He needs quiet moments in which to open his consciousness to the outpouring love of his Father; a time to drink in the awareness of the universal harmony of being as created in the beginning; an opportunity to hear the angels sing, and to quietly know his oneness with his Father. He needs to renew his awareness of the power of the Holy Spirit with him.

Jesus Comes to His Disciples

John 6:16-21 *At nightfall his disciples went down to the sea, and set off by boat to cross to Capernaum. Though darkness had fallen, Jesus had not yet joined them; a strong wind was blowing and the sea grew rough. When they had rowed about three or four miles they saw Jesus walking on the sea and approaching the boat. They were terrified, but he called out, 'It is I; do not be afraid.' With that they were ready to take him on board, and immediately the boat reached the land they were making for.*

Apparently the disciples are very surprised to see Jesus walking on the water to come to them. Even though they are away from the land, and we are not told how far away, they apparently are expecting him. Perhaps they have a planned meeting point along the shoreline. Then suddenly, though the water is rough because of the strong wind, he approaches the boat walking on the water. Thinking it must be an apparition they are seized with terror. Obviously these disciples are not supermen!

Jesus wants to join his disciples. The natural way to get there is to go directly to them. The fact that he has no boat does not thwart him. To one who has dominion as the Christ of God the water is there to obey him, not to hinder him. In this episode we have the evidence of his dominion in that he takes his body where he wants to go; he does not let his body or his surroundings dictate where he can go or cannot go. Jesus "walks" on the waves because through his spiritual knowledge he knows that divine law, controlling physical laws, has the power to support him.

Jesus moves at a level of thought superior to the rest of humanity. That is why he can uplift those willing to share his viewpoint.

Paul writes in Galatians 4:3-5, ..."During our minority we were slaves, subject to the elemental spirits of the universe, but when the appointed time came, God sent his Son, born of a woman, born under

the law, to buy freedom for those who were under the law, in order that we might obtain the status of sons."

Jesus is divinely authorized under the seal of his Father's approval to utilize spiritual power, and to live under the protection of divine law.

Instead of "walking" in the disciples' world, Jesus invokes the laws of Spirit's realm which supersede material law, and these spiritual forces surround him. He literally moves in Spirit.

When the boat is "immediately...[at]...the land," it is because his thought (so aware of the omnipotence of Spirit) embraces the disciples, the boat, and their destination in his realization and application of divine law. The omnipresence of Spirit makes him present with his destination even at the beginning or middle of his journey.

The feeding of thousands illustrates God's provision through God's grace, available through Christ-imparted spiritual understanding. The walk on the water, and the bringing of the boat to land immediately, illustrate divine law superseding every limitation or obstruction that finite law can impose. Jesus trusts his Christ to preserve him from drowning; his continued trust later brings his body through crucifixion and entombment to glorious resurrection.

The People Question Jesus

John 6:22-25 *Next morning the crowd was still on the opposite shore. They had seen only one boat there, and Jesus, they knew, had not embarked with his disciples, who had set off by themselves. Boats from Tiberias, however, had come ashore near the place where the people had eaten the bread over which the Lord gave thanks. When the crowd saw that Jesus had gone as well as his disciples, they went on board these boats and made for Capernaum in search of him. They found him on the other side.*

One can almost see the people standing on the shore, staring across the sea, bewildered as to the form of transportation their benefactor has taken. Determined to find him again, they themselves embark.

John 6:25-27 *'Rabbi,' they asked, 'when did you come here?' Jesus replied, 'In very truth I tell you, it is not because you saw signs that you came looking for me, but because you ate the bread and your hunger was satisfied. You should work, not for this perishable food, but for the food that lasts, the food of eternal life.'*

The spokesman for the crowd reflects their puzzled sense concerning Jesus' method of travel across the sea, and questions him. Instead, Jesus goes right to the heart of the matter and deals with their motives. They follow him because he has fed them. Their human needs have been met — their hunger has been satisfied. They do not follow because they discern the "signs" of his divine origin. Telling them to lift their thoughts to higher, more spiritual considerations, he advises them to "work, not for this perishable food but for the bread that lasts, the food of eternal life."

John 6:27-29 *'This food the Son of Man will give you, for on him God the Father has set the seal of his authority.' 'Then what must we do,' they asked him, 'if our work is to be the work of God?' Jesus replied, 'This is the work that God requires: to believe in the one whom he has sent.'*

Historically, in the Bible, "...as a conveyance of power, the use of a royal seal is attested from ca 850 B.C."[1] The seal, when stamped upon an article, or description of an article, indicates ownership. Jesus belongs to God; all that God requires of him he will do. He has accepted this relationship and this undertaking.

So Jesus, claiming the "seal" of his Father, is in fact saying that "God the Father has conveyed His power to me, the Son of Man, in order that I might teach you the Way of Life." His use of the term "Son of Man" calls attention to the fact that his humanity (Mary's Son) is thus divinely endowed "with the Spirit without measure" which is the Father's seal.

The people then eagerly ask what is required of them, and are told that this involves believing in the one whom God has sent. To believe in him means they must give him full credence, trust the verity of his words, and rely on him with full dependence as one sent from God. This is a big order, for to them his words are controversial.

The Bread of Life

John 6:30 *They asked, 'What sign can you give us, so that we may see it and believe you? What is the work you are doing?'*

At once they have second thoughts; perhaps they should proceed more cautiously!

John 6:31 *'Our ancestors had manna to eat in the desert; as scripture says, "He gave them bread from heaven to eat." '*

The crowd desires another definition of his work; they would like a sign such as Moses gives when he feeds them for forty years in the wilderness. That would be very nice!

John 6:32-34 *Jesus answered, 'In very truth I tell you, it was not Moses who gave you the bread from heaven; it is my Father who gives you the true bread from heaven. The bread that God gives comes down from heaven and brings life to the world.' 'Sir,' they said to him, 'give us this bread now and always.'*

First Jesus corrects their misapprehensions. He lifts their thoughts from stomachs effortlessly filled, to consider a type of bread that God sends from heaven that gives life to the world. The Rabbis teach that bread is a symbol of the Torah, and no doubt Jesus' audience is familiar with this fact, though at this point it is unlikely they even remotely grasp the implications of what Jesus is saying. Again he is faced with the stupendous task of defining spiritual things with words designed to name the things of earth. In response to their insistent demand "give us this bread now and always!" he wisely gives them a taste.

---

[1] *Interpreter's Dictionary of the Bible*, under "Seal," page 255, Number 1, "Delegation of Authority", Abingdon Press.

John 6:35-37 *Jesus said to them, 'I am the bread of life. Whoever comes to me will never be hungry, and whoever believes in me will never be thirsty. But you, as I said, have seen and yet you do not believe. All that the Father gives me will come to me, and anyone who comes to me I will never turn away.'*

Jesus can not have stated his position more plainly: "I am the bread of Life." All he stands for, all he represents, his standpoint and doctrine, his love and compassion, his strength and nobility — all this and much more, as the revelator of God to humans, makes him the very bread that sustains life.

Now he rebukes their preoccupation with food and points to a bread that completely satisfies — a spiritual impartation from God that will satisfy their spiritual and physical hunger. "Whoever comes to me..."; they must come to him, accept him, acknowledge him as the Son of God, conform to his teaching, and, through faith, let his life become their life.

Saul, later called Paul, illustrates this. Though at first he misinterprets God's instructions to him, the foundation of his character in its zeal to do the Lord's will, makes it ripe for harvest. His vision of Jesus when on the road to Damascus becomes the turning point of his life. From that moment on he eats the bread of life. Those ready for the Christ blessing hear the Father call and are attracted to Him; Jesus then becomes their Teacher and the yielding of the human to the divine has begun.

John 6:38 *'I have come down from heaven, to do not my own will, but the will of him who sent me.'*

Even the Son of God has the right to follow his own will, nevertheless his life becomes an illustration of supreme obedience. If it were not essential that our lives follow Jesus' example in every way John would not make this vital point. It is basic to all Jesus' teaching that we be strictly obedient. John includes in his presentation of his Master's years as a Teacher only those words and sayings that will elucidate the divine message.

Jesus is totally committed to carrying out the will of his Father. Being a man of free will he chooses to give his "will" to the service of God. To the degree of our discernment, can we do less?

John 6:39-40 *'It is his will that I should not lose even one of those he has given me, but should raise them all up on the last day. For it is my Father's will that everyone who sees the Son and has faith in him should have eternal life; and I will raise them up on the last day.'*

Jesus speaks of the Father's will three times:

1. He is here to do the will of his Father.

2. The Father's will governs the outcome of his work: that he shall not lose even one.

3. It is the Father's will that those who look (with perception) on the Son will have eternal life: i.e. the outcome of spiritually understanding the Son will be the reward of constant provision and immortality.

God's unqualified control of the results of obedience to Him are clearly stated. Jesus Christ confidently goes forward to carry out his mission knowing the desired result will be inevitable. God wills that he lose not one whom He has brought to Jesus. In the human maturing process, in which the transformation from the mortal to spiritual being takes place, the slowness or rapidity of the individual process depends on the seeker's willingness to yield to the Christ-Ego. We cling to self-determination (self-will) in the misunderstanding that it constitutes identity; whereas the identity of each one is only found when the ego becomes obedient to the Father. Identity is then found in each one's unique expression of his divine Source.

Jesus says he will raise up all at the last day. This day of judgment, this last day will be for each one the last day of transformation. Far from being a black day, it will be one of light and of truly entering into the love of our Lord.

John 6:41-45 *At this the Jews began to grumble because he said, 'I am the bread which came down from heaven.' They said, 'Surely this is Jesus, Joseph's son! We know his father and mother. How can he say, "I have come down from heaven"?' 'Stop complaining among yourselves,' Jesus told them. 'No one can come to me unless he is drawn by the Father* *who sent me; and I will raise him up on the last day. It is written in the prophets: "They will all be taught by God." Everyone who has listened to the Father and learned from him comes to me.'*

It is a human trait to belittle someone we know well when we see him rise to greatness. If he is a sports figure or a political candidate we accept him more readily, even extending adulation to other members of his family. But when a neighbor presumes to speak the Word of God we look upon him with a knowing smile, perhaps some toleration, and occasionally some admiration. But here, Jesus is telling his neighbors that he is the Son of God and that he comes down from heaven. No wonder they murmur! To them he is the son of Joseph. They know his father and mother and have watched him grow up from a small boy into manhood. So how can he make this assertion? It sounds ridiculous.

Jesus knows how it sounds to them. Patiently he reiterates the facts concerning his purpose and mission. He offers salvation through a new teaching. Each one whom the Father sends to him shall receive this new viewpoint, and when receiving it shall know he is taught by God.

Raymond Brown writes of this passage:[2] "If the Jews will desist from their murmuring, which is indicative of a refusal to believe, and will leave themselves open to God's movement He will draw them to Jesus."

John 6:46   *'I do not mean that anyone has seen the Father; he who has come from God has seen the Father, and he alone.'*

Coming from God, as the Son of God, he grows to full comprehension of the Holy Spirit; thus the scope of the Infinite is clear to him. God is not perceptible in the usual sense of looking at something and seeing it. To see God as Christ knows Him involves more than physical sense can include. Our eyes see dimensionally, and we comprehend in that manner. The Son, who has come from God, perceives spiritually and infinitely. He, and he alone, has seen the Father.

John 6:47-50   *'In very truth I tell you, whoever believes has eternal life. I am the bread of life. Your ancestors ate manna in the wilderness, yet they are dead. I am speaking of the bread that comes down from heaven; whoever eats it will never die.'*

This is a very strong statement. Here great emphasis is given to what has already been said: "Whoever believes has eternal life."

Jesus is requiring more than just approval. He demands a faith that is conviction.

My Flesh and Blood

John 6:51   *'I am the living bread that has come down from heaven; if anyone eats this bread, he will live for ever. The bread which I shall give is my own flesh, given for the life of the world.'*

Jesus tells us that believing through comprehending him gives us eternal life — now. Eating manna, though it comes from God, does not preserve life. Very forcefully he speaks of bread from heaven as different from manna or loaves of barley. The bread he speaks of has power to give immortality! Then he comes to the point: "The bread which I shall give is my own flesh, given for the life of the world."

In giving his own flesh as a sacrifice in purity and faith Jesus wins eternal salvation for those who accept him. However, he also gives himself, his life, as a supreme example of living — of right attitudes and divinely motivated actions. His human life is lived for our sake just as he dies for our sake. His supreme sacrifice of dying cannot be divorced from the daily and hourly example of living that Jesus gives us.

John 6:52-55   *This led to a fierce dispute among the Jews. 'How can this man give us his flesh to eat?' they protested. Jesus answered them, 'In very truth I tell you, unless you eat the flesh of the Son of Man and drink his blood you can have no life in you. Whoever eats my flesh and drinks my blood has eternal life, and I will raise him up on the last day. My flesh is real food; my blood is real drink.'*

---

[2] Raymond Brown, S. S., *The Anchor Bible*, Volume 29, page 277, Doubleday & Co., Inc.

He asks his followers to eat his flesh and drink his blood. The bones, sinews, flesh, and blood which constitute his human body exist for one purpose: To convey the Christ message in an acceptable form as the man, Jesus. What Jesus does and what he says and thinks, come from the Christliness that makes him the Son of God. But here in this passage we are asked to eat the flesh and blood of the Son of Man, of Mary's son, Jesus. Therefore, we see that as we partake of his thoughts and actions, and act or live our lives upon his foundation, we indeed eat that which "fleshed" his human identity. His life blood is the surging power of God's love flowing out to others. To eat his thoughts (teachings) is to make them our own. To drink his blood is to feel the inspiration of love and the power of God motivating life. This certainly is real food and real drink — all satisfying.

John 6:56-58 *'Whoever eats my flesh and drinks my blood dwells in me and I in him. As the living Father sent me, and I live because of the Father, so whoever eats me will live because of me. This is the bread which came down from heaven; it is not like the bread which our fathers ate; they are dead, but whoever eats this bread will live for ever.'*

Rising to a more spiritual level of thought in our communion with God we do find ourselves, as we partake of the sacred bread, dwelling continually in Him. Jesus Christ is in constant communion with his Father and lives because of this oneness; so he who eats, accepts, and yields to Spirit shall live because of Jesus Christ. This is our food, our sustenance that comes to us right from heaven. It is not a "manna" designed solely to meet physical hunger, but it can be the means of assuaging human hunger and need of every kind. This bread feeds and perpetuates man as the love of God infuses and confers immortality.

John 6:59-60 *Jesus said these things in the synagogue as he taught in Capernaum. On hearing them, many of his disciples exclaimed, 'This is more than we can stand! How can anyone listen to such talk?'*

At this moment the frustration and agony of Jesus' position becomes acute. His followers have been with him, even crowding close to hear his words. There is a feeling that they approve of his work. Then, because of his choice of words — "Eat my flesh...drink my blood" — he is suddenly bereft. The crowd leaves. Barley loaves and fish are just fine, but flesh and blood? Rabbinnical law forbids consuming blood for it is judged to be life, and now, contrary to all they have ever heard, they are told not only to drink blood, but to drink his blood! Thinking members of the group must realize that Jesus is not promoting cannibalism, but has chosen these terms symbolically. However, the sacrifice of self interest is as abhorrent to these men as the thought of cannibalism. They have had enough!

It is not just Jesus' terminology that shocks his hearers. It is more. It is the underlying necessity to give up self-determination for molding by God in His likeness that brings to the surface the resistance to the Christ power.

Bishop Temple writes: "To 'eat the flesh' and to 'drink the blood' of the Son of Man are not the same. The former is to receive the power of self-giving and self-sacrifice to the uttermost. The latter is to receive, in and through that self-giving and self-sacrifice, the life that is triumphant over death and united to God."[3]

John 6:61-65 *Jesus was aware that his disciples were grumbling about it and asked them, 'Does this shock you? Then what if you see the Son of Man ascending to where he was before? It is the spirit that gives life; the flesh can achieve nothing; the words I have spoken to you are both spirit and life. Yet there are some of you who have no faith.' For Jesus knew from the outset who were without faith and who was to betray him. So he said, 'This is why I told you that no one can come to me unless it has been granted to him by the Father.'*

Is Jesus saying to his disgusted disciples, "What if I go back to where I came from? What if I leave you? The Spirit alone gives life, and flesh will not help you;

[3] William Temple, *Readings in St. John's Gospel*, page 95, Morehouse Publishing.

but the meaning of the words which I have spoken to you are both Spirit and Life. And yet some of you have neither the confidence nor conviction of this fact!"

Some of the disciples are unwilling at this time to lay their all on God's altar. They are unwilling to eat the sacred bread he provides; are unwilling to digest the import and grasp the significance of his words. In the giving of our all, insofar as we are able to do so, in communion and in living we follow the sacrificial steps of our Lord Jesus. Judas and some others are apparently not yet able to take this step forward. The requirement is that men listen to the Father and learn from Him. Then they will be able to come to Jesus' way of thinking and reasoning.

The Holy One of God

John 6:66   *From that moment many of his disciples drew back and no longer went about with him. So Jesus asked the Twelve, 'Do you also want to leave?' Simon Peter answered him, 'Lord, to whom shall we go? Your words are words of eternal life. We believe and know that you are God's Holy One.'*

Even though Jesus' intuitive knowledge is aware of the faithlessness of many, because he is human, just as we are, he must feel a heaviness of heart at suddenly finding himself with few disciples. Many have probably been healed by him, or some loved one may have been healed, and they have joined his followers. Now they are gone. "Do you also want to leave me?" is his plaintive question to the Twelve. Peter's perception saves the hour with his forthright reply! "Lord, to whom shall we go? Your words are words of eternal life. We believe and know that you are God's Holy One."

What warmth of love is conveyed in Peter's spontaneous reply. His words must have touched Jesus as a beautiful benediction.

John 6:70-71   *Jesus answered, 'Have I not chosen the twelve of you? Yet one of you is a devil.' He meant Judas son of Simon Iscariot. It was he who would betray him, and he was one of the Twelve.*

What a bond there is between Jesus and the Twelve, for he does not say Eleven, leaving out Judas! Even though he knows there is one who will fulfill the prophecy of betrayal, there is the wonderful acknowledgment "I have chosen you." Of all in the world, he has chosen them. His love radiates and enfolds each one.

Chapter Seven

The Great Controversy

John 7:1   *After that Jesus travelled around within Galilee; he decided to avoid Judaea because the Jews were looking for a chance to kill him.*

By staying in Galilee Jesus probably remains beyond the jurisdiction of the Jewish authorities in Jerusalem. These men fear his popularity and consider him subversive. It is most likely, too, that Rome adds fuel to the fire. Let the Jews do the dirty work for Rome! The situation has become extreme. Certain men in power, the "Jews," want to kill Jesus.

John 7:2-6   *But when the Jewish feast of Tabernacles was close at hand, his brothers said to him, 'You should leave here and go into Judaea, so that your disciples may see the great things you are doing. No one can hope for recognition if he works in obscurity. If you can really do such things as these, show yourself to the world.' For even his brothers had no faith in him. Jesus answered: 'The right time for me has not yet come, but any time is right for you.'*

This is the rare instance in the New Testament where we find an account of Jesus' conversation with his brothers. Their remarks have a sarcastic feeling as they speak of the "great things" Jesus is doing. They have not awakened to the significance of his life or work. The familiar closeness of their lives must have blinded their eyes. He is their brother, they are one family, so they look no farther.

Explaining his position to them, Jesus says, "The right time for me has not yet come, but any time is right for you." These words are fraught with meaning.

Raymond E. Brown writes:[1] "The answer that Jesus gives his brothers in verses 6-10 is a classic instance of the two levels of meaning found in John. On the purely natural level it appears to the brothers that Jesus does not find this an opportune time to go... Jesus' subsequent behavior in going up to the festival shows us, however, that this was not really what he meant... When Jesus speaks of his 'time' he is speaking on the level of the divine plan. His 'hour,' the hour of passion, death, resurrection and ascension to the Father; and the 'time' is not to come at the festival of Tabernacles... The two levels of meaning were recognized by early commentators."

The fact that "any time" is right for his brothers reveals that Jesus recognizes that he moves in a way unique to him and dependent on the plan of his Father. His every move holds significance for eternity. Their lives move within their human span. It is the very timelessness (see John 6:21) of Jesus' life and action that brings the boat carrying himself and his disciples immediately to shore. As the eternal Christ of God he includes beginning and ending; therefore he can trust the divine Spirit to ensure the success of the work the Father has given him to do. This sphere of timelessness is a spiritually mental or metaphysical (beyond the physical) realm, available to Jesus and to those who "eat his flesh and drink his blood" in its full measure.

John 7:7-10   *'The world cannot hate you; but it hates me for exposing the wickedness of its ways. Go up to the festival yourselves. I am not going to this festival, because the right time for me has not yet come.' So saying he stayed behind in Galilee.*
Later, when his brothers had gone to the festival, he went up too, not openly, but in secret.

Jesus must have been very aware of the world's hatred. During this period he maintains such a "low

---

[1] Raymond E. Brown, S. S., *The Anchor Bible*, Volume 29, page 308, Doubleday & Co., Inc.

profile" that even his unbelieving brothers chide him. They do not feel the oppressive opposition sensed by their brother, Jesus. Nothing they have ever done has stirred their fellowmen, but he has exposed the worldliness and wickedness of men, their meanness and smallness, and his rebuke to these types stirs them all! They begin to lash back at their tormentor.

Knowing full well through his spiritual vision the tremendous ordeal and the demands that will be made upon him in the coming months Jesus is probably using this time at home for long periods of communion with his Father.

Later he goes to the festival, "almost in secret." There is danger, to be sure, but all the hosts of heaven are guarding his holy purpose. Going "in secret" may well mean that he wishes to be alone — alone to tread his own path.

Raymond E. Brown writes:[2] "We say only that John's picture wherein Jesus remains a long period in the Jerusalem area between Tabernacles and the following Passover may well be more accurate than the crowded Synoptic picture where he seems to arrive in Jerusalem a few days before his death. Much of the material, particularly by way of accusation and trial, that the Synoptics pack into those final days is found in John in the chapters that cover the period from Tabernacles to Passover."

Jesus Teaches at the Festival

John 7:11-13   *At the festival the Jews were looking for him and asking where he was, and there was much murmuring about him in the crowds. 'He is a good man,' said some. 'No,' said others, 'he is leading the people astray.' No one talked freely about him, however, for fear of the Jews.*

Here John gives us a sampling of the attitudes towards Jesus. Like a pollster we can read the signs of the times. Trouble is brewing. Even a brave man need not be foolhardy.

These are the very types Jesus would address. What they are thinking is typical of men in all ages,

and what Jesus teaches is designed to accost their thinking and force it into new channels.

John 7:14-18   *When the festival was already half over, Jesus went up to the temple and began to teach. The Jews were astonished: 'How is it,' they said, 'that this untrained man has such learning?' Jesus replied, 'My teaching is not my own but his who sent me. Whoever chooses to do the will of God will know whether my teaching comes from him or is merely my own. Anyone whose teaching is merely his own seeks his own glory; but if anyone seeks the glory of him who sent him, he is sincere and there is nothing false in him.*

Picture yourself in the crowded temple at the festival. Suddenly Jesus appears to teach. All listen. Those who believe him a good man wish to hear his words. Those who hate, listen in order to throw his words back at him. But his learning impresses everyone. Which rabbi was his teacher?

Raymond E. Brown writes:[3] "A knowledge of how to read and write was centered about knowledge of the Scriptures, for this is what the children were trained to read. However, this is more than a question of Jesus' literacy; it is a question about his teaching. Before a man became a rabbi, he normally studied diligently under another rabbi; much of the rabbinical learning consisted of knowing the opinions of famous teachers of the past. Yet Jesus had not undergone any such training."

Jesus humbly tells those who question his teaching source, "It is the teaching of Him who sent me." Anyone who has listened intuitively and prayerfully for instruction by the Spirit will understand the way in which Jesus receives his education. Far from being haphazard or unclear, his understanding comes to him with precision, exactness, and clarity. This great illumination of "instant knowledge" of scripture, coupled with divinely revealed interpretation, again shows the unity of Christ, the wholly divine, and the human Jesus. "Whoever chooses to do the will of God will know whether my teaching comes from him or is merely my own." The profundity of Jesus'

---

[2] Raymond E. Brown, S. S., *The Anchor Bible*, Volume 29, page 309, Doubleday & Co., Inc.
[3] Raymond E. Brown, S. S., *The Anchor Bible*, Volume 29, page 312, Doubleday & Co., Inc.

teaching precludes the possibility of human invention. He speaks the very words of God, his Father.

When our will seeks to do the will of God it requires self-discipline and self-sacrifice. Thus we reach the threshold of life and thereafter enter into the vast immensity of spiritual experience.

In the above quotation Jesus says, "Anyone whose teaching is merely his own, seeks his own glory." In this statement Jesus is speaking on the level of humanity and about human accomplishment. Then, focusing on the spiritual level he states: "But if anyone seeks the glory of him who sent him, he is sincere and there is nothing false in him." Here he pictures man reaching beyond himself in order to honor "Him who sent him."

In the brief passages given in the Seventh Chapter of the Gospel, John has done a masterful work in presenting us with a clear picture of the controversial atmosphere in which Jesus is involved. He has, by this time, antagonized many in authority. John speaks of them as "the Jews"; however, in this chapter in verse 45 "the temple police, ...the chief priests and Pharisees" are enumerated. Even among the priests at this time, high positions can be purchased. The Roman grasp is tight and many buy and sell to better themselves. Jesus and most of his hearers are Jews, so the "Jews" of whom John speaks appear to be a group of men anxious to preserve their own power during the Roman occupation. It is also true that, to the pious Jew, Jesus is breaking all the rules, and he also appears to be inciting others to follow his example. To Jesus, narrow ritualistic worship has robbed the faith of Abraham of its vitality. He knows that those who violate this narrow practice will be put to death. But beyond human death he can see resurrection and the glorification of the Son of Man. Then will follow the ultimate triumph of righteousness in the minds of men. Until his mission is accomplished he knows the "angels of His presence" will protect him.

None of the New Testament writers tell of every healing, wise saying, or marvelous work done by the Master during his stay on earth. John chooses certain of these events to portray the life and teachings of Jesus. This Chapter 7 is particularly interesting. Raymond E. Brown likens it to theater:[4] "Because it is argumentative, this discourse differs in style somewhat from previous discourses, for it is constantly broken up by questions and objections. Nevertheless, the familiar Johannine technique of the double stage appears: while Jesus is arguing with the crowd in the foreground, in the background the authorities are plotting his arrest."

> **John 7:19-20** *'Did not Moses give you the Law? Yet not one of you keeps it. Why are you trying to kill me?' The crowd answered, 'You are possessed! Who wants to kill you?'*

This crowd apparently is unaware of the plots to kill Jesus, and scoffs at the suggestion.

> **John 7:21-24** *Jesus replied, 'I did one good deed, and you are all taken aback. But consider: Moses gave you the law of circumcision (not that it originated with Moses, but with the patriarchs) and you circumcise even on the sabbath. Well then, if someone can be circumcised on the sabbath to avoid breaking the law of Moses, why are you indignant with me for making someone's whole body well on the sabbath? Stop judging by appearance; be just in your judgements.'*

Jesus justifies the sabbath work he has done by comparing it to the act of circumcision on the sabbath, a "lesser evil" that avoids breaking the more important law that a child must be circumcised on the eighth day after birth.

It is interesting that our present term "healing the whole man," meaning the healing of man's body and mind, fits so well with this *Revised English Bible* translation.

"Stop judging by appearances..."

The admonition not to make hasty judgements, or base the conclusion on the outward appearance only, should be a constant reminder to each one.

The people, and the Jewish authorities, see Jesus work on the sabbath. His work on the sabbath violates the Law of Moses and the penalty is death. In

---

[4] Raymond E. Brown, S. S., *The Anchor Bible*, Volume 29, page 315, Doubleday & Co., Inc.

their eyes he has committed a terrible offense against God. Jesus respects the laws that men use to live in an orderly manner, as witness his payment of the tax money; but in this healing he has invoked the law of God which is above that of Moses. He knows himself to be the Son of God, therefore, not above the law, but the very operation of law itself. He is a Priest of God after the order of Melchizedek, so he likens his position to that of the priests who also work when they circumcise on the sabbath. Giving health to a man on the sabbath is as important as circumcision on the sabbath.

Though by birth a Jew, Jesus does not at any time limit himself to their way of thinking. He and his followers are a people apart. Jesus teaches a new viewpoint about God and man. He teaches his followers not to reason about a situation on the mortal level but to lift their thought to the spiritual vantage point. It is necessary to turn completely away from old patterns of thought in order that one not judge superficially. This new teaching becomes the "good news" that we learn about in the books of the New Testament.

John 7:25-27   *This prompted some of the people of Jerusalem to say, 'Is not this the man they want to put to death? Yet here he is, speaking in public, and they say not one word to him. Can it be that our rulers have decided that this is the Messiah? Yet we know where this man comes from; when the Messiah appears no one is to know where he comes from.'*

Here again John shows us another facet of Jesus' life on earth. Here is the man they want to kill, speaking openly and without restraint. Do our rulers now believe he is Messiah? Then the people again doubt, for prophetic requirement states that they will not know where Messiah comes from, and Jesus they know!

How little they realize that they truly do not know where he comes from. No one recognizes his point of origin.

John 7:28-29   *Jesus responded to this as he taught in the temple: 'Certainly you know me,' he declared, 'and you know where I come from. Yet I have not come of my own accord; I*

was sent by one who is true, and him you do not know. I know him because I come from him, and he it is who sent me.'

In a loud voice he again gives the evidence of prophecy that denotes his Messiahship. Speaking first on the human level he says: "Certainly you know me;...you know where I come from." Then, speaking on the spiritual level: "Yet I have not come of my own accord; I was sent by one who is true, and him you do not know."

John 7:30-31   *At this they tried to seize him, but no one could lay hands on him because his appointed hour had not yet come. Among the people many believed in him. 'When the Messiah comes,' they said, 'is it likely that he will perform more signs than this man?'*

Earlier they had questioned his teaching. Here is a nobody — an untrained man — telling the priests, rabbis, and Pharisees that they do not know God, and he does know Him! What an outrage! A sudden surge to seize him comes to naught. This is not his sacrificial hour. How protected he is by God's angels at every point in his experience, and how awe-inspiring the protection of his Messianic mission.

John 7:32-34   *The Pharisees overheard these mutterings about him among the people, so the chief priests and the Pharisees sent temple police to arrest him. Then Jesus said, 'For a little longer I shall be with you; then I am going away to him who sent me. You will look for me, but you will not find me; and where I am, you cannot come.'*

The Pharisees now take action in cooperation with the chief priests and send temple police to arrest the troublemaker.

Only a little longer will he remain with them, then he will leave to be one with his God. In his wholly divine being they cannot find him. Speaking to their very material thought, he says, "Where I AM you cannot come."

The use of *I AM* (in Greek the EGŌ EIMI) is Jesus' statement of his complete identification with God. The EGŌ EIMI is in the statement God makes to Moses when he says "I AM THAT I AM." This sense of I AM is very important to the interpretation of Jesus' identity.[5]

Raymond E. Brown writes:[6] " 'where I am.' One would expect 'where I go...' It is Augustine who captures the atemporality of Jesus' statement, "Christ was ever in that place to which he would return.' "

Jesus stands within the majesty of his Christliness where human hatred can not reach him.

John 7:35-36 *So the Jews said to one another, 'Where does he intend to go, that we should not be able to find him? Will he go to the Dispersion among the Gentiles, and teach Gentiles? What does he mean by saying, "You will look for me, but you will not find me; and where I am, you cannot come"?'*

What problems Jesus poses for human reasoning! The incredible suggestion that Jesus will go to Greece and teach the Gentiles is probably met with laughter; but some years later this happens. The teaching of the Word in Greece is known to the readers of this Gospel, the early Christians!

These quotations of Jesus in Chapter 7 are very reminiscent of Job 28:12: "But where can wisdom be found and where is the source of understanding?" It is not amiss to equate the Christ with the wisdom of God, and Jesus Christ's necessity is to reveal the divine wisdom in action.

The Fountain of Life

John 7:37-38 *On the last and greatest day of the festival Jesus stood and declared, 'If anyone is thirsty, let him come to me and drink. Whoever believes in me, as scripture says, "Streams of living water shall flow from within him." '*

The Feast of Tabernacles holds deep meaning for those who walk the streets of Jerusalem during Jesus' lifetime. Because the underlying significance of Tabernacles is so well known, John obviously finds no need to expound that theme when writing his Gospel.

It is on the last and greatest day of the Festival[7] that Jesus makes his claim. The timing is perfect. The priests and the people have completed the journey from the fountain Gihon and have poured the holy water into the altar. It is probably at this most propitious moment that Jesus stands up. He must tower over those seated on the floor around him. In loud tones he cries, "If anyone is thirsty, let him come to me and drink. Whoever believes in me,..."

All this and more, much more, must have been proclaimed by Jesus on that greatest day of the Festival. Zechariah's prophecy is fresh in the minds of the people. The "waters" are a familiar symbol to them for wisdom and teaching. What an appropriate moment to declare himself the Fountain of Life.

John 7:39 *He was speaking of the Spirit which believers in him would later receive; for the Spirit had not yet been given, because Jesus had not yet been glorified.*

Biblical authorities are divided as to whether this last statement was inserted at a later date, or whether it is an explanation given by John. It seems too limited in its meaning to be genuinely by John. It is true that Jesus is referring to the Spirit to come later; but he also is offering spiritual understanding through his own revelation to us of his Father's nature and his teaching.

John 7:40-44 *On hearing this some of the crowd said, 'This must certainly be the Prophet.' Others said, 'This is the Messiah.' But others argued, 'Surely the Messiah is not to come from Galilee? Does not scripture say that the Messiah is to be of the family of David, from David's village of Bethlehem?' Thus he was the cause of a division among the people. Some were for arresting him, but no one laid hands on him.*

The remarks recorded here show that the people are hopeful that here in their midst is the One of whom prophecy speaks. The confusion concerning

---

[5] Raymond E. Brown, S. S., *The Anchor Bible*, Appendix IV, Volume 29, page 533, Doubleday & Co., Inc.

[6] Raymond E. Brown, S. S., *The Anchor Bible*, Volume 29, page 314, Doubleday & Co., Inc.

[7] Raymond E. Brown, S. S., *The Anchor Bible*, Volume 29, page 326, "Background of the Feast of Tabernacles", Doubleday & Co., Inc.

his place of birth emphasizes this. These prophetic sayings and others like them concerning the coming of Messiah are very well known to the masses.

So the confusion results in a split among them. Should they seize an impostor and desecrater of the sabbath? Should they wholeheartedly follow the Messiah? No one does anything.

John 7:45-50   *The temple police went back to the chief priests and Pharisees, who asked them, 'Why have you not brought him?' 'No one ever spoke as this man speaks,' they replied. The Pharisees retorted, 'Have you too been misled? Has a single one of our rulers believed in him, or any of the Pharisees? As for this rabble, which cares nothing for the law, a curse is on them.'*

What a remarkable instance of disobedience. Defying the authorities who have sent them to arrest Jesus, their only excuse is, "No one ever spoke as this man speaks." The power of the Word holds them at their distance. The permeating divine presence reaches their hearts and minds and changes them. Just as it always happens, the slightest touch of Spirit begins a change in man — a change that overcomes former loyalties and outweighs every material argument. These temple police are never again the same. Their spiritual transformation has begun.

The Pharisees rebuke them with the rhetorical question, "Has a single one of our rulers believed in him, or any of the Pharisees?" This reveals their frustration and desperation. They do not want to see or find any good in Jesus. As for the rabble, the Pharisees admit they do not observe the Law nor give any honor to them (the Pharisees). Therefore, "a curse is on them."

John 7:50-52   *Then one of their number, Nicodemus (the man who once visited Jesus), intervened. 'Does our law,' he asked them, 'permit us to pass judgement on someone without first giving him a hearing and learning the facts?' 'Are you a Galilean too?' they retorted. 'Study the scriptures and you will find that the Prophet does not come from Galilee.'*

Nicodemus intervenes on the side of justice. Earlier, in conversation with Jesus, he has questioned the Master at length and in secret; here he encourages his fellow Pharisees to listen to Jesus and form judgment after that. They turn upon Nicodemus. Sneering, they ask, "Are you a Galilean too?" In their present state of mind this is a supreme insult. Then a further blow — "Study the scripture" (Nicodemus is a famous teacher of the Scriptures) "and you will find that the Prophet does not come from Galilee." With that pronouncement they seem to dismiss all arguments favoring justice for Jesus.

One's thoughts can wander and explore possibilities when we consider the fate of the temple police — were they punished? Severely? Lightly? And does Nicodemus, who obviously has been growing apart from his colleagues, make a break with them at this point? We do not hear of him again until the crucifixion when he claims Jesus' body. Hopefully, as time goes on, he and the police may find kindred spirits among the followers of Jesus. It is hoped they do.

Chapter Eight

An Incident in the Temple

John 7:53-8:1[1] *And they all went home, while Jesus went to the mount of Olives.*

We are not told in this passage where Jesus spends the night. The town of Bethany is on the east side of the Mount of Olives, a little more than a mile and a half from Jerusalem. Simon the Leper lives in Bethany as does Mary, Martha, and Lazarus. Perhaps Jesus is staying with one of these friends. His way will pass through groves of olive trees which show their age in gnarled trunks. Lacy, soft green foliage paints shadows on the warm earth. Such an area can provide a haven for Jesus where he can rest and pray and find the refreshment his busy life demands.

John 8:2-3 *At daybreak he appeared again in the temple, and all the people gathered round him. He had taken his seat and was engaged in teaching them when the scribes and the Pharisees brought in a woman caught committing adultery.*

People who live off the soil, and who live where the midday heat is fierce, learn to be at their tasks in the coolness of early morning. So it is not uncommon to find a crowd at the temple at daybreak: but on this day Jesus sits to teach them. His lecture proceeds until it is rudely interrupted. In walk the Doctors of the Law and the Pharisees and they come straight to the group listening to Jesus. All heads turn in their direction. With them, probably held by temple police, is a woman taken in adultery. "Why have they brought her here?" must be in everyone's mind.

John 8:3-6 *Making her stand in the middle they said to him, 'Teacher, this woman was caught in the very act of adultery. In the law Moses has laid down that such women are to be stoned. What do you say about it?' They put the question as a test, hoping to frame a charge against him.*

The high-handed methods the Jewish authorities use in this instance must be transparently clear to each person seated at Jesus' feet. They do not follow the customary procedures. It is the Sanhedrin that usually try such cases, although during Roman times it is said they lost the authority to pronounce capital punishment. Why do they bring her to an itinerant preacher? Obviously they want to maneuver him into an untenable position.

This is one of the most vicious attacks brought upon Jesus up to this time. Present day attention is almost entirely devoted to the love and wisdom of Jesus' pronouncement — and rightly so. Great value is placed on his words and attitude towards this unfortunate. However, she is merely the tool used, the target is Jesus himself. The Sanhedrin enforce the Law, and they also have the delicate task of placating the Roman authorities, and local politics are not ignored either.

In their eyes, here is a man disobeying the Law of Moses and enticing the people with marvelous works. They have tried to arrest him a number of times without success. Always some power seems to preserve him and extricate him from the prepared trap. How sure they must be that this time he cannot escape! If he declares the woman should be stoned, he will violate Roman law. If he says she should be forgiven, the Mosaic law will be circumvented. He will then be in great peril. The mechanisms of the

---

[1] The Text of Chapters 7:53-8:11 appear at this point in the *King James Bible* and others, but the *Revised English Bible* makes these verses an addition at the end of the Gospel, for some scholars feel it was not part of John's original Gospel. I have put it in its accustomed place at the beginning of Chapter 8, because it seems to belong there, part of the whole scene.

devil to thwart the power of Christ in the world reaches a climax in this contrived and outrageous situation.

The uncomfortable woman stands at the center of the crowd, probably quite close to Jesus. All eyes are on these two. What will he say? They wait in hushed silence.

John 8:6-8   *Jesus bent down and wrote with his finger on the ground. When they continued to press their question he sat up straight and said, 'Let whichever of you is free from sin throw the first stone at her.' Then once again he bent down and wrote on the ground.*

Perhaps when Jesus writes on the ground he is not really writing, for surely some disciple would have recorded the marvelous word. The "writing" may be the cover for deep prayer to his Father and the Holy Spirit that is his constant guide. When Jesus Christ takes on human form he becomes dependent on divine guidance. Because of his purity and complete acquiescence to God there is no barrier of self-will to the unfoldment of ideas coming from his Source. A moment's turning to God brings the needed supply. He gives his judgment, then again he writes.

John 8:9-11   *When they heard what he said, one by one they went away, the eldest first; and Jesus was left alone, with the woman still standing there. Jesus again sat up and said to the woman, 'Where are they? Has no one condemned you?' She answered, 'No one, sir.' 'Neither do I condemn you,' Jesus said. 'Go; do not sin again.'*

This story, told in a few words, is well known. What becomes of her we do not know, nor do we know of those others who leave when they recognize that they cannot throw the stone that their accusation has demanded. Perhaps the fact that they leave without casting a stone shows the first faint glimmer of change in their attitude.

The Light of the World

John 8:12   *Once again Jesus addressed the people: 'I am the light of the world. No fol-*
lower of mine shall walk in darkness; he shall have the light of life.'

The crowd of interested listeners wait for him to speak. He is seated, a compelling presence. His voice, confident in tone, reaches each one as though he speaks to him alone.

A hush falls as he proclaims, "I am the Light of the world."

In his conversation with Nicodemus (John 3:19-21) Jesus says, "This is the judgement: the light has come into the world, but people preferred darkness to light because their deeds were evil. Wrongdoers hate the light and avoid it, for fear their misdeeds should be exposed. Those who live by the truth come to the light so that it may be clearly seen that God is in all they do."

As the "...light which gives light to everyone..." (John 1:9). Christ is the decisive moral force of honesty and uprightness that preserves each one's identity in God's image. Mankind, illumined by Christ, becomes a moral force.

He says, "No follower of mine shall walk in darkness; he shall have the light of life." The goodness and richness of God's wisdom shall be as a cup, full and running over with joy and God's blessing.

It is as though Jesus has said: "Through me the great illumination comes; all there is to know of God shall be revealed. Through me God becomes approachable and knowable. No follower of mine shall be ignorant of Him for he shall have the radiance of my glory to lead him." Of old the glory of the Lord precedes the children of Israel on their flight from Egypt. Christ's glory, his marvelously illuming presence, leads us as we flee the bondage of materialism.

True Witnessing

John 8:13-14   *The Pharisees said to him, 'You are witness in your own cause; your testimony is not valid.' Jesus replied, 'My testimony is valid, even though I do testify on my own behalf; because I know where I come from, and where I am going. But you know neither where I come from nor where I am going.'*

Again the Pharisees dispute with Jesus. Mosaic law requires at least two witnesses. Jesus here upholds his prerogative to witness to himself for he alone knows where he comes from and where he is going. The Pharisees have no comprehension of his origin or his goal.

John 8:15-16 *You judge by worldly standards; I pass judgement on no one. If I do judge, my judgement is valid because it is not I alone who judge, but I and he who sent me.*

Jesus does not judge by worldly standards when he changes the water into wine at Cana, nor when he feeds the five thousand from a few loaves and fishes. He does not judge by worldly standards at the pool of Bethesda, nor when he heals the officer's son. Instead he brings a fresh new standard to the immediate situation in each instance. His standard is given him by his Father and it is the standard of perfection for every man. He sees men at the spiritual level; he sees them in God's image, cared for by God and supported by God. God does not create a man "like Himself" and then leave him without provision. If God's man is left destitute he will be unlike his all-inclusive Creator.

Jesus always accepts the spiritual facts about man to be true about him at that moment. This brings healing or provision to the one he is helping.

This judgment is the restorative judgment sent by God to redeem humanity and restore them to a heavenly estate. The Father bears witness to Jesus' divine standard and upholds his position, for Jesus is doing the Father's will.

John 8:17-19 *'In your own law it is written that the testimony of two witnesses is valid. I am a witness in my own cause, and my other witness is the Father who sent me.' 'Where is your father?' they asked him. Jesus replied, 'You do not know me or my Father; if you knew me you would know my Father too.'*

Now Jesus points out to his accusers the validity of his position, because his Father is his other witness. 'Where is your father?' they ask. Note that the word *father* is not capitalized in this instance. His questioner's thought can only comprehend a human father.

"You do not know me or my Father; if you knew me you would know my Father too." This statement must have dumbfounded them. To us, however, his meaning stands out. We accept Jesus as the Incarnate Declaration of the Father of Creation. Yes, if we know Jesus, we know the Father.

John 8:20 *Jesus was teaching near the treasury in the temple when he said this; but no one arrested him, because his hour had not yet come.*

The last sentence attests again to the divine intervention in the events of Jesus' life-experience. His work must be completed before those opposing him can have their way.

Where I Am Going You Cannot Come

John 8:21 *Again he said to them, 'I am going away. You will look for me, but you will die in your sin; where I am going, you cannot come.'*

Those who look for Jesus Christ but persist in a material viewpoint will not find him. They will die in their sins (their false viewpoint). Where Jesus is going, those who reason from a material viewpoint cannot follow.

John 8:22 *At this the Jews said, 'Perhaps he will kill himself: is that what he means when he says, "Where I am going, you cannot come"?'*

This passage illustrates with great clarity what Jesus calls "judging by worldly standards." One can almost picture them whispering among themselves.

John 8:23-24 *Jesus continued, 'You belong to this world below, I to the world above. Your home is in this world, mine is not. That is why I told you that you would die in your sins; and you will die in your sins unless you believe that I am what I am.'*

Jesus speaks very plainly in this passage. He is addressing a type of thinking that lives within narrow concepts and is of very limited vision. They are born, live, and die — never escaping the confines of this littleness. The spiritually unenlightened individual perishes for he has no vision (see Proverbs 29:18, *King James Bible*). Jesus says of himself that he lives above in a realm appreciated through spirituality, a place of divinely inspired and expanded thought. Such contemplation raises the individual above his present environment to a new and fresh level of life.

These men now speaking with Jesus (an opportunity many would like to have) find no affinity with his views — they do not feel his touch nor accept his reasoning. They literally are at home in this world (materiality) and feel satisfied in it, so they shall die in their sins — the sin of refusing the invitation of Christ, "...unless you believe that I am what I am." This is the pronouncement that could waken them to new existence, or spell their doom. The wording here is closely akin to God's words to Moses: "I AM THAT I AM." Only believe and this whole new universe of Spirit's creating will be yours to explore!

John 8:25-26   *'And who are you?' they asked him. Jesus answered, 'What I have told you all along. I have much to say about you — and in judgement. But he who sent me speaks the truth, and what I heard from him I report to the world.'*

Who are you? This is the great question! Why should he approach them and offer them again that which they are unwilling to consider? One can sense weariness with repetition on his part.

How can Jesus explain his wholly spiritual and divine nature to such dense materiality. Yes, he can have a great deal to say about such a state of mind — and it will all be in judgment.

"He who sent me speaks the truth." This and many other statements point to Christ Jesus' oneness with his Father, and he adds "and what I heard from him I report to the world."

Are we examining his statements in this light?

John 8:27   *They did not understand that he was speaking to them about the Father.*

It is incredible! In truth, why should he speak to them at all!

Lift Up the Son of Man

John 8:28-29   *So Jesus said to them, 'When you have lifted up the Son of Man you will know that I am what I am. I do nothing on my own authority, but in all I say, I have been taught by my Father. He who sent me is present with me, and has not left me on my own; for I always do what is pleasing to him.'*

With infinite patience Jesus speaks again: "When you have lifted up the Son of Man you will know that I am what I am." Here hope is held out to those who think they do not want the Christ.

How do we lift up the Son of Man? When we begin to see Jesus as more than just another mortal. Those to whom he speaks think of him as just another human being. But to many he is much more. Some disciples see him as the Son of God. Jesus is asking that he be seen and accepted as the Son of God and be seen as the Son of Man, the pattern for all men. "When you have lifted up the Son of Man" you will suddenly find barriers to thought evaporating before the effulgence of spiritual illumination.

Speaking of himself Jesus says he does nothing on his own authority, but in all he has been taught by his Father. The willingness of Jesus to follow God's instruction, instead of allowing his human selfhood to assert itself, powerfully illustrates a pattern of life for each of us. Are we willing to follow the path to which God points? Are we listening to Jesus' words? "He who sent me is present with me, and has not left me on my own; for I always do what is pleasing to him." Jesus is a man confident and assured, for he knows the One who sent him is ever with him. It is the Father within him that enables him to heal the sick and redeem the sinner, a Father well pleased with His Son.

John 8:30   *As he said this, many put their faith in him.*

This pattern of obedience to God is in line with Jewish belief and more familiar. Some even dare to trust that this new teaching, so strange to them, may have real meaning in their lives.

Slave or Free?

John 8:31-32   *Turning to the Jews who had believed him, Jesus said, 'If you stand by my teaching, you are truly my disciples; you will know the truth, and the truth will set you free.'*

This is a tremendous undertaking — to stand by his teaching — to dwell within the revelation that Jesus brings — only then shall we be his disciples.

When we learn to look at life with Jesus' instructions to us as our beginning point, instead of our last resort, then we shall learn that our Father and Jesus are always at our side; they have not left us alone. Trusting our Lord's revelation to be The Way, we earn our discipleship. He assures us that we shall know the truth: we shall know the reality of God, learn also the reality of men, and women, and the universe, and this knowledge will bring to us our freedom — freedom from sin, from limitation, and from death as well.

John 8:33-36   *'We are Abraham's descendants,' they replied; 'We have never been in slavery to anyone. What do you mean by saying, "You will become free"?' 'In very truth I tell you,' said Jesus, 'that everyone who commits sin is a slave. The slave has no permanent standing in the household, but the son belongs to it for ever. If then the Son sets you free, you will indeed be free.'*

The Jews who believe in Jesus find this to be a very hard saying, for they, as Abraham's seed, feel freedom to be their true status. But Jesus says that everyone who commits sin is a slave. No exceptions! He continues, "The slave (sinner) has no permanent standing in the household (of God), but the son belongs to it for ever."

Here Jesus compares a contemporary household, in which the son and heir has power to free a slave, with the household of God where the Son fulfills the Father's will in freeing the slaves of sin. He says, "You will know the truth, and the truth will set you free." Equating himself with Truth, he teaches, "If then the Son sets you free, you will indeed be free."

John 8:37-38   *'I know that you are descended from Abraham, yet you are bent on killing*

me because my teaching makes no headway with you. I tell what I have seen in my Father's presence; you do what you have learned from your father.'

Jesus understands better than anyone who has walked this earth the antagonisms produced by a mind unwilling to acknowledge truth; self-righteousness and self-importance increase until rage culminates in violence to the tormentor.

They hate him because his teachings do not please them. What he has to say makes them very uncomfortable.

John 8:39-41   *They retorted, 'Abraham is our father.' 'If you were Abraham's children,' Jesus replied, 'you would do as Abraham did. As it is, you are bent on killing me, because I have told you the truth, which I heard from God. That is not how Abraham acted. You are doing your own father's work.'*

Jesus makes the point in John 8:37 that they are descended from Abraham as Jews, but in John 8:39-41 he disputes that they are Abraham's spiritual descendants. If they are, he says, they will act as Abraham did. If they can accept him in faith, Jesus is saying, then they will indeed be like Abraham, and thus his children in kind. But with their resistance to truth they are following the footsteps of former generations.

Nowhere does Jesus make it clearer than here in this conversation that to be Abraham's children they must attain a spiritual level of thought. At present they are reasoning from a purely mortal level, "doing their own father's work."

John 8:41   *They said, 'We are not illegitimate; God is our father, and God alone.'*

These people are now saying that God father's their thought and action. Abraham's name does not seem to benefit their cause.

John 8:42   *Jesus said to them, 'If God were your father, you would love me, for God is the source of my being, and from him I come.'*

We should keep in mind the concept of inherited traits and character. The nobility of man points to God as his father. It is unthinkable that God can father thoughts antagonistic to Himself or His Son. God does not give man base or evil thoughts. These stem from false concepts of life and being, and gross misconception of God. This profane, vile, evil, and cruel compilation is the opposite of God and His angelic thoughts, and is the Devil spoken of in the Bible. The children of God find compatibility with Jesus, and acceptance and agreement with his teachings. They love God and His Son.

John 8:42-43   *'I have not come of my own accord; he sent me. Why do you not understand what I am saying? It is because my teaching is beyond your grasp.'*

Jesus' speech becomes more and more explicit.

He reiterates that he has been sent — and this statement implies that he has been sent for a purpose. He asks, "Why do you not understand what I am saying?" and answers, "Because my teaching is beyond your grasp."

So the revelation is not beyond the grasp of everyone. But it is beyond the grasp of those who do not love God or acknowledge our Lord Jesus Christ.

While in prayer, before the crucifixion (John 17:4) Jesus states that he has completed the work he has been given to do. There is a massive amount of material in the four Gospels, and in the rest of the New Testament, to guide us and instruct us how we may dwell within the revelation. Paul is given special instruction (Acts 9:15-16) by our Lord Jesus in order that he may become a "... chosen instrument to bring my name before the nations and their kings, and before the people of Israel. I myself will show him...." says Jesus.

God will, through the Holy Spirit, impart to each of us the spiritual knowledge we need to accomplish the work He has given us to do. The revelation will not be beyond the grasp of those who hear the divine commands and assurances — rather, the revelation will enfold them.

False Reasoning

John 8:44   *'Your father is the devil and you choose to carry out your father's desires. He was a murderer from the beginning, and is not rooted in the truth; there is no truth in him. When he tells a lie he is speaking his own language, for he is a liar and the father of lies.'*

Here Jesus utterly rejects this false assertion that God fathers their reasoning! Indeed, God is not their father — their father is the devil and they have chosen to carry out the devil's desires! As a murderer from the beginning the devil undermines, perverts, and attacks by every means available all that is good, loving, and godlike, and this devilish type of thinking seeks those who will lend their minds to do his will. As the opposite of God, his position is founded on lies and falsity. Until we comprehend an infinite God, wholly good and supreme in power, we shall be tempted to trust the false — always to our detriment!

John 8:45-47   *'But because I speak the truth, you do not believe me. Which of you can convict me of sin? If what I say is true, why do you not believe me? He who has God for his father listens to the words of God. You are not God's children, and that is why you do not listen.'*

Jesus speaks the truth and they do not believe him because the lie about God and man are all that the devil's "children" understand. None of them can prove Jesus wrong. Having God as Father means that God is the source of your ideas, and that His truth is the logic of your reasoning.

Do we realize this when we try to impart to another some beautiful spiritual idea? Those who rebuff us are "possessed" by the lies which reject truth. It is hard indeed to have a loved one reject the spiritual truths and love which we keenly feel and accept.

Obey My Teaching

John 8:48-51   *The Jews answered, 'Are we not right in saying that you are a Samaritan, and that you are possessed?' 'I am not possessed,' said Jesus; 'I am honouring my Father,* *but you dishonour me. I do not care about my own glory; there is one who does care, and he is judge. In very truth I tell you, if anyone obeys my teaching he will never see death.'*

The "Jews" are now off on another track. Having failed in their claims to be Abraham's children or God's children, they attack Jesus as heretical — a Samaritan — and claim he is possessed — crazy! Jesus disdains answering the notion that he is a Samaritan. It is very well known that he is not. He patiently tells them that he is honoring his Father.

Though he says he does not care about his own glory, he points out that his Father does care, and judges whether proper honor is paid His Son. The rewards of giving such honor and respect are great, for such a man shall not know the experience of death as he gives up the mortal body, for that man shall never know separation from God, who is his life.

John 8:52-53 *The Jews said, 'Now we are certain that you are possessed. Abraham is dead and so are the prophets; yet you say, "If anyone obeys my teaching he will never taste death." Are you greater than our father Abraham? He is dead and the prophets too are dead. Who do you claim to be?'*

To the Jews, the whole conversation is getting out of hand. Abraham and the prophets are dead. He has made a remarkable assertion; that by obeying his teaching one will not know what it is to die! Who are you? These questions indicate that perhaps a faint glimmer of spiritual light touches them. For standing before them is one greater than Abraham.

John 8:54-59 *Jesus replied, 'If I glorify myself, that glory of mine is worthless. It is the Father who glorifies me, he of whom you say, "He is our God," though you do not know him. But I know him; if I were to say that I did not know him I should be a liar like you. I do know him and I obey his word. Your father Abraham was overjoyed to see my day; he saw it and was glad.' The Jews protested, 'You are not yet fifty years old. How can you have seen Abraham?' Jesus said, 'In very truth I tell you, before Abraham was born, I am.' They took up stones to throw at him, but he was not to be seen; and he left the temple.*

Who do you claim to be? These men claim they know God, but their attitudes and viewpoints prove otherwise. "But I know him," says Jesus, "before Abraham was born, I am."

Jesus does not count his life in years, but in being. "I AM" brings to thought agelessness, timelessness, a perpetuity of existence that knows neither beginning nor ending — an always presence. Dependent on and obedient to his Father, it is the Father who glorifies Jesus, honors him, anoints him, and chooses him to reveal to all the world their Father in heaven, and who establishes His reign on earth.

This is too much for their puny minds to grasp, so picking up stones from among the building blocks of the temple they seek to stone him. But the same blindness that makes it impossible for them to understand Jesus renders him invisible to their eyes, and he escapes their fury.

Chapter Nine

The whole of this chapter is devoted to telling the story of a man blind from his birth whom Jesus heals. The greater part of Chapter 8 of this Gospel is an illustration of the world's blindness to the presence of God's Son, who himself declares, "I am the Light of the World." Chapter 9 shows how acceptance of Christ in our hearts heals this blindness. Chapter 9 also relates the controversy and opposition which arises as a result of this healing. Underlying all this is the broader application of the term "blindness" to which Jesus addresses himself. Both presentations are closely interwoven and beyond these two extremes there is the pattern of the great individual spiritual experience of being "born again," of which Jesus speaks to Nicodemus (John 3:7).

Healing a Man Born Blind

John 9:1-3 *As he went on his way Jesus saw a man who had been blind from birth. His disciples asked him, 'Rabbi, why was this man born blind? Who sinned, this man or his parents?' 'It is not that he or his parents sinned,' Jesus answered; 'he was born blind so that God's power might be displayed in curing him.'*

Again, as in the case of the man at the pool of Bethesda, Jesus offers his help to one who needs him, a man blind from birth. It is the belief of many that blindness from birth is the result of sin. Such being the case, only God can heal the affliction. Jesus quickly informs his disciples that neither the parents nor the man are sinners, and that "he was born blind so that God's power might be displayed in curing him."

In this world where men find it difficult to know God, all people can be termed "born blind." In this statement Jesus is probably alluding to this broader concept of "blindness," though the healing of the man will illustrate both the release from his physical handicap as well as his spiritual awakening.

This passage is remarkable also because Jesus flatly states: "It is not that he or his parents sinned, he was born blind so that God's power might be displayed in curing him."

To declare this Jesus must see beyond the physical appearance to the spiritual identity. We only begin to glimpse this real nature after the Holy Spirit has opened our thought to the glories of God. Then we become aware of the original sinless spiritual man and woman. By degrees, this spiritual identity then becomes manifested in human lives. To illustrate: Jacob's nature is progressively transformed through communion with God and he is henceforth called Israel, and lives a more righteous life.

John 9:4-5 *'While daylight lasts we must carry on the work of him who sent me; night is coming, when no one can work. While I am in the world I am the light of the world.'*

As the "light of the world" Jesus brings both the power and the presence of God to every situation he experiences. Jesus well knows that his work will soon be ending and may feel some pressure to fill each minute with his valuable instruction and example. Because the gift of the Holy Spirit — the baptism of fire — has not yet been given, when Jesus departs through the crucifixion experience, then it will indeed be a time of great darkness "when no one can work."

And let us also note that Jesus does not speak of what he is doing as "healing." He calls it his "work" — "we must carry on the work of Him who sent me..." This is the job he has come to do. While he is on earth it supports him — and feeds him. Remember, at the time of his talk with the Samaritan at Jacob's well, when his disciples bring him food he says, "I have food to eat of which you know nothing" (John 4:32).

John 9:6-7 *With these words he spat on the ground and made a paste with the spittle; he spread it on the man's eyes, and said to him, 'Go and wash in the pool of Siloam.' (The name means 'sent'.) The man went off and washed, and came back able to see.*

Bible scholars are very intrigued by the paste made with spittle with which Jesus anoints the man's eyes. It has even been linked to superstitious beliefs of the curative power of spittle that were then prevalent. But spitting is also a sign of contempt — and the wiping of the paste on the man's eyes can have registered Jesus' contempt for the blindness — for he is in the process of releasing the man from that handicap. Having applied the spittle mixed with dust he sends him to wash in a pool of water whose prior greatest claim to fame is the name "Sent" (Siloam), for it is a reservoir, its water coming from another source. John is so anxious to have us realize the significance of this pool that he gives the translation in an aside. Jesus is the one sent by the Father. He also is the Fountain of Life. By calling our attention to the pool Siloam, John begins to show us that this story has many spiritual lessons.

The blind man obediently carries out Jesus' instructions just as carefully as do Abraham and Moses in their time, and the result of this accepting and obedient attitude is that he comes back seeing!

John 9:8-12 *His neighbors and those who were accustomed to see him begging said, 'Is not this the man who used to sit and beg?' Some said, 'Yes, it is.' Others said, 'No, but it is someone like him.' He himself said, 'I am the man.' They asked him, 'How were your eyes opened?' He replied, 'The man called Jesus made a paste and smeared my eyes with it, and told me to go to Siloam and wash. So I went and washed, and found I could see.' 'Where is he?' they asked. 'I do not know,' he said.*

Here is a perplexing happening — one born blind has received his sight! Is this the man — or this one? His appearance is changed with intelligent eyes illuming his face. "I am the man," he admits. When questioned he makes no attempt to do other than state his case plainly; "...I went and washed, and found I could see." But he does not know where to find his Lord.

The Pharisees Doubt

John 9:13-17 *The man who had been blind was brought before the Pharisees. As it was a sabbath day when Jesus made the paste and opened his eyes, the Pharisees too asked him how he had gained his sight. The man told them, 'He spread a paste on my eyes; then I washed, and now I can see.' Some of the Pharisees said, 'This man cannot be from God; he does not keep the sabbath.' Others said, 'How could such signs come from a sinful man?' So they took different sides. Then they continued to question him: 'What have you to say about him? It was your eyes he opened.' He answered, 'He is a prophet.'*

Wherever Jesus goes his influence stirs the lives of men. He touches one man to heal him and the lives of all are affected. This is true today. When our lives are touched with God's power there radiates a current of divine force which touches the lives of others. Those open to God are blessed. But in some there rises a furious antagonism.

Because Jesus has again healed on the sabbath in violation of their law, the Pharisees go into action to protect their teachings. The man who has been healed is summoned and they interview him. He describes what Jesus did and how he came to see. This information results in an argument among themselves. How can a sinful man who does not keep the sabbath perform such signs? And on the other hand, "How could such signs come from a sinful man?" So they reasoned. Finally they ask the man, "What have you to say about him? It was your eyes he opened." "He is a prophet," he said. A prophet is one who voices the Word of the Lord. The man's insight discerns the hand of God in what Jesus did for him and fearlessly he declares his conviction to them.

John 9:18-23 *The Jews would not believe that the man had been blind and had gained his sight, until they had summoned his parents and questioned them: 'Is this your son? Do you say that he was born blind? How is it that he can see now?' The parents replied, 'We know that he is our son, and that he was born blind. But how it is that he can now see, or who opened his eyes, we do not know. Ask him; he* *is of age; let him speak for himself.' His parents gave this answer because they were afraid of the Jews; for the Jewish authorities had already agreed that anyone who acknowledged Jesus as Messiah should be banned from the synagogue. That is why the parents said, 'He is of age; ask him.'*

The Pharisees take the easiest way out of their predicament: they simply refuse to believe a man blind from birth has been healed. But when they call the man's parents for verification, they agree with their son — he now sees. Ask him all about this!

John 9:24-29   *So for the second time they summoned the man who had been blind, and said, 'Speak the truth before God. We know that this man is a sinner.' 'Whether or not he is a sinner, I do not know,' the man replied. 'All I know is this: I was blind and now I can see.' 'What did he do to you?' they asked. 'How did he open your eyes?' 'I have told you already,' he retorted, 'but you took no notice. Why do you want to hear it again? Do you also want to become his disciples?' Then they became abusive. 'You are that man's disciple,' they said, 'but we are disciples of Moses. We know that God spoke to Moses, but as for this man, we do not know where he comes from.'*

His statement, "I was blind and now I see," is conclusive and without argument.

Repeating their former questions the Pharisees want him to tell them again what Jesus did to him. But the statement the man has just made to them shows us he really can see now, for he sees his questioners in a new light — he no longer is in awe of them. He has already described what Jesus has done, but, he points out, they have taken no notice. Why do they want him to recount it? Do they want to become disciples?

The progression of the man's thinking is very instructive. He grows very bold in his speech. This last question rouses the authorities to abuse. They accuse him of being a disciple of Jesus. Perhaps for the first time this possibility comes to him.

The Pharisees retreat to safe ground: "We are disciples of Moses. We know that God spoke to Moses..." But where "that fellow" comes from, they

know not. And that is the core of their mental darkness. They can not conceive that Jesus is from God.

Let us consider one of the points made by the man; that the Pharisees have taken no notice of his statement. They perform as people do even today. If one relates a healing, or some other occurrence that reveals the power of God, there will be those who ask for more information and then they do not listen to the answer. How accurately John paints this picture of the devil trying to reverse the work of God.

John 9:30-34   *The man replied, 'How extraordinary! Here is a man who has opened my eyes, yet you do not know where he comes from! We know that God does not listen to sinners; he listens to anyone who is devout and obeys his will. To open the eyes of a man born blind — that is unheard of since time began. If this man was not from God he could do nothing.' 'Who are you to lecture us?' they retorted. 'You were born and bred in sin.' Then they turned him out.*

This man shows insight and courage. He is also very articulate. These three gifts may be the reason Jesus seeks him out to heal him for the glory of God. The man recognizes divine purpose in his healing: "If this man was not from God he could do nothing." His perception of the source of Jesus' power reveals that more than his eyes are healed of blindness. He is particularly brazen in pointing out to the Pharisees that "We know that God does not listen to sinners; he listens to anyone who is devout and obeys his will." All this results in his expulsion from the synagogue.

The Man Finds Christ

John 9:35-38   *Hearing that they had turned him out, Jesus found him and asked, 'Have you faith in the Son of Man?' The man answered, 'Tell me who he is, sir, that I may put my faith in him.' 'You have seen him,' said Jesus; 'indeed, it is he who is speaking to you.' 'Lord, I believe,' he said, and fell on his knees before him.*

This scene is intimate and touching for now the man who had been blind comes to know his benefactor. John tells a beautiful story.

Having located the man Jesus asks, "Have you faith in the Son of Man?" Do you believe in the Son of God?

"Tell me who he is," is the reply. The man thinks: "You have opened my eyes physically — this can only be the power of God — now give me the revelation that I may believe."

"You have seen him...indeed, it is he who is speaking to you." His Helper, the very one who has shown such compassion, is the Lord! As the depths of this truth dawn in his consciousness and the wonder of it all becomes real to him, he whispers, "Lord, I believe," and kneels before him.

Three Lessons

John 9:39-41 *Jesus said, 'It is for judgement that I have come into this world — to give sight to the sightless, and to make blind those who see.' Some Pharisees who were present asked, 'Do you mean that we are blind?' 'If you were blind,' said Jesus, 'you would not be guilty, but because you claim to see, your guilt remains.'*

There are three aspects to be considered in this story.
1. The healing of the blind man.
2. The blindness or disbelief of those who do not accept Jesus Christ.
3. The "newborn" of Spirit.

This little drama may be applied to humanity as a whole. From the time of Adam people have been blind. Rays of spiritual light pierce this darkness from time to time. Prophets, whose spiritual eyes (understanding) are opened by the Word of God, speak in His name. Divine revelation, woven through Jewish history, reaches its pattern of glory in Jesus Christ. Those who accept the Son of God in their hearts receive the anointing by his touch. Through obedience to his precepts, they are freed from their blindness and come to know their Savior. But always, like the Pharisees of the story, lurking at hand are all the arguments and persuasions of those who oppose and reject God and His love.

Jesus' statement: "It is for judgement that I have come into this world — to give sight to the sightless and to make blind those who see," really points to types of thinking, attitudes, and convictions held by

men and women. This is the area that needs healing. "No follower of mine shall walk in darkness," Jesus says earlier (John 8:12).

The blind man typifies a heart willing to yield to God. In the Pharisees we have the opposite type — stubborn, self-righteous, and power-conscious. These "Jews" are antipathetic to Christ. These are the ones Jesus comes "to make blind." They need to learn that looking towards self is blindness — this very judgment will heal them ultimately.

The world's blindness is greatest by reason of its claim to knowledge — We see! We know! We are! And all the while they see only their own thoughts and never know the vast and limitless range of God's universe. Preoccupied with self-engrossing plans and pursuing happiness at their own level, they are content with their own littleness until calamity startles them — then they ask, "Who shall lead me in my blindness?"

A third lesson can be drawn from the story, that of the earnest follower of our Lord who suddenly finds heaven opened to him and the glory of the Lord revealed. Never again can he return to the womb of his former self. He has been born again, born into a larger concept of God, Christ, and the Holy Spirit.

When thought is touched by Divine Power, the individual who responds is washed in the outpouring love of our Lord — and having been washed in this Heaven-sent water his vision is opened to the new light of Christ. Friends and neighbors see a change in him but are not really sure of their conclusions about him. Is he the same man? And who performs this change? The one who sees in this new dimension does not yet know.

Following this new birth comes a period of doubt. It is akin to Jesus' forty days in the wilderness when he is tempted by Satan. Audibly from friends, and from whisperings in his own consciousness, come thoughts to plague him. "Were you really blind? Maybe you only thought you could not see! Surely the power you think touched you cannot have been God!"

Step by step the newly born must learn to hold his own against these specious arguments. He knows he was blind! He knows he now sees! He finally rests in the realization that the power that touched him is divine.

Chapter Ten

The Good Shepherd

John 10:1   *'In very truth I tell you, the man who does not enter the sheepfold by the door, but climbs in some other way, is nothing but a thief and a robber.'*

"In very truth I tell you," this beautiful method of emphasis cannot help but arrest our attention.

We must remember (in spite of the fact that Chapter 10 has commenced) that Jesus has been, and apparently still is, talking to the leaders of the Jewish synagogue. He has just told them that they are spiritually blind, and that therein lies their sin. They are guilty!

He now starts a parable — and it is a story that reveals the contrast between the God-appointed leader of the faithful and the self-assertive "leader" who "climbs" over all others to take the highest seat. Such a man is nothing but a thief and robber says Jesus.

Those who attempt to lead men's minds, and do not walk the path of the Holy Spirit, are indeed thieves and robbers. They take from the faithful the Gift of God, their Good Shepherd.

John 10:2-5   *'He who enters by the door is the shepherd in charge of the sheep. The door-keeper admits him, and the sheep hear his voice; he calls his own sheep by name, and leads them out. When he has brought them all out, he goes ahead of them and the sheep follow, because they know his voice. They will not follow a stranger; they will run away from him, because they do not recognize the voice of strangers.'*

The man who enters by the door is he who is sent by the Father. He is the Shepherd in charge of the sheep, the Pastor divinely appointed to minister to the faithful.

The door-keeper is the guardian of the things of God. He knows God's Son who is the Shepherd for his Father's sheep.

The sheep hear his voice. They listen to him for he calls them by name. He knows them and they know him. He has a special message for each one.

Instead of sending them out into the world alone the Shepherd leads them out. He goes before "...to prepare a place..." (John 14:2). The sheep, the faithful, follow the leading of the Chosen One, because they understand and trust him.

They do not follow a stranger — because they do not recognize his voice. The Shepherd always voices the Word of God. The stranger does not know God's Word and cannot utter it. When the stranger speaks the faithful run away, for he offers nothing to attract them.

John 10:6-9   *This was a parable that Jesus told them, but they did not understand what he meant by it.*
So Jesus spoke again: 'In very truth I tell you, I am the door of the sheepfold. The sheep paid no heed to any who came before me, for they were all thieves and robbers. I am the door; anyone who comes into the fold through me will be safe. He will go in and out and find pasture.

"I am the door of the sheepfold." Jesus Christ is the point of "entering-in" to the joy of our Lord. He is the Beginning. He is the Judgment, the Separator. For the door is the divider of one side from the other, of the in and the out, of those who cleave to God and those who shun Him.

It is interesting that God has given those faithful who wait for the coming of their Lord the gift of discrimination. They do not follow the strangers.

Having entered the door into the fold, having accepted Jesus Christ, and through him become sons of God (John 1:12) they are secure, safe; they shall live their lives, both in the world and in the fold, and everywhere they shall find pasturage, they shall find God's continuing provision for them.

John 10:10-13   *A thief comes only to steal, kill, and destroy; I have come that they may have life, and may have it in all its fullness. I am the good shepherd; the good shepherd lays down his life for the sheep. The hired man, when he sees the wolf coming, abandons the sheep and runs away, because he is not the shepherd and the sheep are not his. Then the wolf harries the flock and scatters the sheep. The man runs away because he is a hired man and cares nothing for the sheep.*

The thief, the false leader or so-called "Messiah," comes to take instead of to give, to kill pure worship and to destroy moral integrity. Jesus Christ comes to give life in all its fullness and joy — a cup running over with spiritual fulfillment.

To provide this good and full life for all men the Good Shepherd will even lay down his life. He gives all for the sheep to keep them safe. There is never a time when he gives "too little and too late." The full measure of divine presence always is at hand to rescue, safeguard, and provide.

When he sees the "wolf" coming (the specter of useless lives, envy, and want), the hired man abandons the sheep for he has no resources with which to save them. He is not the one to whom the sheep have been given, for he is not the chosen shepherd.

The wolf then harries the sheep. Envy and fear separate them from each other and scatter the flock.

The man runs away because he is a false leader who has no love to give the faithful. It is he who deserts his flock when their need is greatest.

John 10:14-15   *'I am the good shepherd; I know my own and my own know me, as the Father knows me and I know the Father; and I lay down my life for the sheep.'*

Identifying himself as the Good Shepherd, Jesus now brings out the closeness and intimacy of his relationship with his sheep by comparing this to the closeness he has with his Father "as the Father knows me and I know the Father."

Earlier he said, "The Father loves the Son and has entrusted him with complete authority" (John 3:35) and "For the Father loves the Son and shows him all that he himself is doing, and will show him even greater deeds,..." (John 5:20).

These words speak of the close interchange of love, authority, and direction between Father and Son.

He stresses here that he knows the sheep and the sheep know him. There is an interchange of ideas, love, and dominion with the faithful, an enabling power that sets them apart as his own. And he gives his very life for them. His sacrifice is not only in dying to save his own, it is also his day by day, moment by moment dedication to the redemption of the sheep.

John 10:16   *'But there are other sheep of mine, not belonging to this fold; I must lead them as well, and they too will listen to my voice. There will then be one flock, one shepherd.'*

It seems obvious here that Jesus considers his immediate followers the sheep, but the other sheep "not belonging to this fold" looks ahead to the calling of the Gentiles to his teachings.

Victory Over Death

John 10:17-18   *'The Father loves me because I lay down my life, to receive it back again. No one takes it away from me; I am laying it down of my own free will. I have the right to lay it down, and I have the right to receive it back again; this charge I have received from my Father.'*

This is the third time he says "The Father loves me" and this time it is "because I lay down my life, to receive it back again." Jesus' willingness to do the "work" his Father charges him to do blesses him with love that sustains him and gives him courage.

God's love is sustaining and supporting. It is the central force of life. The constant love of the Father for the Son is the vibrant source of Jesus' power. It enables him to experience death as the man Jesus and it enables him to take up his life again after death.

One frequently thinks of Jesus as the victim of prejudice and politics; a victim of misunderstanding; a man betrayed by Judas; but from the beginning Jesus is aware of the final scene of his earthly career. No one can take his life in any way. He can lay it down for all men everywhere, but none can take it from him, and he will do this through his own choice, because he always does that which is pleasing to his Father. This is his joy, his responsibility, his obligation, his charge.

The importance of the crucifixion and the necessity for this final sacrifice, in his life of complete self-sacrifice, is to win for God's people two equally significant aspects of salvation.

First: He comes to reveal the reign, or sovereign power, of his Father on earth. It will show, when he overcomes death, that the works he now does are stepping stones towards this "mightier work." His multiplication of food, changing water to wine, the healings he does, his control of wind and wave, as well as every other sign he has wrought, proves the power and correctness of his teachings for all time. From the first "sign" he reveals to the raising of Lazarus from the dead, there is the clear pattern of the Father's power operating in him, and it is supreme in every instance.

Second: He comes to redeem men from sin.

By assuming human form he takes upon himself the sins of mankind. He takes the inborn wrath, vileness, cunning, duplicity, greed, vengeance, and cruelty, as well as the doubt, fear, hesitancy, and distrust that also besets mankind; in this manner he truly bears our sins and he overcomes their corruption through the outpouring to all of his Father's great life. His life shows that it is from within a man's mind and heart and feelings that the victory over evil must come. The stream of holy life ever flowing through his consciousness purifies his human identity of all unlike his spiritual identity as the Son of God, thus "lifting up" his humanity to its place as the Son of Man. As one both human and divine he provides in his sacrifice the necessary target, or focal point, for evil to unleash its pent-up hatred of the God he stands for. Evil, in the fury of its effort to destroy the power and presence of God in the world, nails Jesus to a cross. He is battered, naked, and helpless in the eyes of all; yet at this climax he quietly prays, "Father,

forgive them; they do not know what they are doing." (Luke 23:34).

On the cross, with this brief prayer of forgiving love, he nullifies for himself and all victims of sin the destructive power of sin. He pays the price that evil demands: that the Son and Heir of God be killed so that the earth may remain the domain of all evil. But Jesus has taught the prayer:

"Our Father...Thy kingdom come on earth as it is in heaven..."

Killing the Son and Heir does not win the day. He is an innocent victim and the pangs of death can not hold him. Nothing in him responds to evil's thrusts.

John 10:19-21   *These words again caused a division among the Jews. Many of them said, 'He is possessed, he is out of his mind. Why listen to him?' Others said, 'No one possessed by a demon could speak like this. Could a demon open the eyes of the blind?'*

The stir that the words of Jesus always cause in the minds of men is very evident here. Their thoughts concerning him are in turmoil. They want to come to some conclusion regarding his position.

John 10:22-24   *It was winter, and the festival of the Dedication was being held in Jerusalem. As Jesus was walking in the temple precincts, in Solomon's Portico, the Jews gathered round him and asked: 'How long are you going to keep us in suspense? Tell us plainly: are you the Messiah?'*

Winter in Jerusalem brings piercing cold winds. What more comfortable place to be walking than in the sheltered side of the temple court. The colonnade of arches is open to the courtyard but has a solid wall to the east which keeps off the bitter cold wind. Converging on Jesus a group of Jews ask him the thought uppermost in their mind — "Tell us plainly: are you the Messiah?"

Study shows that Jesus consistently avoids this specific title for himself. Possibly the political overtones mentioned earlier in this writing influence his thought about this. The Messiah is to come to throw off the yoke of oppression. But obviously Jesus' concept of the Messiah, and the concept of the populace of a warrior king who will reestablish Israel, are far apart.

John 10:25-30 *'I have told you,' said Jesus, 'and you do not believe. My deeds done in my Father's name are my credentials, but because you are not sheep of my flock you do not believe. My own sheep listen to my voice; I know them and they follow me. I give them eternal life and they will never perish; no one will snatch them from my care. My Father who has given them to me is greater than all, and no one can snatch them out of the Father's care. The Father and I are one.'*

"I have told you already," says the man born blind to the questioning Pharisees. "I have told you," said Jesus. Those interrogating the blind man and those now pleading with Jesus are not willing to listen. In John 1:12 we learn that the necessity is a willingness to believe and an act of yielding allegiance to Jesus Christ. Neither the Pharisees nor these Jews to whom Jesus speaks are really willing to listen and hear him with mind and heart.

It is recognized as valid in Jesus' time that one who is delegated authority by another is his legal representative. He can do business and in every way stand in the stead of the one he represents.

So when Jesus says he does his "deeds" in the name of his Father and that the works are his credentials, he is standing on the foundation of recognized procedure.

Jesus says that because they are not sheep of his flock they do not hear. They are not of his flock because they are not willing to listen to him nor permit their thoughts to come into agreement with him. The willingness to listen is a characteristic of his own sheep. "I know them," he says. This is not an unknown leader; he knows his flock, each one. This intimacy and closeness gives them eternal life, (i.e., all needed to support them comes from the Shepherd) and none can snatch them away. Once found, this relationship is permanent; the care is for eternity. The Father has given the Shepherd the flock, and He is the Supreme Power. No one can snatch them out of the Father's care, nor from His representative, the Shepherd, because, as Jesus says, "My Father and I are one."

Hitherto Jesus claims to be God's Son, but never before has he claimed oneness with God. "My Father and I are one" reveals a concept of his self-sameness with the Great Cause, the I AM. The divine Being and its Word are One, and I AM is its declaration. The Holy Spirit, the power of God, is the third member of the Trinity.

John 10:31-33 *Once again the Jews picked up stones to stone him. At this Jesus said to them, 'By the Father's power I have done many good deeds before your eyes; for which of these are you stoning me?' 'We are not stoning you for any good deed,' the Jews replied, 'but for blasphemy: you, a man, are claiming to be God.'*

As he is about to be stoned, Jesus points out the many good deeds he has done by his Father's power. Never, in any of his statements, does he ever claim a single act is done by his own power. He is there to work in the Father's name to glorify the Father. And it is his Father who glorifies him.

They are about to stone him for claiming to be God, utter blasphemy in their eyes, for they see him as a mere man. This is very important for us to recognize. In every human sense he is a "mere man." If he is solely divine he has no body to sacrifice to atone for mortal sin. His humanity and divinity make him the common denominator for God and man.

John 10:34-36 *Jesus answered, 'Is it not written in your law, "I said: You are gods"? It is those to whom God's word came who are called gods — and scripture cannot be set aside. Then why do you charge me with blasphemy for saying "I am God's son," I whom the Father consecrated and sent into the world?'*

Psalm 82:6 is the probable scripture Jesus refers to in this passage. It alludes to the Judges who, in rendering verdicts, are speaking for God; and, as previously stated, they are legally recognized as "being" God. "Now here am I," says Jesus, "consecrated and sent into the world by my Father, and you do not give me the benefit of the definition given in your law!" Under Jewish law, one "consecrated" is set apart to become wholly devoted to the pursuit of the specific duty, or devotion.

John 10:37-38 *'If my deeds are not the deeds of my Father, do not believe me. But if they are, then even if you do not believe me, believe the deeds, so that you may recognize and know that the Father is in me, and I in the Father.'*

It is as though Jesus says, "If I am not doing the kind of works you think my Father would do, then do not believe me. But if I am representing Him correctly, then accept the evidence of these works as proof of the Father's presence and power with you even if you cannot accept me. Having taken this step you may then be able to recognize and understand that the Father is operating in and through me, and that I abide — stay within the jurisdiction of my Father's power — always."

John 10:39 *This provoked them to another attempt to seize him, but he escaped from their clutches.*

It is as though they want nothing to do with him.

John 10:40-42 *Jesus withdrew again across the Jordan, to the place where John had been baptizing earlier, and stayed there while crowds came to him. 'John gave us no miraculous sign,' they said, 'but all that he told us about this man was true.' And many came to believe in him there.*

We can only feel a great sense of peace and quiet when reading of Jesus' return to the familiar and more friendly area where John baptized with water and preached his great evangelism of repentance. Crowds now come to Jesus and because of the Baptist's work their thought can accept his presence and his message and feel the benediction of his saving love. Many open their hearts to him and find their new birth in believing in him. Jesus must feel loved at last.

At this point most of the years of his ministry are behind him. This interlude of warm friendliness that is implied in this passage must bring blessed refreshment to Jesus and his followers. It is the hush before the dawn when his greatest battle will be fought and his greatest victory will be won.

Chapter Eleven

Lazarus is Ill

John 11:1-6   *There was a man named Lazarus who had fallen ill. His home was at Bethany, the village of Mary and her sister Martha. This Mary, whose brother Lazarus had fallen ill, was the woman who anointed the Lord with ointment and wiped his feet with her hair. The sisters sent a message to him: 'Sir, you should know that your friend lies ill.' When Jesus heard this he said, 'This illness is not to end in death; through it God's glory is to be revealed and the Son of God glorified.' Therefore, though he loved Martha and her sister and Lazarus, he stayed where he was for two days after hearing of Lazarus' illness.*

This is our first introduction to this family, even though we are told that Jesus stays somewhere on the Mount of Olives. Bethany is there and it is likely that he stays with these good friends, Mary, Martha, and Lazarus.

How very natural that they send a message to him when Lazarus becomes ill. It is a very concise message that tells all that is needed. Apparently sharing this news with some disciples, he assures them Lazarus' illness will not end in death, but that it will reveal God's glory and bring glory to the Son of God.

Then he stays for two days where he is. No reason is given for this delay, but, knowing the outcome we can surmise that he waits for the death and entombment of his dear friend. Just as the changing of the water into wine seems to hark back to some similar occurrence in Jesus' earlier experience which Mary knows about, so this death and burial, at a time when Jesus is so keenly aware of his coming crucifixion and death, may rehearse its spiritual significance for him and act as a point of reassurance to him to comfort him during his own trying experience. Surely all can agree that this wait before going to Lazarus is very deliberate.

John 11:7-10   *He then said to his disciples, 'Let us go back to Judaea.' 'Rabbi,' his disciples said, 'it is not long since the Jews were wanting to stone you. Are you going there again?' Jesus replied, 'Are there not twelve hours of daylight? Anyone can walk in daytime without stumbling, because he has this world's light to see by. But if he walks after nightfall, he stumbles, because the light fails him.'*

The suggestion that they return to Judaea astonishes and dismays his disciples. They remind him of the strong emotions he has roused in Judaea, for they had been about to stone him when he departed.

Jesus replies with a question, "Are there not twelve hours of daylight?' Earlier, when he announces himself as the "Light of the world' (John 8:12), he also claims that none of his followers shall wander in the dark. The consciousness that is illumined will unerringly choose the right path designated by God. But the unillumined will encounter failure and difficulties. Jesus knows himself to be the Light, and that as long as he is in the world there are certain works that he must do, for this is his Father's plan.

John 11:11-16   *After saying this he added, 'Our friend Lazarus has fallen asleep, but I shall go and wake him.' The disciples said, 'Master, if he is sleeping he will recover.' Jesus had been speaking of Lazarus' death, but they thought that he meant natural sleep. Then Jesus told them plainly: 'Lazarus is dead. I am glad for your sake that I was not there; for it will lead you to believe. But let us go to him.' Thomas, called 'the Twin,' said to his fellow-disciples, 'Let us also go and die with him.'*

Much is made of the term that "Lazarus has fallen asleep." Not for even a moment does Jesus imply that Lazarus' condition is less than death. Even though he says he will wake him, it is the rousing from death, not sleep, of which he speaks. It has been suggested that Lazarus suffers a deep coma. Seemingly those interested in this episode are unable to bring themselves to believe that one dead four days can be roused from that state. All things are possible to God.

Jesus is a teacher. This experience with Lazarus serves to illustrate many of the wonderful teachings he imparts privately to his students. It also serves to strengthen him.

"Let us also go and die with him," said Thomas. The times must be very dangerous for them if the disciples have to face death themselves by reason of their association with Jesus.

Lazarus is Dead

John 11:17-20   On his arrival Jesus found that Lazarus had already been four days in the tomb. Bethany was just under two miles from Jerusalem, and many of the Jews had come from the city to visit Martha and Mary and condole with them about their brother. As soon as Martha heard that Jesus was on his way, she went to meet him, and left Mary sitting at home.

Martha goes to Jesus. He has come at last! Perhaps, because the authorities are searching for him, Jesus has stayed away from Martha and Mary's house. He seems to have waited somewhere in the vicinity of Lazarus' tomb. It is logical for him to stop there first. Mary, her grief great, is with her friends at home, unaware of Jesus' arrival.

John 11:21-27   Martha said to Jesus, 'Lord, if you had been here my brother would not have died. Even now I know that God will grant you whatever you ask of him.' Jesus said, 'Your brother will rise again.' 'I know that he will rise again,' said Martha, 'at the resurrection on the last day.' Jesus said, 'I am the resurrection and the life. Whoever has faith in me shall live, even though he dies; and no one who lives and has faith in me shall ever die. Do you believe this?' 'I do, Lord,' she answered; 'I believe that

you are the Messiah, the Son of God who was to come into the world.'

If only you had been here this would not have happened! This has ever been the cry of the grief-stricken.

"God will grant you whatever you ask of him." Martha's spiritual eyes have not yet seen the Messiah, the Christ of God. She still sees only a good man who is so close to God that his every prayer is answered. He reassures her that Lazarus will rise again, but she answers with the traditional Jewish phrase "I know that he will rise again at the resurrection on the last day." Then Jesus speaks very plainly to her, "I am the resurrection and the life." He goes on to explain this statement to her. "Whoever has faith in me, shall live even though he dies; and no one who lives and has faith in me shall ever die." We can almost see his earnestness, his hands on her shoulders as he faces her with loving eyes and tender consideration. Perhaps he even gives her a bit of a shake as he asks, "Do you believe this?" She needs to be roused to a larger concept of life and God's all-inclusive management of life. "I am the resurrection" means that he, Jesus Christ, Son of God, is the inbreathing power, the indwelling presence of those who accept him. As life, his living presence within men is the perpetual life or "resurrection-action" to his followers. And to one who is alive in the Spirit and has faith, the living God within shall keep him from the experience of death. "Do you believe this?" Jesus asks.

Piercing the darkness of her grief and human reasoning with his truth and spiritual power she takes her first footstep in the new dimension Jesus has just opened to her, the realm where Spirit reigns. "I do, Lord," she answers; "I believe that you are the Messiah, the Son of God who was to come into the world."

John 11:28-31   So saying she went to call her sister Mary and, taking her aside, she said, 'The Master is here and is asking for you.' As soon as Mary heard this she rose and went to him. Jesus had not yet entered the village, but was still at the place where Martha had met him. When the Jews who were in the house condoling with Mary saw her hurry out, they went after her, assuming that she was going to the tomb to weep there.

Quietly, to ensure Jesus' safety, Martha tells her sister of Jesus' arrival and gives her the heart-warming message that he "is asking for you." But Mary is to have no privacy with him because the many friends who come to support them in their grief for Lazarus misinterpret her sudden departure.

John 11:32-37 *Mary came to the place where Jesus was, and as soon as she saw him she fell at his feet and said, 'Lord, if you had been here my brother would not have died.' When Jesus saw her weeping and the Jews who had come with her weeping, he was moved with indignation and deeply distressed. 'Where have you laid him?' he asked. They replied, 'Come and see.' Jesus wept. The Jews said, 'How dearly he must have loved him!' But some of them said, 'Could not this man, who opened the blind man's eyes, have done something to keep Lazarus from dying?'*

This little account of tragedy in the life of two sisters who are devoted to Jesus is full of love and warmth. Jesus knows before he starts his journey to Bethany, that Lazarus will die, and he also knows that he will restore him through his prayers. It is no wonder he weeps tears of love and frustration to see such dear friends go through torment. Jesus is human, although blessed with God's unlimited gift of the Spirit; so in his humanity he must grieve due to Mary's and Martha's suffering.

Those Jewish friends who follow Mary to the tomb are correct in both their perceptions. Jesus does love Lazarus and he can save him. But in obedience to the Spirit, his constant guide, he does that which glorifies his Father. He waits for Lazarus to die.

Take Away The Stone

John 11:38-41 *Jesus, again deeply moved, went to the tomb. It was a cave, with a stone placed against it. Jesus said. 'Take away the stone.' Martha, the dead man's sister, said to him, 'Sir, by now there will be a stench; he has been there four days.' Jesus said, 'Did I not tell you that if you have faith you will see the glory of God?' Then they removed the stone.*

Jesus' sighing springs from the oppressive weight of his friends' despair that cries out to God for help when their loved one dies. The great moment has arrived when the barrier of death will be pierced and one dead four days will return to be loved anew.

The sisters and their friends show their faith and trust in Jesus by removing the stone as he requests. If they feel otherwise they can laugh at him and return to the house!

John 11:41-44 *Then Jesus looked upwards and said, 'Father, I thank you for hearing me. I know that you always hear me, but I have spoken for the sake of the people standing round, that they may believe it was you who sent me.' Then he raised his voice in a great cry: 'Lazarus, come out.' The dead man came out, his hands and feet bound with linen bandages, his face wrapped in a cloth. Jesus said, 'Loose him; let him go.'*

Let us imagine this scene: Jesus stands at the mouth of the cave. This is no hasty prayer he utters; for more than four days he has lived with the assurance that God will preserve Lazarus.

His prayer is thanksgiving. Thanks that he has been heard; thanks that his prayers are always heard. But he speaks also for the sake of the people standing witness, that they might believe that God has sent him. This is his constant and great concern, that it be known that he is sent by his Father.

With divine authority he utters the cry that shatters forever the finality of death, "Lazarus, come out."

The spiritual power that rouses Lazarus also must bring him forth from the tomb, for his body is swathed in linen bands as is customary.

But let us go back a bit to the moment before Jesus calls Lazarus forth. What of the watching people?

Jesus faces the tomb, raises his hand with authority, and cries: "Lazarus, come out!" For a moment the cold dread of anticipation grips each one, even Mary and Martha. An awe, even terror of what might be, touches them all. They are to see what none before has seen. Yes! He comes! Lazarus comes from the tomb! There he is, all bound in linen.

Then the command, "Loose him; let him go!" Eager hands made short work of the task. Then, that which has been deepest grief a moment before suddenly becomes glorious joy. And what of Jesus? This is his dear friend. Does he stand apart — or does he join in the rejoicing?

Conspiracy

John 11:45-46   *Many of the Jews who had come to visit Mary, and had seen what Jesus did, put their faith in him. But some of them went off to the Pharisees and reported what he had done.*

The great event these people have witnessed affects them deeply. To some this is the great power of God. To others this event confirms that here is a man dangerous to the "status quo" and one who can very easily tip the delicate balance the Pharisees maintain to keep some freedom of worship in spite of Roman conquest. A great deal is at stake, the very life of the nation.

John 11:47-53   *Thereupon the chief priests and the Pharisees convened a meeting of the Council. 'This man is performing many signs,' they said, 'and what action are we taking? If we let him go on like this the whole populace will believe in him, and then the Romans will come and sweep away our temple and our nation.' But one of them, Caiaphas, who was high priest that year, said, 'You have no grasp of the situation at all; you do not realize that it is more to your interest that one man should die for the people, than that the whole nation should be destroyed.' He did not say this of his own accord, but as the high priest that year he was prophesying that Jesus would die for the nation, and not for the nation alone but to*

gather together the scattered children of God. So from that day on they plotted his death.

Caiaphas, as high priest, is an instrument of God's purpose and furthers the plans that makes it possible for the Lamb of God to pay the price for the redemption of God's people. Jesus' sacrifice will save, not only God's people in the Jewish nation, but also the scattered children of God in other nations.

John 11:54   *Accordingly Jesus no longer went about openly among the Jews, but withdrew to a town called Ephraim, in the country bordering on the desert, and stayed there with his disciples.*

Common sense brings Jesus and his disciples to the edge of the desert. Here they have a measure of safety and Jesus can have the peace of quiet communion with his Father. Trying days lie ahead.

The Passover in Jerusalem

John 11:55-57   *The Jewish Passover was now at hand, and many people went up from the country to Jerusalem to purify themselves before the festival. They looked out for Jesus, and as they stood in the temple they asked one another, 'What do you think? Perhaps he is not coming to the festival.' Now the chief priests and the Pharisees had given orders that anyone who knew where he was must report it, so that they might arrest him.*

Jesus is well known, with a large following.

The word has gone out to arrest Jesus. They wait only for the opportune moment.

Chapter Twelve

The Lasting Gift

John 12:1-2   *Six days before the Passover festival Jesus came to Bethany, the home of Lazarus whom he had raised from the dead. They gave a supper in his honour, at which Martha served, and Lazarus was among the guests with Jesus.*

Some Bible scholars feel that this dinner takes place at the home of Simon the Leper. There is agreement on the part of some scholars, as well, that he is the father of Martha, Mary, and Lazarus. Jesus is very fond of this family and apparently frequently stays with them. This is the circle of friends in Bethany, the little town on the Mount of Olives.

John 12:2-3   *Then Mary brought a pound of very costly perfume, pure oil of nard, and anointed Jesus' feet and wiped them with her hair, till the house was filled with the fragrance.*

Jesus is the guest of honor at the dinner, and Mary singles him out to perfume his feet. Much conjecture and puzzling comments have arisen, and magnificent sermons have been preached, concerning the selfless giving of the fragrant gift. One would think at first reading that she uses the entire pound of nard for "the house was filled with the fragrance." But later Jesus says, "Let her keep it till the day when she prepares for my burial."

Why does Mary do this? In Mark 14:8 Jesus is quoted as saying, "She has done what lay in her power; she has anointed my body in anticipation of my burial." In Mark's account she anoints his head; in John's account she anoints his feet. Each rendering has little differences. Perhaps the copyists of Mark's Gospel thought of Jesus sitting in a chair at a table, in which case his feet are under the table and inaccessible. In John's Gospel it is likely that the Roman custom is followed, in which the guests recline on couches, their feet away from the table. In fact, if this is so, his feet are the only part of his body near her.

Again, why does she do this?

Anointing Jesus' feet with oil of nard shows the great depths of gratitude Mary feels for the recovery of her brother. It also pledges her love for Jesus as she anoints his feet and wipes them with her long hair.

What lovelier symbol of overflowing love can there be than this perfume. Used in burials its lasting sweetness conveys the continuing love of sorrowing relatives and friends for the departed.

It is absurd to think that this family, whom Jesus knows so well, is unaware of his coming destiny. With the knowledge that Jesus will be taken from them at some time, and further anticipating that it will be unlikely that she can give her precious gift at that time, Mary offers it now. Jesus is being honored by her father as well as the whole household and guests. This is her special and perfect gift of love and thanksgiving.

Lazarus and Judas Iscariot

John 12:4-8   *At this, Judas Iscariot, one of his disciples — the one who was to betray him — protested, 'Could not this perfume have been sold for three hundred denarii and the money given to the poor?' He said this, not out of any concern for the poor, but because he was a thief; he had charge of the common purse and used to pilfer the money kept in it. 'Leave her alone,' said Jesus. 'Let her keep it for the day of my burial. The poor you have always among you, but you will not always have me.'*

Here is Judas interrupting what is a most touching scene, with a venal note — ugliness takes the stage. Even John feels constrained to tell us why he has made such an outburst; one of Jesus' disciples is a thief! But we also see Judas' littleness! The stench of jealousy is striving to compete with the beautiful fragrance of love. Mary's offering is pure. Lazarus is receiving great attention for he is a man returned from the dead; and Judas is simply ignored. If Judas is small enough to steal from the common purse in the past, he can be seen as capable of seizing any opportunity to attract attention to himself, especially at this feast where selfless love is so evident. So much for this outrage at Mary's expense. Presumably Jesus reads the picture very clearly.

John 12:9-11   *Learning he was there the Jews came in large numbers, not only because of Jesus but also to see Lazarus whom he had raised from the dead. The chief priest then resolved to do away with Lazarus as well, since on his account many Jews were going over to Jesus and putting their faith in him.*

Word spreads rapidly and the restoration of Lazarus becomes very well known. People, by nature being very curious, gather to see Jesus and to see Lazarus as well.

Hosanna!

John 12:12-18   *The next day the great crowd of pilgrims who had come to the festival, hearing that Jesus was on the way to Jerusalem, went out to meet him with palm branches in their hands, shouting, 'Hosanna!' Blessed is he who comes in the name of the Lord! Blessed is the king of Israel!' Jesus found a donkey and mounted it, in accordance with the words of scripture: 'Fear no more, daughter of Zion; see, your king is coming, mounted on a donkey's colt.' At the time his disciples did not understand this, but after Jesus had been glorified they remembered that this had been written about him, and that it had happened to him.*
The people who were present when he called Lazarus out of the tomb and raised him from the dead kept telling what they had seen and heard. That is why the crowd went to meet him: they had heard of this sign that he had performed.

Scriptural Evidence

Biblical prophecy can be found underlying almost every phase of the account of Jesus. His birth, events in his life, his victory over death, and finally, that he will sit at God's right hand, have all been foretold. Jesus is well acquainted with the Scriptures that concern his coming and his work. He considers it enormously important that he be seen by his contemporaries, as well as by people now, within the context of Scripture.

In the Scriptures we find the prophecies of God, and to find within them the description of Jesus and his mighty works, as well as prophecies of specific events, (such as riding the ass into Jerusalem) makes his coming, his life, and his influence more believable as the power-of-God-in-action to succeeding generations. Mainly, however, this foretelling acts as God's seal of approval of His Chosen.

Traveling to Jerusalem, Jesus rides on a young ass. Maybe it is one of the beautiful little animals so loved by visitors to the Near East — those with dark hair along the spine and across the shoulders, forming a cross. Today tradition says this donkey wears the cross in remembrance of the Holy One he carried long ago.

On the day of Jesus' triumphant entry to Jerusalem the young ass carries a burden more precious than any little donkey before or since.

Mark's Gospel is slightly different from John's account in its detail of this event. In it we learn Jesus instructs his disciples where to find a young ass. They spread their cloaks upon the animal which Jesus mounts and rides to the temple.

"Many people carpeted the road with their cloaks, while others spread greenery which they had cut in the fields; and those in front and those behind shouted 'Hosanna! Blessed is he who comes in the name of the Lord!" (Mark 11:8-9).

John's description tells us the populace carries palms which they wave as they shout their praise.

The One who rides the ass so confidently is indeed triumphant. He has come into the world for one purpose — to reveal the Father in his own selfhood, and to redeem humanity. He has obediently followed his Father's plan and fulfilled his purpose thus far, and he is content. Facing him is his greatest sacrifice. Only the great love he bears humanity can equip him for this next step.

Jesus is acclaimed for only this very short period as he rides to Jerusalem.

His kingdom has been given him by his Father; Spirit has equipped him to rule; instead of a king's regalia, he comes clothed in humility; and he rides, not on a prancing steed, but upon a little ass!

To the materialist and the worldly this little procession is ridiculous! But this same procession shows the thoughtful that God works through the humble, and through what the world calls the insignificant.

Paul writes (1 Corinthians 1:27-29) "Yet, to shame the wise, God has chosen what the world counts folly, and to shame what is strong, God has chosen what the world counts weakness. He has chosen things without rank or standing in the world, mere nothings, to overthrow the existing order. So no place is left for any human pride in the presence of God."

We should also be aware that this small devoted group, walking to Jerusalem and to the temple, prefigures the way in which Christianity will be made known through the coming ages. The acceptance of Jesus in this particular instance is largely based on Lazarus' recent resurrection. The apostles and Paul will later preach the acceptance of Jesus through his crucifixion and resurrection.

John 12:19   *The Pharisees said to one another, 'You can see we are getting nowhere; all the world has gone after him!'*

Helpless before God's plan for His Son, the Pharisees are unable to arrest Jesus. His "time has not yet come." All the plans they make are frustrated and to these guardians of the law it seems that all the world is now following this troublemaker!

John 12:20-21   *Among those who went up to worship at the festival were some Gentiles. They approached Philip, who was from Bethsaida in Galilee, and said to him, 'Sir, we should like to see Jesus.'*

It is natural that they contact Philip, for he has a Greek name and comes from a community where Gentiles live. They want to see Jesus, who has just completed his triumphal ride and has received the acclamation of the crowds.

This Gentile group, perhaps representing others who stay at home, feel their need urgent enough to present their request even during this tumultuous hour. Now Jesus' message is going to be heard by the Gentiles, the "other sheep"[1] of whom he speaks.

John 12:22   *Philip went and told Andrew, and the two of them went to tell Jesus.*

Philip probably is in a quandary when he hears the Gentiles request to see Jesus; for until now there has been no indication, other than their Master's reference to "other sheep," that the teaching they have been receiving will be for any except the nations of Abraham's descendants. Should he take a Gentile, a non-Jew, to Jesus? He shares his concerns with Andrew. "Not only," he might have said, "are these people Gentiles, but they are requesting to see our Master now when so many demands are being made upon him!" Together they take the problem to Jesus.

The Hour Has Come

John 12:23-24   *Jesus replied: 'The hour has come for the Son of Man to be glorified. In very truth I tell you, unless a grain of wheat falls into the ground and dies, it remains that and nothing more; but if it dies, it bears a rich harvest.'*

The hour of the Son of Man's glorification is at hand. The triumphal entry discloses it; the acknowledgment of Jesus by the Gentiles declares it; and in his statement to the crowds Jesus explains it.

And it is well he does. Using wheat as a symbol, he teaches through nature's process, that death is not the final point of life. The "rich harvest" comes after death in his parable. Thus he gently turns the thought of his hearers out of the usual ruts of reasoning into the area beyond physical life.

---

[1] John 10:16 (other sheep)

He is telling them very plainly that the time has come for him to die; but his tender love cushions this grim news with a parable of a grain of wheat. He does not elaborate at this time on the "rich harvest," but the emphasis in his announcement is not on his death but on that which will happen after his death.

John 12:25   *'Whoever loves himself is lost, but he who hates himself in this world will be kept safe for eternal life.'*

Our focus at this moment is on the triumphant Jesus, yet his message cautions us of the danger of such a position. Our Lord teaches that we must love God with our mind and heart and soul, and our neighbor as ourselves. In this statement he is not contradicting his earlier teaching, but is calling attention to the great danger of accepting any glorification, or rewards, as though earned by one's own excellence.

Jesus constantly states, as John records, "I speak (and I do) only as my Father directs me to do." Jesus loves God so completely that his regard for himself can almost be likened to disregard, or "hatred." However, this pure love provides a condition that enables the Father to glorify his Son.

When shouts of praise are heaped upon Jesus he quickly states that such glory and honor belong to his Father, not to him, for he is here to reveal the Father.

"Whoever loves himself is lost." He who is pleased with accomplishments and thinks them of his own making is lost. Why? Because he has turned away from God as the great Cause in his life and being. He does not give God all glory but has taken it upon himself.

"But he who hates himself in this world will be kept safe for eternal life."

With hatred there frequently comes the desire to obliterate the one hated. When we allow our sense of self to grow less and less important, and find Jesus Christ growing larger and larger in our lives, then we are accomplishing the type of "hatred" of ourselves that our Lord knows is important for eternal life.

As long as thought is centered on God as the Source and the author of every act and thought, then we will continuously be an open fount for divine expression for performing the will of God — and this is life eternal.

John 12:26   *'If anyone is to serve me, he must follow me; where I am, there will my servant be. Whoever serves me will be honoured by the Father.'*

In order to serve Jesus, we must follow him. We must look in the direction in which he looks. We must have his viewpoint. We must see that his Father is also our Father who loves us as tenderly as He loves His own Jesus. It is the Father who provides him with power and dominion to do mighty works in His name, and this Father is making it possible for us to serve God and Jesus by doing mighty works in His Son's name.

Just as Jesus stands in God's stead with full credentials to act for God, so we who serve our Lord are equipped to act in the name of Jesus Christ. Following him we will serve him, and will be with him. We will be honored by the Father through the glorification of him whom we serve, the Son of God.

John 12:27-28   *'Now my soul is in turmoil, and what am I to say? "Father, save me from this hour?" No, it was for this that I came to this hour. Father, glorify your name.'*

We are told that Jesus is sensitive in every human way. At this moment he must have an overwhelming dread of his coming execution. It is the first time we have shared the horror that presses in upon him. He knows the ransom price he has to pay. For that purpose he has come into the world. Facing a terrible death, that many before him and after him will also suffer, it is understandable that he will recoil. He prays, "Father, glorify your name." He petitions his Father to strengthen his humanity in the face of his awesome responsibilities. He asks that the Father's selfhood be revealed in even greater glory; that the "I AM" be the dominant selfhood within him instead of his fear-filled human self. He asks that the Son of Man yield completely to the Son of God, that only Divinity's selfhood be seen.

Jesus and the men and women of his time are very familiar with the process of crucifixion. It is a slow, agonizing torment, sometimes lasting days. The victim is naked and exposed to weather as well as the jeers of the populace. It is very cruel and carries a curse.

So it is no wonder that Jesus is suddenly overcome by the thought of the events to come that will sweep him to his mighty sacrifice. Only through the strength of his Father's glorification can he walk this chosen path of obedience. "Father, glorify your name," is Jesus' prayer.

John 12:28-29 *A voice came from heaven: 'I have glorified it, and I will glorify it again.' The crowd standing by said it was thunder they heard, while others said, 'An angel has spoken to him.'*

His Father answers his prayer. The turmoil leaves and his calmness and dominion return. He is able to continue his statements to those who come to hear.

In his continuing triumph over human self, the voice of his Father is heard approving His Nature as seen in Jesus. Jesus is glorified, for his divinity shines forth in his decisive stand and in the integrity of his obedience to His Father. Jesus also is given the great assurance that His Father will glorify him again.

Differing stages of thought are illustrated by the comments of the people, some thinking the voice to be thunder. Those more spiritually-minded conceive it to be an angel they hear. But Jesus hears God's Voice, and one of his disciples also hears it as the Voice of God and is able to repeat the message as well, for we have John's account.

John 12:30 *Jesus replied, 'This voice spoke for your sake, not mine.'*

Since the people do not understand, how can he mean that the voice speaks for the crowd's sake? His next words give the answer.

When I Am Lifted Up

John 12:31-32 *'Now is the hour of judgement for this world; now shall the prince of this world be driven out. And when I am lifted up from the earth I shall draw everyone to myself.'*

When the great Voice from heaven speaks the divine commendation and glorification of Jesus, it correspondingly pronounces the hour of judgment for all conduct and teaching contrary to Jesus' position. For in Jesus' glorification the human yields to the divine Presence. The Voice thunders that all righteousness comes from God.

Accepting Jesus we must accept his line of reasoning. The judgment comes to the worldly-minded through their failure to follow him.

The prince of this world is driven out when men are responsive to God alone. There is nothing left for the devil to use.

When the Father glorifies Jesus He "lifts up" his humanity. Under the pressure of the grim hours and days ahead of him, Jesus asks that his human self-control yield to the control of God, and the people see him regain composure.

His prayer for himself is all-inclusive in his desire to glorify God. "Glorify your name," he asks. He asks that the glory permeate his entire individuality.

This prayer asks that his fears and confusion be replaced by the glory of God's peace and a vision that transcends human events.

He asks that he be given the continuing endurance of spiritual strength to replace the weakness of his body under torture.

These visible proofs of his Father's presence in him, and his Father's love for him, glorifies God's name.

As we allow the glory of our God to strengthen and uplift our humanity, by replacing frailty with spiritual strength, we will be lifted above this lower level of thought and drawn to our Lord Jesus Christ.

Jesus says, "When I am lifted up from the earth I shall draw everyone to myself."

Through the centuries this has been interpreted as a reference to his elevation on the cross. It also can mean that his crucifixion will be the overcoming of death — the defeat of death — and that this overcoming will be not only for himself but for all those whom he loves, for, as Peter tells us: "Christ too suffered for our sins once and for all, the just for the unjust, that he might bring us to God..." (1 Peter 3:18). Having ascended to his place on the right hand of the Father he draws all men to himself.

"The right hand of the Lord" is a Biblical term expressing the power of God. To be on the right hand of the Father is to share the power of God.

Having been lifted up from the earthly dimension to the infinitude of Spirit, Jesus exercises the love that enfolds all who love him and his Father, gathering his own to himself.

John 12:33   *This he said to indicate the kind of death he was to die.*

This editorial remark is interesting. It obviously refers to Jesus being lifted up on the cross with arms outstretched to all humanity. But this statement does not preclude the reference from having a broader meaning.

It is not known whether such editorial remarks are original or the addition of a copyist.

John 12:34   *The people answered, 'Our law teaches us that the Messiah remains for ever. What do you mean by saying that the Son of Man must be lifted up? What Son of Man is this?'*

The crowds want a David-like king as Messiah. A Savior on a wholly spiritual basis seems incomprehensible. Their law is correct in that God's Savior will remain forever with His people. But they misinterpret the law and this beclouds their vision of Jesus. The Prophet says, "where there is no vision the people perish.'[2]

John 12:35-36   *Jesus answered them: 'The light is among you still, but not for long. Go on your way while you have the light, so that darkness may not overtake you. He who journeys in the dark does not know where he is going. Trust to the light while you have it, so that you may become children of light.' After these words Jesus went away from them into hiding.*

Jesus knows he is the light, or enlightenment, of men and that in his flesh he will be with them only a little longer. He urges them to take the glimmering of truth that they have understood and to go their way, to make it their own. This they should do lest

doubt and unbelief overtake their tenuous hold of his teachings.   Then he leaves them.

Biblical Prophecy

John 12:37-41   *In spite of the many signs which Jesus had performed in their presence they would not believe in him, for the prophet Isaiah's words had to be fulfilled: 'Lord, who has believed what we reported, and to whom has the power of the Lord been revealed?' And there is another saying of Isaiah which explains why they could not believe: 'He has blinded their eyes and dulled their minds, lest they should see with their eyes, and perceive with their minds, and turn to me to heal them.' Isaiah said this because he saw his glory and spoke about him.*

John again stresses Biblical prophecy. The very unbelief of the people has been foretold. He again quotes Isaiah: "He (the Devil) has blinded their eyes and dulled their minds..."   A Bible footnote tells us some witnesses read: "Isaiah said this when he saw his glory and spoke about him." Isaiah's vision spans the centuries and brings him close to Jesus.

John 12:42-43:   *For all that, even among those in authority many believed in him, but would not acknowledge him on account of the Pharisees, for fear of being banned from the synagogue. For they valued human reputation rather than the honour which comes from God.*

So Jesus is believed. He is accepted, but furtively, for these men live in dangerous times. And that which happens to displease those in authority, whether Jew or Roman, can be utterly disastrous to individuals and families. Stoning and crucifixion are all too commonly the punishment given. It is not easy to be a martyr for one's faith.

Jesus' Eight Points

John 12:44-50   *Jesus proclaimed: 'To believe in me, is not to believe in me but in him*

---

[2] Proverbs 29:18, King James Bible.

who sent me; to see me, is to see him who sent me. I have come into the world as light, so that no one who has faith in me should remain in darkness. But if anyone hears my words and disregards them, I am not his judge; I have not come to judge the world, but to save the world. There is a judge for anyone who rejects me and does not accept my words; the word I have spoken will be his judge on the last day. I do not speak on my own authority, but the Father who sent me has himself commanded me what to say and how to speak. I know that his commands are eternal life. What the Father has said to me, therefore — that is what I speak.'

Eight points are made by Jesus. He has voiced them at various times when speaking to the multitudes and to his students.

1. To believe in me, is not to believe in me but in Him who sent me.

2. To see me, is to see Him who sent me.

3. I have come into the world as light, so that no one who has faith in me remains in darkness.

4. If anyone hears my words and disregards them, I am not his judge. I have not come to judge the world but to save the world.

5. There is a judge for anyone who rejects me and does not accept my words; the word I have spoken will be his judge on the last day.

6. I do not speak on my own authority, but the Father who sent me has Himself commanded me what to say and how to speak.

7. I know that His commands are eternal life.

8. What the Father has said to me, therefore — that is what I speak.

In these eight points in the final paragraph of the twelfth chapter John summarizes Jesus' preaching. He writes this as though Jesus is still speaking, as indeed he is to each one of us. In succinct, clear phrases Jesus declares his purpose and his presence.

Each statement has previously been expounded. He closes with: "What the Father has said to me, therefore — that is what I speak!"

Chapter Thirteen

The Farewell Discourses

Jesus the Servant

John 13:1 *It was before the Passover festival, and Jesus knew that his hour had come and that he must leave this world and go to the Father. He had always loved his own who were in the world, and he loved them to the end.*

Passover commemorates the time written about in Exodus 12. It is the hour when the Lord "passes over" and does not harm the Israelites as His vengeance fights for their liberation.

It is the eve of the commemoration of the great exodus from Egypt. A week of preparation, including the consumption of ritualistic food, precedes the remembrance of that dreadful hour when the first born of every living thing in Egypt, men and animals, are struck down. Fearing complete annihilation, the Egyptians have relented and urged the Israelites to leave, giving richly to them of all they ask, even gold and jewels.

The time of Jesus' death will also be Passover. This time it is the First Born of God who is to be killed. The devil believes that if God's first born dies, he, the devil, will turn the tables, and that he will forever more possess God's people for his own. The snuffing out of that light (Jesus Christ) will leave him in command.

That pretender to power, the one our Lord calls "a liar and the father of liars," connives to silence God's Word, and to betray and vilify him who speaks it.

Jesus has to come into the world, for it is here on earth, right where evil boasts having full control, that God's people need to be set free. Only by being one of these people, and by overcoming evil from the level of human weakness, can Jesus destroy the roots of the bondage that hold men separate from God and His beneficent influences.

John 13:2 *The devil had already put it into the mind of Judas son of Simon Iscariot to betray him.*

Here is a captive, a slave, ready to do the bidding of his master, the devil. Though he is a key figure in the crucifixion drama that is unfolding, it is to redeem such as Judas that our Lord makes his sacrifice.

John 13:2-5 *During supper, Jesus, well aware that the Father had entrusted everything to him, and that he had come from God and was going back to God, rose from the supper table, took off his outer garment and, taking a towel, tied it round him. Then he poured water into a basin, and began to wash his disciples' feet and to wipe them with the towel.*

Our key phrase here is "well aware that the Father had entrusted everything to him." The word "entrusted" tells us of his Father's approval and confidence as well as the fact that his control is complete. It all belongs to him.

Knowing his position was secure, because he knew where he came from and where he was going to return, he took a basin and towel and began to wash his disciples feet. This was a living parable designed to convey deep meaning to his immediate disciples, and those who would come later. Though holding the reins of government he was the Servant Isaiah foresaw. In the most humble way he would serve each one. No matter what his service required of him, it would not shame nor degrade him.

John 13:6-9 *When he came to Simon Peter, Peter said to him, 'You, Lord, washing my feet?' Jesus replied, 'You do not understand now what I am doing, but one day you will.' Peter said, 'I will never let you wash my feet.' 'If I* *do not wash you,' Jesus replied, 'you have no part with me.' 'Then, Lord,' said Simon Peter, 'not my feet only; wash my hands and head as well!'*

Peter is embarrassed and uncomfortable when his Lord comes to him to wash his feet. Sandals are worn and feet become easily soiled with dust. It is the task of the lowest servants in a household, or the privilege of a wife who wishes to demonstrate her great love for her husband, to perform this service. Jesus' reply to Peter's protest, "You do not understand now what I am doing, but one day you will," implies that Peter's further spiritual growth will reveal the meaning to him.

John 13:10-11   *Jesus said to him, 'Anyone who has bathed needs no further washing; he is clean all over; and you are clean, though not every one of you.' He added the words 'not every one of you' because he knew who was going to betray him.*

But Peter still has a wrong notion about what Jesus is doing, for Jesus corrects him saying that one who has bathed, or been baptized, needs no further washing; he is clean.

So what is Jesus' purpose? He is facing a time when he will have to drain to the dregs a bitter cup. Crucifixion is designed to shame and degrade, and carries with it a Biblical curse as well.[1] Is he not illustrating to his disciples that service to others, no matter how degrading the worldly think it to be, cannot remove one from one's God-given place?

The passage starts off telling us that Jesus is "well aware" that the Father entrusts everything to him; and he knows he comes from God and will return to Him. Therefore, nothing that transpires can supersede this fact. Jesus has ended his ministry. Many have either failed to listen or have let selfish goals, and sometimes timidity, stand between them and the Christ message. The hour has come when Jesus is to enter another sphere of activity. The removal of the dust from the disciples' feet symbolizes that they too, have finished the first phase of the work.

---

[1] Deuteronomy 21:22-23

There is significance also in his earlier instruction to his disciples when he sends them out, two by two. John does not include this episode in his account, but in Matthew 10:14-15 we learn that Jesus instructs them to shake the dust of the place off their feet if they are not received and listened to.

Washing their feet removes the dust, just as the "shaking" does, when the disciples are not well received. Rather than a cleansing, this is the act of separating one's self from those attitudes which prevent people from opening their hearts to Christ. Only by separating ourselves from the reasoning used by those who refuse to accept Jesus can we be in fellowship with Jesus Christ, in communion with him. We should love and help these misguided ones, but we are not to let the dust of their arguments, no matter how clever, soil our robes of righteousness.

John 13:12-17   *After washing their feet he put on his garment and sat down again. 'Do you understand what I have done for you?' he asked. 'You call me Teacher and Lord, and rightly so, for that is what I am. Then if I, your Lord and Teacher, have washed your feet, you also ought to wash one another's feet. I have set you an example: you are to do as I have done for you. In very truth I tell you, a servant is not greater than his master, nor a messenger than the one who sent him. If you know this, happy are you if you act upon it.'*

One can picture our Lord as he resumes his position at the table where all recline. Utter quiet prevails. He looks round on them all searching their faces, then asks, "Do you understand what I have done for you? Note he says: "what I have done for you." This is no idle gesture but a specific deed done for them. "I have set you an example," he goes on to say. They are to do as he has done for them. Here his great emphasis is upon his role as Servant. His disciples are to serve their fellows for his and his Father's sake. Evidently they do understand him, for foot washing is not practiced by the early fathers of the church, but serve they do. They understand the lesser position they occupy and are able to let the

Word and the Spirit speak through them, effacing their "self" to become a transparency for their Lord's message.

Judas

John 13:18-20   *'I am not speaking about all of you; I know whom I have chosen. But there is a text of scripture to be fulfilled: "He who eats bread with me has turned against me." I tell you this now, before the event, so that when it happens you may believe that I am what I am. In very truth I tell you, whoever receives any messenger of mine receives me; and receiving me, he receives the One who sent me.'*

Again Jesus cites scripture stressing its great importance in his mission. This citation foretells the break in the family of twelve. Though they have eaten bread together there is one who will turn upon him. Wishing to clarify further what he has been saying, he says he is speaking "before the event, so that when it happens you may believe that I am what I am." Jesus relies on his credentials (his works) and the scriptures to verify him and his place. He further states: "He who receives any messenger of mine receives me; receiving me, he receives the One who sent me."

As we have stated earlier (see notes for John 10:34) it is acceptable in Jewish law to have someone conduct business in your stead. Such agents are recognized and accepted today. Jesus is telling his disciples — and this right after demonstrating to them his self-effacing service, that those who receive them as his messengers will, if they are truly getting "self" out of the way, in reality be receiving him; and, receiving him they will be in the presence of and receive the One who sent him.

This reality of the presence and closeness of the Son and Father, as the Holy Spirit speaking through an individual, is so wonderful that one finds this difficult to grasp at first reading. This momentous information becomes lost in the record of the events of that night.

John 13:21-22   *After saying this, Jesus exclaimed in deep distress. 'In very truth I tell you, one of you is going to betray me.' The disciples looked at one another in bewilderment: which of them could he mean?*

This is a chilling statement! Though he has just quoted scripture in verification of the words he now utters, the disciples find it hard to believe — or do they? Perhaps their bewilderment comes from not knowing who is the traitor.

They are reclining, Roman fashion, at this dinner, as is the custom when the meal is more than a casual gathering.

John 13:23-27   *One of them, the disciple he loved, was reclining close beside Jesus. Simon Peter signalled to him to find out which one he meant. That disciple leaned back close to Jesus and asked, 'Lord, who is it?' Jesus replied, 'It is the one to whom I give this piece of bread when I have dipped it in the dish.' Then he took it, dipped it in the dish, and gave it to Judas son of Simon Iscariot. As soon as Judas had received it Satan entered him. Jesus said to him, 'Do quickly what you have to do.'*

The disciple whom Jesus loves, tradition says it is John, reclines close to Jesus so is in a perfect position to quietly ask, "Who is it?" Jesus tells John how he will identify him then proceeds to give Judas the bread sop.

No longer is Judas hidden. He has opened his thought to evil. Satan enters him. By giving him the sopped bread, Jesus symbolically hands him his body and his life. He dismisses him saying, "Do quickly what you have to do."

John 13:28-30   *No one at the table understood what he meant by this. Some supposed that, as Judas was in charge of the common purse, Jesus was telling him to buy what was needed for the festival, or to make some gift to the poor. As soon as Judas had received the bread he went out. It was night.*

To those who have not observed the interchange between Peter and John, and John's whispered inquiry of Jesus — the giving of the sop, and Jesus' admonition to Judas, hold no significance. But Judas, at that moment, must feel he has Jesus in the palm of his hand. His spiritual littleness is incapable of recognizing more than his immediate necessity of getting back at Jesus for the imaginary affront he has suffered when Lazarus is the center of interest. He departs with Jesus' words ringing in his ears.

"It was night." It is indeed night because of the time, and it is deepest night for Judas who is so self-centered that the love of the Light of the world cannot penetrate his thinking.

John 13:31-32   *When he had gone out, Jesus said, 'Now the Son of Man is glorified, and in him God is glorified. If God is glorified in him, God will also glorify him in himself; and he will glorify him now.'*

Through his action in giving Judas the token of food, Jesus knows that he has at that moment given his consent to the death that is to come. "Now the Son of Man is glorified, and in him God is glorified" means that the Son of Man, the human and divine Jesus, has given up every material resource and henceforth will be wholly dependent on his Father. The Son of Man will be glorified by the radiant majesty of God which will abide with him, and see him through, and lift him above the experience. And in the eyes and hearts of all for all time God will thus be glorified. And because God will be a visible power with and in Jesus, this will be the beginning of his return to his Father; and God's glory and presence will be seen as majesty and strength in Jesus, outshining the indignity and shame of the cross.

John 13:33   *'My children, I am to be with you for a little longer; then you will look for me, and, as I told the Jews, I tell you now: where I am going you cannot come.'*

Gently, as he has done once before in alluding to his coming death, Jesus tells his disciples that he will be with them only a little while longer. The events in his life have reached a climax and where he is going they cannot come. As David fights Goliath alone, so Jesus is to go alone to meet all the combined evil that represents the world's indifference to and hatred of God. Through his death and resurrection he will

overcome and refute the so-called power of evil, and he will open wide the door of revelation so that God's will and God's power will be known on earth. He is going beyond death, but his disciples are not yet equipped to follow him there.

John 13:34-35   *'I give you a new commandment: love one another; as I have loved you, so you are to love one another. If there is this love among you, then everyone will know that you are my disciples.'*

Heretofore their Lord has directed their thought to God and His Son. Now they are commanded to love one another.

Jesus' love for his disciples is unique. He well knows their faults and limitations. Even Judas has a purpose, for he is an instrument of Jesus' consent to his death (for remember he states he can lay down his life but no one can take it from him). Jesus also knows the spiritual potential of his disciples, and it is to cultivate this potential that the warmth of his love tenderly embraces each one, and the sting of his rebuke excises the unrighteous attitudes of his twelve.

The love Jesus wishes to see will be a strong, steadfast love, constant and pure, empowered by Spirit to heal and bless all who come near them. It will be their proof of discipleship.

John 13:36-38   *Simon Peter said to him, 'Lord, where are you going?' Jesus replied, 'I am going where you cannot follow me now, but one day you will.' Peter said, 'Lord, why cannot I follow you now? I will lay down my life for you.' Jesus answered, 'Will you really lay down your life for me? In very truth I tell you, before the cock crows you will have denied me three times.'*

Simon Peter must find it very hard to accept death as the way of Jesus' departure. He who has healed the sick and raised the dead; he, the Son of Man, the Son of God; surely he must be speaking of some journey! When Jesus tells Peter he can not follow him now, but that someday he will, he peevishly declares he will even lay down his life! Jesus knows Peter better than Peter knows himself. Though named the

Rock (Petros), at this time in his unfolding life he is less than solid. Though well intentioned, his spiritual strength and spiritual understanding have not reached maturity.

Knowing all this, Jesus fondly asks, "Will you indeed lay down your life for me?... Before the cock crows you will have denied me three times."

This is inconceivable to Peter!

Chapter Fourteen

The Farewell Discourses, continued

Trust In Me

John 14:1 *'Set your troubled hearts at rest. Trust in God always; trust also in me.'*

Jesus again tells his beloved Twelve that he will soon leave them. Only now have they begun to grasp the fact that he will soon die — very soon — and they are greatly grieved. Ever the Comforter, Jesus immediately gives them reassurance, "Set your troubled hearts at rest. Trust in God."

Raymond E. Brown's[1] translation of this passage uses "faith" in place of "trust." Speaking of this, he says: "The Hebrew word for 'faith,' from the root *'mn*, has the concept of firmness; to have faith in God is to participate in his firmness — an appropriate note in the present context."

A dictionary[2] defines "participate" as "to have a share in common."

Participation in God's firmness takes away all apprehension, all dismay; one finds security instead of fear and weakness. It enables one to advance spiritually with vigor even in the face of what seems to be impending disaster.

"Trust also in me," says Jesus. To participate in Jesus' strength, love, and insight is to become part of his progress.

My Father's House

John 14:2-4 *'There are many dwelling-places in my Father's house; if it were not so I should have told you; for I am going to prepare a place for you. And if I go and prepare a place for you, I shall come again and take you to myself, so that where I am you may be also; and you know the way I am taking.'*

The Psalmist tells us "He that dwelleth in the secret place of the Most High shall abide under the shadow of the Almighty... He will cover me with his feathers and under his wings shall I trust" (Psalm 91). In the 23rd Psalm he sings, "The Lord is my shepherd, I shall not want. He maketh me to lie down in green pastures beside the still waters" (*King James Bible*). And in Isaiah the prophet tells us, "And the Lord will create upon every dwelling place of mount Zion, and upon her assemblies, a cloud and smoke by day, and the shining of a flaming fire by night: for upon all the glory shall be a defense" (Isaiah 4:5, *King James Bible*).

Our dwelling place is in God's love, the "secret place of the Most High." It is a place exalted above all earthly desires. Here every need is supplied — not meagerly, but as a lush pasture is bountiful for those who feed there. Our dwelling shall be beside still waters, close to the deep flow of God's goodness and love. And over every dwelling shall be the visible evidence of God's presence; and wherever there is glory, there will be security.

Jesus is going to the house of his Father, to the full awareness of the glorious presence of God. Here is safety and love, shelter and provision. In the ascension he will preserve his identity, his body, and rise with it into Spirit. Soon the final evidence of his dual nature will appear as he is perceived anew in his place in the Trinity — Father, Son, and Holy Spirit.

---

[1] Raymond E. Brown, S. S., *The Anchor Bible*, Volume 29A, pages 617-618, Doubleday & Co., Inc.

[2] By permission. From *Webster's Ninth New Collegiate Dictionary* © 1990 by Merriam-Webster Inc., publisher of the Merriam-Webster® dictionaries.

The transition from the human to the divine is the process of "preparation" of which our Lord speaks. It begins with the embracing of his humanity — the Son of Man — by his Christ nature, the Son of God.

Jesus allows his humanity to be so completely identified with the Son of God that the two are one. Thus his human will early yields to the divine will. The complete incorporation of human and divine shatter precedent and opens the way, through the human will yielding to God, for the translation of all the people of God.

This mighty achievement can be likened to a space vehicle which needs special thrust to escape earth's gravitational field. Jesus, in his final hours on earth, suffers the torture and mockery of the anti-Christ, but pours forth pure thought and divine love to all those opposing him and his mission. This love is the mighty thrust of God-power that enables him to rise above and beyond the hatred and limitation of opposing concepts, and allows him to move freely in the wholly spiritual infinite.

In this way Jesus breaks the barriers that restrict mankind and opens the way for them to follow him. Thus the resurrection of Jesus Christ is the pattern, the "way" that brings God's people to Him.

In the place that Jesus prepares, God's people will be "at home," compatible with all that surrounds them — content; for to reach that home they will follow "the way," they will take the steps of thought and action that Jesus teaches them.

They will dwell in the house, or love and care of God, forever.

"I shall come again and take you to myself" Jesus is tenderly reassuring them. Although he will go away for a little while he will come again and welcome them. He will receive them into himself as part of the body of Christ. This indwelling in Jesus Christ will be possible because earlier, through baptism, they begin to partake of him — and later, through his atonement in the sacrificial death, he will die once, for all. Because he welcomes those who "yield" to him (John 1:12), the disciple is able to participate, or share, in common with him, his spiritual accomplishments for them, before "death," and afterwards.

"So that where I am you may be also." His progressive overcoming will lift each one to his level, for we are to be where he is.

This does not mean that the disciple can sit back and "let Jesus do it all." The student must learn to yield himself; to accept and assimilate all that Jesus Christ is asking him to accept. He must begin to think from the new standpoint that is offered him, and to the degree that he is able to do this he will become aware of his oneness with his Lord.

"My way there is known to you." The disciples all learn from his progress — from the day of the wedding feast in Cana to the momentous instant of Lazarus' resurrection — in each instance there is a lesson to learn.

Jesus wins our salvation giving us God's way of "life to life" as opposed to evil's condemnation of "dust to dust." It is only after Adam eats the forbidden fruit of the "tree of knowledge of good and evil" that men are under the condemnation of "dust to dust." As long as man is singleminded, seeking only the gifts of God, he lives in Paradise. It is to restore mankind to this primal purity of thought and experience that Jesus comes to destroy erroneous knowledge with his divine revelation, thus enabling us to share his vision and being. In this way God's people participate in the body of Christ.

"There are many dwelling-places in my Father's house." He is saying, "When you go to my Father's house — heaven — you will find you have an identity and a place there. You will feel at home, content, and you will know the beauty of the place where you have come to dwell."

"And my way there is known to you." His way, or method of returning to the Father, is his legacy to those who will practice his teachings in all time to come. He establishes the foundational truths for all to understand and master. He spends three years with his Twelve, tutoring, testing, admonishing, and loving them. Now he and his Twelve are about to be put to the greatest test.

I Am The Way

John 14:5-6 *Thomas said, 'Lord, we do not know where you are going, so how can we know the way?' Jesus replied, 'I am the way, the truth, and the life; no one comes to the Father except by me.'*

Faced with the loss of the shepherding Jesus, Thomas seems to become obtuse. He seems unable to face the inevitable moment when he will be required to "follow through" — or put into practice — all he has been taught. He feels confused and helpless. His perception is dulled.

Now, Jesus, the very one he is clinging to, answers his need. "I am the way." "Do as I do." Follow me in your thoughts, your living. "I am the truth." Seek me and my Father and do not be fooled by other teachings. "And I am life." In following me as the Way and Truth you will be filled with Spirits' energies which lift you up to my Father. "No one comes to the Father except by me."

"But to all who did accept him, to those who put their trust in him, he gave the right to become children of God" (John 1:12).

John 14:7-11 *'If you knew me you would know my Father too. From now on you do know him; you have seen him.' Philip said to him, 'Lord, show us the Father; we ask no more.' Jesus answered, 'Have I been all this time with you, Philip, and still you do not know me? Anyone who has seen me has seen the Father. Then how can you say, "Show us the Father"? Do you not believe that I am in the Father, and the Father in me? I am not myself the source of the words I speak to you: it is the Father who dwells in me doing his own work. Believe me when I say that I am in the Father and the Father in me; or else accept the evidence of the deeds themselves.'*

If we think of God as physical like the human Jesus it is hard to believe that Jesus is in the Father and the Father in him. But when we consider God as Spirit it is comprehensible that Jesus Christ is in the Spirit and that Spirit is in Jesus.

It is the Father (Spirit) who is the source of Jesus' works and deeds. "It is the Father who dwells in me doing his own work," says Jesus.

Then Jesus says, "If you cannot accept that fact on my say so, then accept the evidence of the deeds themselves — the blind see, the lame walk, and the dead are raised."

---

[3] See Elijah and Elisha: 2 Kings 2:1-15.

Ask In My Name

John 14:12-14 *'In very truth I tell you, whoever has faith in me will do what I am doing; indeed he will do greater things still because I am going to the Father. Anything you ask in my name I will do, so that the Father will be glorified in the Son. If you ask anything in my name I will do it.'*

Here again the tremendous earnestness of Jesus shows in his "In very truth I tell you, whoever has faith (is strong, firm) in me will do what I am doing." It is this faith in Jesus that opens wide the doors of consciousness to God — to accept fully and completely the fact that Jesus, Son of God, brings the Gift of God to us! The indwelling Father, Spirit, comes to us and fills us and enfolds us. Then the Father acts in us through Christ. And the works that Jesus does we will do; and we will fulfill his prophecy with greater works, "because I am going to the Father," The Ego will be the Father.

In his ascension and return to his Father, the human Jesus will no longer be visible to men on earth because, as it "was in the beginning before the world was," the Word and God will be found One. No longer will the Son need to strive to be obedient to the Father's will; instead the Son's will shall be the Father's will; one will only shall be evidenced. God has visited His people and provided them with a way to return to the place they lost.

"Anything you ask in my name I will do, so that the Father will be glorified in the Son." Jesus is saying that the response to the petition will be only for the Son's glorification of the Father. Under those conditions "If you ask anything in my name I will do it." He is saying: "As you assume my mantle[3] and in my nature ask in my name, I will do it."

Jesus Christ expects us to grow spiritually and to assume — take up — the legacy of responsibility he gives us — to glorify the Father in the Son's name. His promise to us is in effect today.

The Advocate

John 14:15-17   *'If you love me you will obey my commands; and I will ask the Father, and he will give you another to be your advocate, who will be with you for ever — the Spirit of truth.'*

This statement is predicated on love — agape love. It is this selfless spiritual love that becomes the reception area for the Father's provision. With consciousness attuned through selfless love the disciple is ready. Jesus indicates that he will ask the Father to give another to instruct and advise. He will be the Spirit of Truth and not a corporeal being as is Jesus. This "Advocate" will reveal Jesus' nature just as Jesus in his career reveals his Father's nature.

The Greek word "Paracletus" is translated as follows:

Revised English Bible — Advocate

King James Bible — Comforter

Modern Language Bible — Helper

Living Bible — Comforter

New Revised Standard Bible — Advocate

The Spirit of Truth embodies all the definitions given in the various translations of the New Testament.

John 14:17   *'The world cannot accept him, because the world neither sees nor knows him; but you know him, because he dwells with you and will be in you.'*

Speaking of the Advocate — the Spirit of Truth — we learn again that worldly thought is incapable of discerning the Spirit of Truth. There is no response or desire in such a consciousness to become acquainted with God or Jesus Christ. Such types are quite satisfied to continue to believe in powerful evil and helpless good! But those whose baptism has been genuinely of God have eyes that see and ears that can hear. The things of Spirit have reality for them, and it becomes a thing of joy to obey the will of God! And why is this? Because, Jesus tells us, the Spirit of Truth dwells with and is in those who love

God. Because His love is active in us we are able to be active in His love

John 14:18-20   *'I will not leave you bereft; I am coming back to you. In a little while the world will see me no longer, but you will see me; because I live, you too will live. When that day comes you will know that I am in my Father, and you in me and I in you.'*

Though addressing his disciples Jesus is speaking to Christians everywhere in all time.

Jesus is not going to leave his disciples without guidance. Informing them in advance of his resurrection experience, he assures them he will come back. In a short time he will disappear to the world's view, but they will see him again. He will live because he will have overcome death and the grave. Because he lives they too will live. At this time it will become clear to them that Jesus is in the Father, that they are One in being, and that they, the disciples, will have the relationship with Jesus Christ that he has with his Father. One in being and one in expression, "You in me and I in you." Can words depict a closer relationship?

Why will they live because Jesus lives? As the Light of the world, as the Fountain of Life, Jesus is the mediator between the universe of Spirit and the concepts of the unspiritual. The universe of Spirit is the substance of Spirit, holy concepts, and pure ideas; the world of the corrupt is comprised of its opposite, the self-centered, the power-hungry, and the iniquitous.

Jesus has just said that the world cannot know Spirit; but Jesus, as Son of Man, can exist in the world in a form recognizable to men. He can continue to speak and to exhort — and can love God's own with an infinitude of love heretofore unknown to man. Because his disciples (Judas Iscariot is not with them at this time) have reached beyond limited horizons of thought, because they have accepted him as coming from God, and because they have repented, or turned away, from their former concepts and teachings about man and God, therefore they can partake of his resurrection and follow him in passing from life to life eternal. At the time he gives them his blessing, after his resurrection, there will pour out upon them the clear knowledge of Jesus' relationship with the Father, and of their relationship with him and the Father.[4] All they need to know will come from within — from the Spirit of Truth, who can reveal him and the Father through each one.

Loving Jesus

John 14:21 *'Anyone who has received my commands and obeys them — he it is who loves me; and he who loves me will be loved by my Father; and I will love him and disclose myself to him.'*

Wholehearted joyous surrender and obedience, obedience that is natural and spontaneously happy, only such a one really loves Jesus. The Father will love the one who so blissfully loves and yields to Jesus. And further, says Jesus, "I will love him and disclose myself to him." We enter the joy of our Lord and know his presence in the fullness of commitment.

John 14:22 *Judas said — the other Judas, not Iscariot — 'Lord, how has it come about that you mean to disclose yourself to us and not to the world?'*

Well might Judas ask this pertinent question. Until now Jesus has addressed his words to the multitudes. All of a sudden he becomes very selective.

John 14:23-24 *Jesus replied, 'Anyone who loves me will heed what I say; then my Father will love him, and we will come to him and make our dwelling with him; but whoever does not love me does not heed what I say.'*

"Loving" Jesus is a very inclusive position. It not only involves ardent feelings and deep admiration, respect, trust, and humility, even a love that sacrifices everything — including life — for Jesus' sake; but also includes understanding and fully accepting Jesus as the Son of God and Son of Man; that he comes from God and returns to Him, and that his human body in resurrection bridges the "worlds" of flesh and Spirit.

The student will have to ask and seek for the coming of the Holy Spirit. Filled by the Spirit, the understanding, love, and appreciation of Jesus will become the wellspring of his being. It is in this receptive state that the disciple "heeds" Jesus.

"Then," says Jesus, "my Father will love him and we will come to him and make our dwelling with him." Such is Immanuel — God with us!

The thought that is able to accept and fulfill loving and listening to Jesus with understanding, finds he has entered the very presence of the Most High. The love God pours out upon him is the essence of God and Christ at the center of his being — God dwelling with man, abiding at the heart of man, speaking from the consciousness of man.

"But whoever does not love me does not heed what I say."

The man who seeks not his Lord; who feels no warmth in his Lord's presence; who decries the time spent searching the Gospel, loves not Jesus. He does not heed what Jesus says. What a sorry state. A closed mind, self-centered, world-oriented instead of God-oriented, unwilling to pay the price of listening to and obeying Jesus; these will not hear the Father's voice!

John 14:24 *'And the word you hear is not my own: it is the word of the Father who sent me.'*

Step by step, closer and closer, Jesus takes his students to the crux of his message. He has the perfect relationship with the Father, for the Father loves him and dwells with him. God even speaks as Jesus speaking. It is in reality the Father who gives the words and whose voice is heard. God's people are to be given this same close relationship through Jesus. The oneness of Father and Son is to be revealed in the oneness of God's people and the Trinity. This holy union of Christians with Jesus includes the Son's oneness with the Father, and the Holy Spirit.

The perfect unity of will of Father and Son, voiced by Jesus among men, is the pattern of the relationship Jesus has with those who love and heed him. When

---

[4] See John 20:22

men speak, doing God's work, then in reality, the voice is that of Jesus speaking the Father's words.

Do we believe this? Are we humble enough to realize and recognize this irrepressible holiness with us? Do we pause to contemplate how our acceptance of our Lord's presence with us alters our life course? Are we ready to stand in the mainstream of God's purpose? Let us rejoice that "hitherto the Lord has helped us" (1 Samuel 7:12, *King James Bible*).

John 14:25-26 *'I have told you these things while I am still with you; but the advocate, the Holy Spirit whom the Father will send in my name, will teach you everything and remind you of all that I have told you.'*

One cannot help but visualize eleven earnest and very concerned men who are listening — and loving — and are fearful of what is to come. Each word their Teacher speaks is very precious. Jesus is anxious to have them grasp what he is saying, for time is running out. His friends are endeavoring to memorize the message, to store up the love they see in his eyes; and they cherish the life that fills his active body. All that is Jesus, their dear friend, they want to keep forever. But the end is near! The human emotions felt by all at this intimate feast of love are being refined and purified by their Lord.

He tells them of the dwelling places he will prepare for them in his Father's house, that he is the Way, the Truth, and Life, that seeing him they see the Father, and that the very words he speaks are the Father's own words. Those who have faith in him will do what he does; those who obey his commands show their love for him. If you ask anything in my name I will do it, Jesus says — that the Son may glorify the Father. This he tells them while being with them. But in the future there will be a difference. Henceforth the Advocate, who will come in his name, will communicate the message to them. All they need to know will be supplied them — and all they are told when Jesus is with them will be remembered.

Peace

John 14:27 *'Peace is my parting gift to you, my own peace, such as the world cannot give.*

Set your troubled hearts at rest, and banish your fears.'

"Peace..., my own peace..." Love and peace are more desired by mankind than any other condition. Sacrifices have been made for loved ones since time began. But peace, the elusive, indefinable necessity, is given by Jesus as his parting gift! Let us recognize that peace is not of our own making, nor of our own achieving. It is a spiritual gift — a power and presence that speaks of God with us. No worldly forces can win it nor bring it about; neither can they dispel it!

Peace comes to those who love the Lord, who follow His way, and who obey His requirements. Peace belongs to the thought that is able to soar to spiritual heights and dwell in "the secret place of the most High" (Psalm 91). The gift of peace is the crown of man's serenity and the glory of this Sovereign Power. It is the quiet sanctuary wherein to worship the Father, Holy Spirit, and Christ Jesus. It is a place where love meets love, where Wisdom speaks, and, for men who must cope with the world's problems, it ensures clear thinking.

Does not Jesus say, "Set your troubled hearts at rest, and banish your fears"? How is this accomplished? By accepting Jesus' gift of peace. Always, always, we must be humble enough to accept. To give up our way and accept his way! To give up distress and accept peace!

Here is the assertive power of peace at work. Here is man achieving dominion over a "troubled heart," and able to banish fear.

John 14:28-29 *'You heard me say, "I am going away, and I am coming back to you." If you loved me you would be glad that I am going to the Father; for the Father is greater than I am. I have told you now, before it happens, so that when it does happen you may have faith.'*

"If you love me you will be glad that I am going to the Father." This is a very gentle rebuke. Jesus knows full well the tremendous emotional struggle his friends are having because of their immanent separation. He gives them his Peace — but, like all spiritual gifts it must be appropriated by each one and used for the purpose God intends. His Peace will settle on and enfold them in its security once they grasp its presence and power. It is something the world cannot give nor take away.

If the disciples can rejoice that Jesus is going to the Father, what support Jesus will feel! Perhaps much of the horror of his last ordeal will be avoided. If they are able to achieve the kind of peace he has given them (and later they do); had they been more faithful during his tutelage; if they can rise with spiritual power — but they do not, and their Lord will die without their support.

But, one may say, since he is the Son of God, why cannot he step down from the cross and avoid its torture?

Jesus is overcoming the crucifixion. But he is not doing it in the way the onlookers think he will. He is not loosening his hands and feet to get off the cross, but he is spiritually separating himself from that odious condition. He is obeying his Father in fulfilling the purpose of his mission. He is allowing his humanity to yield completely to Spirit, though the suffering he undergoes must tempt him to believe he lives physically instead of wholly in Spirit.

As a human he has all the inherent human fears and deficiencies to overcome. It is for this very reason that he can be the "way" for mankind. As one "trapped" in the flesh he shows us how to receive spiritual power and exercise dominion. The overcoming he accomplishes in the crucifixion is the essential lesson for humanity. The "Principalities" and "Powers" which boast they can destroy God's Son are proved to be incapable of doing so. Death is destroyed instead. Jesus "breaks the ice" and "blazes the trail" for all of us. In his direst moment the power of his thought is in his love and forgiveness instead of resentment and revenge.

The great redemptive act of Jesus in the cross-experience is in returning to men the grace of yielding to God that they have lost through disobeying God. The power of yielding to God with love is the key to man's dominion. Only by obeying his Father's demand that he love (thus pouring forth divine power) throughout the supremely difficult time of suffering, can he nullify the damage done by man to

himself when he chooses not to obey God. It has to be proven by a man that he can be faithful to all that the Father can ask of him — to die in love and forgiveness instead of hate and resentment — and thus return to life in Spirit (see Hebrews 2:10-18).

"If you loved me you would be glad I am going to my Father; for my Father is greater than I." Jesus constantly holds the power, supremacy, authority, and greatness of his Father before his disciples. Jesus, exalted though he is, does not compare himself to God as witness his statement, "My Father is greater than I." Yet he can say, "I and my Father are One."

1. Christ Jesus is the individualized expression of the infinite One.

2. The Holy Spirit is the evidence of the Father's everywhere-abiding presence and influence.

3. The Father is the One and All, the infinite source who provides ideas and life to man and the universe.

4. The Trinity is one in being and three in purpose: Father — wholeness and Allness; Son — individualized Divinity; Holy Spirit — all-pervading Presence.

In giving his tender utterances of comfort and support, and at the same time forewarning his disciples of events to come, he strengthens and prepares them for the coming dark days. He well knows the weakness of human faith and the effect the finality of the crucifixion will have on them.

John 14:30 *'I shall not talk much longer with you, for the prince of this world approaches. He has no rights over me; but the world must be shown that I love the Father, and am doing what he commands; come, let us go!'* [5]

The prince of this world approaches — the authorities, those with the authority to take a man into custody, are coming for him. But who is this "prince of this world" who is coming for Jesus? Is it not the selfish, self-willed, envious, conniving, and cruel elements of human nature that find in Jesus' holiness their unbearable torment? The perverters of goodness and truth, the criminal and the lewd, those

---

[5] Some accounts read: 'let us go forward to meet him!' (*Revised English Bible*)

who live by word and guile — these are the dupes who constitute the worldly army of him whom he calls the "prince of this world." This is the element that cannot tolerate divinity in its midst.

It is to the slaves of this "prince" that Jesus comes to bring redemption and visibly manifest God's love for men. It is for these as well as the righteous that he dies a death to liberate sinners and to show them the better way of love. It is not that God plans a cruel death for His Son, but that He knows that the reaction of the worldly, to the love and the close relationship that He offers, will be the violence of crucifixion. The resurrection reveals to the spiritually minded the reward of Jesus' faithfulness.

Of this "prince" Jesus says, 'He has no rights over me." What a statement when he is about to be taken roughly in hand, convicted, and crucified. In Jesus' calmness and courage we see the evidence of his "peace" in operation. At no time does the evil element have power over God's Favored. It has no "rights" over him. The permission to take Jesus has to come from Jesus. He gives that permission when he hands Judas the bread and says to him, "Do quickly what you have to do" (John 13:21-30).

"The world must be shown that I love the Father and am doing what He commands." Ever mindful of his mission, he is anxious to show proof to the world that he loves his Father. To him this proof rests in his obedient expression of his Father's true nature — Love!

"Come, let us go forward to meet the prince of this world." The force of Jesus' peace must be felt by those with him. Jesus perceives, even though his disciples may only glimpse, that the power and presence of the Most High is meeting head-on the "prince of the world" and that the "prince" will be defeated. Later, each one of his disciples will be the prince's target, and through the love of their Lord each one will rise in victory.

Chapter Fifteen

Farewell Discourses, continued

The True Vine

John 15:1 *'I am the true vine, and my Father is the gardener.'*

Psalm 80:8-10, 17

You brought a vine from Egypt;
you drove out nations and planted it;
you cleared the ground for it,
so that it struck root and filled the land.
The mountains were covered with its shade,
and its branches were like those of mighty cedars.
Let your hand rest on the one at your right side,
the one whom you have made strong
for your service.

Archbishop J. H. Bernard,[1] writing on the *Gospel According to St. John*, says, "Always in the Old Testament where Israel is compared to a vine, the comparison introduces a lament over her degeneracy, or a prophecy of her speedy destruction.... And it has been thought that when Jesus said 'I am the True Vine', the comparison in view was that between the degenerate vine of Israel and the Ideal Vine represented by Himself. That is to say, the True Vine is now brought before the disciples as the new ideal of the Spiritual Israel."

When Jacob is renamed by God as "Israel" a whole new nature is ascribed to him. Israel of the Spirit means "He will rule as God." The name Israel comes from two root words meaning "to prevail" or "have strength" as God, a divine gift of dominion.

Jesus' statement "I am the true vine" sets him completely above all earthly conditions. He declares himself to be Israel of the Spirit, coming from God and returning to Him, and at all times under the care of the Father.

It is the Israel of the Spirit that exercises dominion over all the earth, the One whom God has made strong in His service.

The Gardener who cares for this Vine maintains it at the peak of perfection.

John 15:2 *'Any branch of mine that is barren he cuts away; and any fruiting branch he prunes clean, to make it more fruitful still.'*

Because the branches cohere with the Vine, the vital forces of being course to furnish each branch fresh life, vigor, and vitality. As we accept the flow of Christ's power in our lives we are transformed spiritually to live productive Christian lives. In leaving all for Christ we return to our native element, Spirit.

Those who do not respond to the life-giving elements flowing through the Vine, who are barren of love and joy, who know no life but self interest, deprive themselves of God and His universe. They are in a cut-off state. They do not know God.

But if a sin encumbers one who is part of the true Vine let him take heart. God will not allow that corrupting spot to remain. He cuts it away in order that the fruiting branch may bear even more fruit.

John 15:3-4 *'You are already clean because of the word I have spoken to you. Dwell in me, as I in you. No branch can bear fruit by itself, but only if it remains united with the vine; no*

---

[1] *Gospel According to St. John* by the Most Rev. and Right Hon. J. H. Bernard, D.D., edited by the Rev. A. H. McNeile, D.D. (in two volumes) Volume II, page 478. Edinburgh, T. & T. Clark, 59 George Street.

more can you bear fruit, unless you remain united with me.'

In a vineyard care is taken that no branches are snapped from the central vine. They and their fruit will quickly wither if this occurs. Here Jesus is impressing on the Eleven the necessity for oneness with him. There can be no wandering from him, for he and his teaching are one; therefore, those who accept him and his new way of thought become one with him.

His men are truly cleansed by the Word he speaks to them — their whole outlook on life is changed from their previous standpoint; their natures are now different as proof, or evidence, of their acceptance of the Christ in their friend Jesus. From him, the real Vine, flows the love, truth, and energy of Spirit that has wrought their transformation. As mortal men touched by the divine they have broken from the chrysalis of limitation to begin their journey heavenward. The streams of spirituality flowing through the "Jesus Vine" feeds the branches of discipleship and brings their fruition. Jesus' love and spiritual understanding, which he communicates to his trusted friends, feeds them with hope and strength at this time. The fruits of this experience will be manifested later. Their great necessity, their Leader counsels, is that they be aware of his indwelling with them.

John 15:5-6   *'I am the vine; you are the branches. Anyone who dwells in me, as I dwell in him, bears much fruit; apart from me you can do nothing. Anyone who does not dwell in me is thrown away like a withered branch. The withered branches are gathered up, thrown on the fire, and burnt.'*

Here Jesus is emphasizing what in a later time was written by Brother Lawrence and known as the "Practice of the Presence of God." [2]

By allowing thought to be open to Jesus Christ that he may speak and be heard — and by silencing self in order to be governed by divine will alone — this daily and hourly practice bears much fruit. Thus men conscientiously bring their will in accord with God's will that they be one in motive and action. The day dreamer, the idler, the person who prefers to credit "opportune" events to "coincidence" rather than give recognition to the action of God in his life — such types are withering branches — these individuals will indeed be consumed by the nothingness they accept.

John 15:7-10   *'If you dwell in me, and my words dwell in you, ask what ever you want, and you shall have it. This is how my Father is glorified: you are to bear fruit in plenty and so be my disciples! As the Father has loved me, so I have loved you. Dwell in my love. If you heed my commands, you will dwell in my love, as I have heeded my Father's commands and dwell in his love.'*

"By achieving this perfect oneness with me you will find that you are also at one with that for which you ask — it will be at hand — for," says Jesus, "this is my Father's glory, that you may bear fruit in plenty, and so become like me.

"I have loved you with the same love with which the Father has loved me. Dwell in this love. Be aware of it, realize it continually, feel the warmth and power of my love. Attend to my counsel and you will dwell in my love, as I have paid attention and been obedient to my Father's instructions — and I dwell always in His love." [3]

Complete Joy

John 15:11   *'I have spoken thus to you, so that my joy may be in you, and your joy complete.'*

Joy! Perfunctory reading of this passage indicates the natural conclusion that if the disciples follow his instructions he will be pleased with them — will have joy in them — and they will be pleased or joyous in his pleasure.

---

[2]   Brother Lawrence, *The Practice of the Presence of God*, translated by E. M. Blaiklock, Thomas Nelson Publisher.

[3]   Archbishop J. H. Bernard writes: 'In the Synoptists "faith" is the prerequisite for efficacious prayer...But in John faith in Christ is more than belief in His message, or fitful attraction to His Person; it is a continual abiding "in Him." ' *A Critical and Exegetical Commentary on the Gospel According to St. John* by Archbishop J. H. Bernard, Volume 2, page 482. Edinburgh, T & T Clark, 59 George Street.

But more is in the passage. In so speaking to them of his perpetually indwelling presence, Jesus is telling them he has given them the gift of joy! "...that my joy may be in you." That the joy they experience is a Christ-joy — strong, enduring, spiritual in origin, not flimsy or based on evanescent events. This joy comes straight from God and radiates throughout their whole experience. This holy gift is their strength in trials, and their witness to His own presence with them.

You Are My Friends

John 15:12-13   *This is my commandment: love one another, as I have loved you. There is no greater love than this, that someone should lay down his life for his friends.'*

Now that he will no longer be with them in the flesh, his instruction is that they love — be concerned in shepherding one another as he has done. He will dwell in them as their love-in-action. And there is to be no limit to this love and the lengths they should go to in giving of this divine love — even to laying down their lives. This selfless love alone can manifest his love with them.

John 15:14-15   *'You are my friends, if you do what I command you. No longer do I call you servants, for a servant does not know what his master is about. I have called you friends, because I have disclosed to you everything that I heard from my Father.'*

All these reiterative phrases show the great effort of John to clearly present the marvelous and intimate kinship that Jesus understands his relationship with the disciples to be. Biblically, Jesus is called Servant, and he earlier instructs his students to serve. But here the emphasis is on the status between Jesus and the disciples. They, in their acceptance of him as Son of God, are friends — equals in mutual trust and mutual love. What can be more private than God's disclosures to him! Yet Jesus shares with them all he has heard from his Father! They are elevated, through spiritual revelations and transformation, to the level of Jesus the Son of Man — and are his friends.

John 15:16-17   *'You did not choose me: I chose you. I appointed you to go on and bear fruit, fruit that will last; so that the Father may give you whatever you ask in my name. This is my commandment to you: love one another.'*

Friends, chosen from the multitudes by Jesus, and for the great purpose of carrying on his work, now he asks that they "go on and bear fruit, fruit that will last." Asking the Father in Jesus' name establishes them in the Body and as the Body of Christ; and in this Body — later knows as "ecclesia" or "church," they are to be a gathering of spiritually disciplined men and women following the teachings of their Lord and Master. This church will be the "fruit" that will last, for it is destined to declare the loving presence of the Son of God with men forever. The dominion of spiritual Israel will be theirs.

I Have Chosen You Out of the World

John 15:18-19   *'If the world hates you, it hated me first, as you know well. If you belonged to the world, the world would love its own; but you do not belong to the world, now that I have chosen you out of the world, and for that reason the world hates you.'*

Do not be surprised, our Lord tells us, if the world hates us. It is because we have come out of the world! "And recollect," he adds, "they hated me first." We have left the limited, puny, self-centered world and have become strong through being God-centered. The world only cares for those of like mind. In choosing us he has lifted us out of this morass of self-indulgent people. In following him we have accepted the hate and trials that he must bear. The introverts would like to have the great blessings that will be ours but they are unwilling to pay the price for them. Therefore in their frustration they lash out at every evidence of the Christ presence. They hate us because they are so uncomfortable in our presence. They are uncomfortable because with us they feel their own shame and guilt.

John 15:20-21   *'Remember what I said: "A servant is not greater than his master." If they persecuted me, they will also persecute* *you; if they have followed my teaching, they will follow yours. All this will they do to you on my account, because they do not know the One who sent me.'*

Expect persecution — expect few results from your teaching — expect to be ill-treated — all this will be your experience. He reminds them that "a servant is not greater than his master." Jesus is saying, "If there is no way I can avoid trials and persecutions, then how can you hope to escape some vicissitudes? All this comes upon us because the world does not accept that I am sent by God!"

This glorious shaft of divine radiance comes to shine in a world that feels it does not need God or His Christ.

John 15:22-23   *'If I had not come and spoken to them, they would not be guilty of sin; but now they have no excuse for their sin: whoever hates me, hates my Father also.'*

How many people have said — "Oh, if I could but see and touch my Lord Jesus"! But even when they do experience the power of God with them in healing, or are spiritually made aware of an action to take, there is great reluctance to give God all credit for the assistance received.

Jesus is speaking of those who come face to face with reality and turn their back on it. Before, they are ignorant of the Lord Christ — now that he is revealed to them and they refuse him, their sin is great. It is great because they do recognize Jesus, and even acknowledge him as sent by God — but his demands are too costly in effort, self-discipline, and humility. They elect to live the life they have with the devil they know, rather than chance life with a little known God who makes great demands upon them.

Because Jesus' perfection makes them seem, by contrast, so very imperfect, they hate him and end up in the untenable position of hating his Father as well.

John 15:24-25   *'If I had not done such deeds among them as no one else has ever done, they would not be guilty of sin; but now they have seen and hated both me and my Father. This text in their law had to come true: "They hated me without reason."'*

What is Jesus' work? He preaches his Father's kingdom come, and the fact of His will done on earth as in heaven. He reveals in himself the nature of God for all to see. He heals the sick and raises the dead; and now his work will continue when he takes upon himself the sins of the world and is the sacrificial lamb, offered to God. His work will be complete with his resurrection and ascension.

And what is the reaction of these people to the mighty works of Jesus? Apathy, disdain, shallow acceptance that quickly turns to disbelief. Their God comes to them and they have rejected Him! Yes, this sinful guilt is upon them. They hate Jesus and all he stands for! This is truly an unreasoning hate.

In this passage again Jesus teaches Biblical fulfillment in his experience.

The Witnesses

John 15:26-27   *'When the advocate has come, whom I shall send you from the Father — the Spirit of truth that issues from the Father — he will bear witness to me. And you also are my witnesses, because you have been with me from the first.'*

The purpose of the Advocate is to bear witness to Jesus Christ — to say, "this is his presence, his word, his life," — Those who listen spiritually will hear him. His disciples are also given the order to "bear witness to him," for they have been with him from the first.

Matthew and John each write a Gospel — and each one of the little band seems to faithfully carry out their work until the time comes when they walk the earth no more.

Just as the healings and other works he performs are Jesus' "credentials" supplied by his Father, so the Advocate's credentials are the proofs of his followers true witnessing: hearts are uplifted, lives transformed, and illness healed.

The world asks for material proofs of spiritual facts. In the face of more than adequate evidence of the hand of God in the affairs of men, they still ask for a sign. Their guilt is upon them for in looking they have looked and not seen, and this blindness is a sin, for they have rejected the Holy One!

Chapter Sixteen

The "Farewell Discourse" continued

John 16:1 *'I have told you all this to guard you against the breakdown of your faith.'*

Jesus is fortifying his men so that they will not lose faith when they most need it. He recognizes that their faith is fragile for it is based upon their awakening apprehension of him and his teachings. The coming events will severely test their spiritual position.

John 16:2 *'They will ban you from the synagogue; indeed, the time is coming when anyone who kills you will suppose that he is serving God. They will do these things because they did not know either the Father or me.'*

Being banned from the synagogue means being cut off from that traditional place of worship and it also is a form of social ostracism.

The performance of religious duties is uppermost in the minds of devout Jews. Strict adherence to these beliefs leads to the persecution of early Christians.

Jesus' prophetic words come true all too soon. A young man named Saul later is witness to Stephen's stoning, and afterwards he is found "harrying the church; he entered house after house, seizing men and women and sending them to prison" (Acts 8:3).

John 16:4-5 *'I have told you all this so that when the time comes for it to happen you may remember my warning. I did not tell you this at first, because then I was with you; but now I am going away to him who sent me.'*

The whole "Farewell Discourse" may be seen as Jesus' final attempt to strengthen his followers with comfort and guidance to protect and deliver them in the ensuing days. His main emphasis is that they love, for love is needed to counteract the great hatred being poured out at them. Jesus also tells them what they must do, and what he will do, what the Father will do, and what the Spirit of Truth will do. Hedging them about with knowledge of things to come will answer some of the questioning doubts concerning his spiritual powers, for such doubts will assail them during the coming dark days.

The Advocate

John 16:5-7 *'None of you asks me, "Where are you going?" Yet you are plunged into grief at what I have told you. Nevertheless I assure that it is in your interest that I am leaving you. If I do not go, the advocate will not come, whereas if I go, I will send him to you.'*

One can easily sense the great despair gripping the minds of the disciples. They think that little could be worse than this announcement of their Lord's immanint departure. They dare not ask "Where are you going?" for fear of what they will hear! How can his departure be for their good? He is leaving to send the Advocate! One can almost hear the comparison being made between Jesus, whom they love, and the unknown Advocate.

It is good for us to try to plumb the depths of their despair. In so doing the Discourse becomes clearer, its repetition logical. Jesus has given them two parting gifts, peace and joy, as well as a third, the Advocate whom the Father will send. Yet in their present state of mind there is neither enthusiasm nor gratitude for this unknown Counselor. Small wonder!

Jesus says that if he does not go the Advocate will not come, and "if I go I will send him to you."

Jesus is physical to those who see him. He is a man like themselves. To receive the Advocate each one of them will have to lose the conviction that the Son of God is wholly physical, or mortal. Unless Jesus returns to his spiritual substance and essence, his oneness with the Father, the disciples will never rise to the glorious apprehension of his spiritual omnipresence and power, nor will they be enabled by the Spirit of Truth to fulfill the purposes to which they are called. It is the Spirit of the man Jesus, his Christ, which attracts them to him; it is this same Christ who will teach them and love them.

Only by relinquishing Jesus' physicality will they find their Comforter and Advisor to be spiritual substance and wholly satisfying. It is this One they know so well who will convey the message.

John 16:8-11 *'When he comes, he will prove the world wrong about sin, justice, and judgement; about sin, because they refuse to believe in me; about justice, because I go to the Father when I pass from your sight; about judgement, because the prince of this world stands condemned.'*

Jesus is very concerned about three things: he wants mankind to accept him as the Son of God, but the sin of the world is their unbelief. He wants them to realize that he has accomplished his purpose and that in justification he will be placed at his Father's side. The people think God has condemned him. Third, he wants all to know that he has defeated the prince of this world thereby rescuing himself and God's children from death.

John 16:12-15 *'There is much more that I could say to you, but the burden would be too great for you now. However, when the Spirit of truth comes, he will guide you into all the truth; for he will not speak on his own authority, but will speak only what he hears; and he will make known to you what is to come. He will glorify me, for he will take what is mine and make it known to you. All that the Father has is mine, and that is why I said "He will take what is mine and make it known to you."*

1. He will guide you into all truth.
2. He will not speak on his own authority but will speak only what he hears.
3. He will make known to you the things that are coming.
4. He will glorify me for he will take what is mine and make it known to you.

Here is the great assurance, that all ideas that are imparted by the Spirit of Truth come from Jesus Christ, the Son of God.

To do their work after Jesus leaves them, the disciples need to be free from fear and doubt concerning his teaching. The populace generally may not believe for various reasons, but the disciples cannot afford to take in one iota of their mistaken beliefs. The Spirit of Truth operates within the thoughts and lives of those who receive the Advocate. Suggestions that undermine true perception and faith, under the influence of the Advocate, will be seen as fraudulent by the disciples and followers of Christ, and they will be rejected.

The Advocate will be to them an armor to keep out weakening and harmful assaults on their faith. Following the resurrection Jesus says, "I am sending on you the gift promised by my Father; wait here in this city until you are armed with power from above" (Luke 24:49).

The Spirit of Truth within each disciple is the separator of truth from falsehood. This shows spiritual discrimination and an ability to conform to the standard and precepts taught by Jesus. The works done by the disciples and their followers are their credentials and the proof that Jesus Christ is working with them. He earlier says, "My deeds done in my Father's name are my credentials."

In this revelation the Advocate glorifies the Father through the glorification of Christ Jesus, because he reveals all that is his and makes it known to those that believe. The Advocate is the protector, the deliverer, the promoter, the director — he is the voice of inspiration and the closeness of Christ, the Father, and the Holy Spirit. He is the Spirit within that only hears God's voice.

John 16:16-18 *'A little while, and you see me no more; again a little while, and you will see me.' Some of his disciples said to one another, 'What does he mean by this: "A little while, and you will not see me, and again a little while, and you will see me," and by this: "Because I am going to the Father"?' So they asked 'What is this "little while" that he is talking about? We do not know what he means.'*

Because the disciples do not yet really grasp the fact that Jesus will die, his statement "you will not see me, and [later] you will see me" brings bewilderment. We, in retrospect, can see a meaning — his death and entombment, and then his reappearance to them.

By this time the disciples are thoroughly upset and this results in the dulling of their spiritual perception. Though clad in the flesh, the Jesus who reveals the Father can only be discerned spiritually and intuitively. It is the illumined senses of the disciples that first perceive something about him that they must follow. They feel within them a response to a glorious presence that requires their full allegiance. The "little while," when these loyal followers will not see him, will be the period when their thoughts are darkened and disturbed by all the tormenting and disheartening events soon to come. "Because I am going to the Father," means the exaltation of the Son — the resumption of his place with the Father.

John 16:19-20 *Jesus knew that they were wanting to question him, and said, 'Are you discussing that saying of mine: "A little while, and you will not see me, and again a little while, and you will see me"? In very truth I tell you, you will weep and mourn, but the world will be glad. But though you will be plunged in grief, your grief will be turned to joy.'*

Weeping and mourning will be the lot of the disciples when they see him no more, but the world, on the other hand, will feel a great good has been accomplished. A troublemaker will be out of the way! But Jesus clearly says to them — though your grief is overwhelming, it will turn to joy.

If these men had not been so distressed they might remember Jesus stilling a great storm that arose when they were sailing with him: "With that he got up and rebuked the wind, and the sea, and there was a dead calm" (Matthew 8:23-27). Though the surging of human emotions during the crucifixion and entombment will engulf them all, when he "comes again" their joy will blot out all pain of such a tragedy.

John 16:21-22 *'A woman in labour is in pain because her time has come; but when her baby is born she forgets the anguish in her joy that a child has been born into the world. So it is with you: for the moment you are sad; but I shall see you again, and then you will be joyful, and no one shall rob you of your joy.'*

Unwilling to have his disciples shocked by the events now looming, Jesus prepares their thought to accept the crucifixion from the standpoint from which he accepts it. Using the illustration of a woman in labor he teaches that Christian steadfastness can make of death a new birth. Progressive spiritual victories before death fill thought with heavenly joys, for the Christ viewpoint permeates all areas of the experience. The vision achieved through this kind of spiritual resurrection operates to translate the individual beyond the power of death. The disciples, though still imperfectly grasping the deep meaning of Jesus' teachings, have already started their heavenward journey. Never again can they return to their immature perspective. Like sprouting seeds they have cracked the cover that shrouds their lives. Now they have expanded beyond the confines of their beginnings. The disciples' productive period draws closer. It will be a time of fruitage that will benefit generation after generation of those who want to follow Jesus.

Ask in My Name

John 16:23-24 *'When that day comes you will ask me nothing more. In very truth I tell you, if you ask the Father for anything in my name, he will give it you. So far you have asked nothing in my name. Ask and you will receive, that your joy may be complete'*

This is the second time John quotes Jesus' instruction to ask the Father in his name. The first is in John 14:13-14. Now Jesus is pointing out that it is when he leaves them that they should petition the Father in his name. They are to ask, and receive, that their joy may be complete.

We are apt to think of early Christians as without joy because of their many persecutions — but these final words of Jesus show the importance of joy in a Christian's life: "That your joy may be complete." Do we accept this assurance — that our joy may be complete? Our Master is speaking to us!

John 16:25-27   *'Till now I have been using figures of speech; a time is coming when I shall no longer use figures, but tell you of the Father in plain words. When that day comes you will make your request in my name, and I do not say that I shall pray to the Father for you, for the Father loves you himself, because you have loved me and believed that I came from God.'*

No longer will Jesus be the intercessor for the disciples. They will be able to go directly to the Father as they pray in the name of Jesus Christ. They may do this because they accept Jesus as Son of God and love him — therefore the Father loves them.

"Asking in his name" demands more than the mouthing of this phrase. A new Christian will find that the acceptance of the Son, Jesus, is sufficient and the Father will honor such a petitioner. But to be a progressive Christian demands greater dedication — the full commitment of desire and purpose that by degrees will present to all the Person of Christ revealed in individual thought and action.

To ask the Father in his name is to yield gently to the divine will and be the instrument for the will, purpose, and love of Christ. Nothing contrary to the nature of our Lord shall occupy thought when petitioning in his name and presence.

John 16:28   *'I came from the Father and have come into the world; and now I am leaving the world again and going to the Father.'*

Thus plainly and simply Jesus comes to the point — he will leave the world — and return to the Father.

John 16:29-30   *His disciples said, 'Now you are speaking plainly, not in figures of speech! We are certain now that you know everything, and do not need to be asked; because of this we believe that you have come from God.'*

Embarrassed because they are not understanding the one whom they love, and wishing perhaps to please him, they exclaim "Now you are speaking plainly!" They add "we are certain now that you know everything and do not need to be asked." This

eager reply does show their grasp, even though in a limited way, of Jesus' spiritual discernment. In those times the ability to discern a man's thoughts is generally considered to be an attribute of divinity.

John 16:31-32   *Jesus answered, 'Do you now believe? I warn you, the hour is coming, has indeed already come, when you are to be scattered, each to his own home, leaving me alone. Yet I am not alone, for the Father is with me.'*

Jesus must have easily seen through their eagerness to please him, for they know so little and he knows all. One translator of this passage phrases Jesus' remark thus: "at this moment you believe!"[1]

Jesus is in effect saying: "You are going to experience a terrible time and under such duress you will be scatter-brained — you will return to your old ways of thinking and will forget all about me. And yet, at this time I will not be alone." Jesus immediately refutes the temptation to think of himself as alone. He does not permit his humanity to suffer in this way — though to human sense Jesus will be totally bereft — absolutely alone except that his Father will always be with him.

John 16:33   *'I have told you all this so that in me you may find peace. In the world you will have suffering. But take heart! I have conquered the world.'*

The instructions, comforting counsels, encouragement, and fortifying thoughts that their Master is endeavoring to give them, to support them until he will see them again, have all been said. The hour of expectation and holy purpose is almost at hand. He has told them all this so that in him they may find peace. But there is a condition to the peace — they must be in him. Here again the implication is that all that he has to give them depends on their willingness and persistence to abide in him. "In the world," he says, "you will have trouble."

Abiding in the world's viewpoint will bring trouble. Preserving one's outlook according to Jesus'

[1] *The International Critical Commentary, St. John*, Volume 2, page 522.

teachings will bring peace. Thus John's favorite theme is again emphasized: the great necessity is to strictly adhere to the spiritual viewpoint, the level which acknowledges God's love as supreme, to see the continuous outpouring of His blessings; and to perceive God's laws operating always to preserve the harmony and order of the universe, with the individual the center of His affection.

Those who "abide in the world" find evil looming ominously, righteousness is depreciated, humans depend on themselves rather than God, and trouble is ever present.

Throughout the centuries Jesus' words have been a clarion call to his standard: "Take heart! I have conquered the world!" In other words: "Take a strong position in me. The victory is mine to give to you. I have overcome, or conquered, the world's viewpoint at each step of our pilgrimage together. I gave the wine of Spirit at Cana to illustrate my Father's love and blessing. I healed the withered arm, freed the paralytic, and opened the eyes of the blind so that they came seeing. The lepers were cleansed, the storms stilled, five thousand fed, and Lazarus was raised. All this I have done in order that you may realize the results that may be yours if you abide in me. As the Father abides in me, so I abide in Him. This is my peace and this is my victory!"

Chapter Seventeen

The Hour

John 17:1   *Then Jesus looked up to heaven and said: 'Father, the hour has come.'*

Having completed his instructions and comforting words, Jesus turns from his disciples. He looks up to heaven, not only with his eyes but with his whole being. His longing and his love are now wholly occupied in his prayer to his Father. The hour has come.

This is the hour of climax to which he has alluded so many times. In his complete humanity he cannot help but know the dread and emptiness of despair shared by all humans when an anticipated time arrives and one must immediately face all its consequences. "The hour" is no longer next year, next month, but NOW.

Looking up to heaven Jesus enters into satisfying communion with his God. This is evident as he pours out his love in inspired utterance.

He does not enter the last period of his earth-life with a sense of coming defeat. He looks up to heaven, thus strengthening his motivation with the spiritual vision of his Father's purposes. In this short statement it is as though he is saying, "Father, I yield to Your will, I accept all as You have planned it. I am prepared to undergo this ordeal to prove that no one can be separated from Your love. I am willing to be put to the test to silence forever the temptation to reject You. I am ready to let You, Spirit, as manifested in my identity, overcome all the sins I bear for humanity's sake. I have overcome the ills and distress of humanity and I am ready to do battle against basic evil."

By laying down his life Jesus places himself at the mercy of his enemy. He does this in the full understanding that his Father will ultimately deliver him.

It is his life of obedience to his Father that gives him supremacy in the overcoming of sin and death. He has never been unyielding to God. He says: "I seek to do not my own will, but the will of him who sent me" (John 5:30). This continual yielding of the human ego to the divine Spirit protects him and lifts him above and beyond the grasp of evil. Only in the furtherance of this overcoming will cruelty and hate be able to touch his humanity. The glory of the Father shines in him and surrounds him at all times. Jesus is aware always of his Father's all encompassing love.

John 17:1   *'Glorify your Son, that the Son may glorify you.'*

In asking that his Father glorify him, Jesus is asking for the appearance of the full measure of his Christ nature. He is affirming his oneness with his Father in order that his Father may be glorified in his earth presence. His petition asks that the mantle of his Father fall upon him as the glory, or visible manifestation, of the divine presence.[1]

John 17:1   *'For you have made him sovereign over all mankind, to give eternal life to all whom you have given him.'*

John earlier writes (John 1:11-12): "He came to his own, and his own people would not accept him. But to all who did accept him, to those who put their trust in him, he gave the right to become children of God,..."

Here Jesus is reaffirming his position as sovereign over all mankind with the right to bestow eternal life, and thus to incorporate those who love God into God's family as "children of God."

---

[1] Kings 2:1-15

John 17:3 *'This is eternal life: to know you the only true God, and Jesus Christ whom you have sent.'*

Jesus' prayer is structured in a very positive manner. He is invoking divine law that it may operate in his life. This law is the functioning of divine will — God's cause and effect.

Humanly he is well aware that events are rushing him towards destruction. Lifting his thought above these events he prays to his Father, saying, "This is eternal life," and then he declares how this is achieved: "to know you the only true God, and Jesus Christ whom you have sent."

Holding his gaze unwaveringly on the spiritual reality, he is asserting the fact that knowledge of God, as he has revealed Him, gives eternal life. Thus, he will not die, but will live. This has been the theme of his teaching and his prayers from the beginning.

In these brief statements Jesus is lifting his vision beyond material events, to the realm of his Father and his Christ. It is in this realm he visualizes, or finds, himself and his men.

The inseparability of the nature of Christ and of Jesus have never been more emphatically stated than in these passages. It is the divine Son or Christ, or Word of God, who is begotten in the flesh as Jesus, son of Mary. This united divinity-and-humanity of our Lord is essential to holy purpose, the babe-and-man-Jesus being the threshold of understanding for mankind. Through this fleshly door of open forgiveness emanates the Father's love and power manifested as Christ in action.

John 17:4-5 *'I have glorified you on earth by finishing the work which you gave me to do; and now, Father, glorify me in your own presence with the glory which I had with you before the world began.'*

Jesus acknowledges the completion of the work which glorifies his Father: he came to reveal the Father, to make Him known, and to do works that show the nature of the Father and Son. The healings he performs, the control he exercises over wind and wave, the feeding of multitudes, and the raising of the dead reveals a God of benign sovereignty.

Having completed his work Jesus now asks his Father to glorify him "in your own presence with the glory which I had with you before the world began." This request can only be made by one who has uplifted his humanity. This he has done step by step as he has increasingly shown in his life a fuller revelation of his Father. He is now fast approaching the time of his ascension to his Father where the completeness of the revelation will show the glory of the combined divine presence — a unity they had before the world began.

John 17:6 *'I have made your name known to the men whom you gave me out of the world. They were yours and you gave them to me, and they have obeyed your command.'*

Living with Jesus, working with him, sharing his joy in their day by day travels, the men given him out of the world see the Father as none else on earth see him. As "the Savior," Jesus reveals the transforming power of the beauty of holiness which in turn his men reveal in their changed lives.

John 17:7-8 *'Now they know that all you gave me has come from you; for I have taught them what I learned from you, and they have received it: they know with certainty that I came from you, and they have believed that you sent me.'*

Every statement that Jesus makes in this, his great final prayer, is positive. He is summing up his life work — work that has proceeded according to his Father's instruction and implementation every step of the way.

Long ago he had said "I can of mine own self do nothing — The Father who dwelleth in me, He doeth the work." The disciples are now aware that the Father-with-Jesus manifests the various gifts, the gifts of insight, healing, dominion, love, spiritual knowledge, and many other talents.

Jesus states that he has taught them all that he has learned from his Father. This acknowledgment of constant instruction and guidance by his Father should answer, once and for all, the general inquiry made through the ensuing ages, "who was Jesus' teacher?"

"They know with certainty that I come from You." The preparation of the disciples' hearts through the daily association and continual teaching by their Master distills within them the conviction that Jesus comes from the Father and that he is purposefully sent by the Father. "They have believed that You sent me."

Jesus Prays for the Disciples

John 17:9-10   *'I pray for them; I am not praying for the world but for those whom you have given me, because they belong to you. All that is mine is yours, and what is yours is mine; and through them is my glory revealed.'*

"I pray for them." Jesus' positive statements are prayers that position his disciples in a framework of spiritual relationship similar to his own.

His prayer is recognition:

1. — that the disciples are gifts of God to him.
2. — that God has chosen them out of the world.
3. — that God imparts knowledge to them through Jesus Christ, His Son.
4. — that God has prepared them so that his knowledge is acceptable to them.
5. — that the disciples now know with certainty that Jesus comes from the Father.
6. — that the disciples have the gift of faith to know that he, Jesus, has been sent by the Father. This faith also involves recognition of Jesus' place in Biblical prophecy.
7. — that he, Jesus, declares that the disciples now belong to God; they are no longer mortals seeking God; they have found Him.
8. Jesus avows "All that is mine is Yours" — these men, dear Father, are really Yours.
9. "And what is Yours is mine" — and because they are Yours they are also mine, for through them my glory shines. Jesus has glorified the Father in his life; now Jesus' life is to be glorified by the disciples' lives.

The outcome of this great prayer is the implementation of God's plan for the continuity of the visible presence of Spirit with men. All is a gift of God. All comes from the Father to glorify Him and His Son. The scepter, or symbol of divine authority, has been handed from Father to Son to disciple — with the promise "from generation to generation of your descendants from now on" being fulfilled (Isaiah 59:21).

In no instance will the disciple be more than a point where Spirit itself can be known. He will not be another Messiah. If he yields his "ego" or "self" in sufficient measure the glory will be given to God.

Why does Jesus so clearly declare, in his prayer, the interrelationship of Father, Son, Spirit, and disciple? Because this prayer is one of healing — a prayer of healing for the human Jesus that will preserve him during the forthcoming experience, and it is also a prayer for his beloved followers, the faithful ones, that they may be secure in their faith and healed of hurt.

Spiritual facts must be introduced into the realm of men by the accepting thought of the one who prays in order that the human mind may open to the divine Presence and allow the will of God and the harmony of God to operate. God cannot be known where He is not welcomed. The Christ knocks at the door of each one. Even a tiny crack in a seemingly closed mind allows the light of Christ to bless, uplift, and heal. The process of salvation has begun.

John 17:11   *'I am no longer in the world; they are still in the world, but I am coming to you.'*

"I am no longer in the world." Jesus' work is finished — but his disciples will remain in the world carrying on the divine purpose for which he came. "I am on my way to Thee." His hour of triumph is immediately ahead.

John 17:11-12   *'Holy Father, protect them by the power of your name, the name you have given me, that they may be one, as we are one. While I was with them, I protected them by the power of your name which you gave me, and kept them safe. Not one of them is lost except the man doomed to be lost, for scripture has to be fulfilled.'*

"Holy Father, protect them by the power of Your name" — protect them by Your name (or nature) shown forth in their transformed lives, now Spirit-filled "that they may be one, as we are one."

Is he not asking that his disciples be held in closest rapport, or communion, with the Father, even as he and his Father are one in constant communion? His men need the continuous outpouring of Spirit as a supportive presence with them.

When Jesus is with them he provides in his person the brooding presence of Spirit's nature. He personifies the greatest love and the most tender care, and through his spiritual dominion he delivers them from dangers unseen and undefined. Jesus is able to walk through crowds undetected, even though the crowds are viciously roused against him. Soon the disciples will face equal resistance to their new way of life.

In the acknowledgment of work well done and brought to completion Jesus points out that no disciple has been lost "except the man doomed to be lost, for scripture has to be fulfilled."

Here again he stresses the need to fulfill the scriptures.

John 17:13 *'Now I am coming to you; but while I am still in the world I speak these words, so that they may have my joy within them in full measure.'*

Jesus equates joy with his coming to the Father, and though still in this world, he is voicing this contentment and happiness, that his disciples may also know this holy ebullience in "full measure." They will recognize it as divine joy and rejoice in it.

John 17:14-16 *'I have delivered your word to them, and the world hates them because they are strangers in the world, as I am. I do not pray you to take them out of the world, but to keep them from the evil one. They are strangers in the world, as I am.'*

Jesus has given God's Word to his disciples — and because of its transforming power the disciples are now recognized as strangers in the world, even as he is a stranger. The vitalizing action of the Word in the lives of men operates on those who yield to Christ to so spiritualize their lives that they literally no longer have earthly roots, but become instruments of Spirit. Attitudes, convictions, assessments, viewpoints — all change gradually under the influence of the Holy Spirit — until the Christian becomes a stranger in a strange land. He finds his roots in Heaven and a place in his Father's house warm and inviting.

"The world hates them"...that which the worldly finds unacceptable for itself it hates in another.

When an individual turns to our Lord and accepts Him without reservation he asks the Holy Spirit to enter his life and govern it in the harmony of love. As long as he yields to Spirit and its impulses he is carried with the current of divine will. However, the opposite attitudes of resistance to Spirit separate him from these spiritual forces of righteousness.

Jesus prays that his men may be protected from the Evil One — that their new understanding and life be firm and strong, and that attitudes and customs not influence nor affect them as they continue this work in the world.

The Consecration

John 17:17-19 *'Consecrate them by the truth; your word is truth. As you sent me into the world, I have sent them into the world, and for their sake I consecrate myself, that they too may be consecrated by the truth.'*

This word translated "consecrate" in this passage clearly means that the disciples will be set apart in holiness through their teachings of truth. Theirs is a most sacred task — to declare and teach the very Word of God to coming generations. These men have the unique experience of seeing God "face to face" in the life and works of their Master, and they are taught the inspired Word of God in close intimacy with the Son of God as he does the work his Father has sent him to do. Their consecration is both their ordination and commission.

"As you sent me into the world, I have sent them into the world." Here the emphasis is in the similarity of Jesus' relationship to his Father — as the express image of His being — and the relationship of the disciples to Jesus in conveying Jesus' message "first hand." In their lives and their words and works they begin to spread the Good News.

"And for their sake I consecrate myself, that they too may be consecrated by the truth."

It has been said that "Jesus is both priest and victim." As priest, in his consecration of himself by

Truth, he invokes the continuing power and glory of God to support and sustain him throughout his coming ordeal and victory. As victim on God's altar he is placing himself in the security of his Father's love. As victim his self-offering trust becomes the ultimate gift.

As priest he manifests the Father's love. As God's victim he knows he can never be taken from his Father's care.

This perfect consecration, made valid by Truth itself, embraces the disciples who love Jesus and are willing to let their lives glorify his Father. Like ripples from a pebble tossed in a pool this holy consecration continues to include hearts given to God.

John 17:20-21   *'It is not for these alone that I pray, but for those also who through their words put their faith in me. May they all be one; as you, Father, are in me, and I in you, so also may they be in us, that the world may believe that you sent me.'*

Jesus' prayer embraces in love "those also who through their words put their faith in me." The hearers of the Word he sees as those beloved by the Father and himself. The all-seeing and all-knowing God pours out comfort and love in advance of the need. The supply will be at hand when required — an overflowing cup of blessing.

The vision held by Jesus for those others who put their faith in him continues as he visualizes them as having one mind and one spirit united in purpose and faith and acceptance of Jesus Christ; thus he acknowledges "even as the Father is in me and I in the Father, so "these others" through their acceptance and complete yielding find themselves in the likeness and nature of the Father and Son. This state of communion is not intermittent and cyclical but a permanent spiritual coalescence. Through this mighty faith with its spiritually transforming power comes the Spirit of Truth proving the world wrong (John 16:8) with the overwhelming evidence of the power of Jesus, Son of God, sent by God.

John 17:22-23   *'The glory which you gave me I have given to them, that they may be one, as we are one; I in them and you in me, may they be perfectly one.   Then the world will*

know that you sent me, and that you loved them as you loved me.'

Jesus perceives faith in him as the gift of oneness with the Father and himself. Now he visualizes the glory which the Father gives him as being also the manifest power with these others, that they may be one with him as he is one with the Father — in full dependence on the Father — and he savors this perfect unity and sharing of glory.

And finally he sums up the fruitage of this vision — that "the world will know that you sent me, and that you loved them as you loved me."

Over and over Jesus stresses the importance of understanding that God has sent him.

There is a longing for fulfillment, to be detected in his words, as well as an underlying assurance: the world will learn that he was sent by the Father because He loves them.

The Gift

John 17:24   *'Father, they are your gift to me; and my desire is that they may be with me where I am, so that they may look upon my glory, which you have given me because you loved me before the world began.'*

Jesus prays that these men, his disciples, "who are Your gift to me" be lifted to such a spiritual level that they may see his glory — his identity as found with the Father before the world was. He prays that they may see him, not with mortal eyes, but with clear spiritual vision, and asks that in this realization they will perceive God's great enfolding love for him.

John 17:25   *'Righteous Father, although the world does not know you, I know you, and they know that you sent me.'*

With an overflowing heart Jesus pours out his love for the Father in unequaled fervency. "Righteous Father,...I know you, and they know that you sent me..." as though he is comforting and reassuring his wholly loving Father in His sorrow over the distance between Him and His children.

John 17:26   *'I made your name known to them, and will make it known, so that the love you had for me may be in them, and I in them.'*

"I showed them Your nature, and through them will continue to make Your nature known, so that the love with which You have loved me may be fully realized in them, for I will be in them."

Jesus ends his prayer in fullness of love — love for his righteous Father, love for his men, and an out-pouring of love for the world in his continuing work of glorifying the Father.

The vision ends and the present becomes the immediate concern.

We are indeed privileged to have this inspired record of our Lord's thoughts prior to his arrest.

Are they his true words? Perhaps not, but John writes them as an integral part of the message his Gospel reveals. Because they are given by the Holy Spirit, can we do less than accept their spiritual import?

Chapter Eighteen

Gethsemane

John 18:1   *After this prayer, Jesus went out with his disciples across the Kedron ravine. There was a garden there, and he and his disciples went into it.*

These events start when Jesus meets with his twelve in an upper room provided for his use by a friend. There he washes their feet, counsels and instructs them, there they eat, and afterwards he prays.

It is the night before the eve of Passover. The hour grows late. It is time to leave. Jesus, and those with him, cross the Kedron ravine and enter a familiar garden known as Gethsemane.

The time scale implied in this Gospel does not seem to permit a lengthy or even a short period for Jesus' prayerful agony while his disciples sleep.[1] John makes no mention of it. Rather he conveys the image of a man whose spiritual vision and awareness of his oneness with his Father enables him to stride to his destiny, secure in the knowledge of his ultimate victory over death. John grows in his spiritual understanding to perceive Jesus' vision; he is "with him" (John 17:24), as Jesus prays his disciples will be, beholding his glory at the time these events are finally recalled. They convey the fact of a triumphant spiritual sense that has overcome the agony of human fears. Is it not possible that the perception of the other writers has not reached this degree of understanding? From the human level they see a man in agony. John witnesses Divinity enfolding His own in triumphant love.

John 18:2   *The place was known to Judas, his betrayer, because Jesus had often met there with his disciples.*

The garden is a familiar meeting place that must have comforted each one on that fateful night as a chill, colder than the dampness of the night, presses upon them.

John 18:3   *So Judas made his way there with a detachment of soldiers, and with temple police provided by the chief priests and the Pharisees; they were equipped with lanterns, torches, and weapons.*

Judas, impelled by dark forces beyond his comprehension, takes the revenge his jealousy and hurt feelings demand. Betraying the one who could have helped him, he leads soldiers and police to the place he is sure to find Jesus. He guides a formidable force consisting of armed Roman soldiers and temple police. This time the chief priests and Pharisees will not let Jesus slip away. They even have one of Jesus' own men to lead them!

It is interesting to picture these soldiers, disciplined men in armor, equipped with weapons for whatever emergency they meet. The temple police also are armed. It is dark; torches and lanterns light their way as they leave the confines of Jerusalem to follow a country road. Their object is to arrest a renegade named Jesus of Nazareth.

John 18:4-5   *Jesus, knowing everything that was to happen to him, stepped forward and asked them, 'Who is it you want?' 'Jesus of Nazareth,' they answered. Jesus said 'I am he.' And Judas the traitor was standing there with them.*

Jesus comes forth from the garden to meet those who seek him. He sees Judas leading the detachment of soldiers and police.

---

[1]   Matthew 26:36, Mark 14:32, Luke 22:39

John tells all in his dramatic and simple statement: "and Judas the traitor was standing there with them."

Stark and alone Judas faces his Master. The enormity of his actions strike his thought with terrifying illumination.

At this moment the inadequacy of mortal man meets the grandeur of the Son of God. Perhaps Judas really sees his Savior for the first time. Prior to this moment he has been unable to yield to Jesus Christ because he is too full of self-interest. But it is at this moment that his redemption begins.

John 18:6   *When Jesus said, 'I am he,' they drew back and fell to the ground.*

Jesus makes the announcement "I am he" from the summit of his Christliness. John writes this as "I AM he" the *ego eimi* — the same pronouncement that Moses hears Jehovah say "I AM THAT I AM."[2]

To the men seeking a sinful renegade the pronouncement is a blast of divine power, and they fall before it. Even though Jesus is willingly giving his human life into their hands, the holiness of his being makes itself felt.

The Arrest

John 18:7-11   *Again, he asked, 'Who is it you want?' 'Jesus of Nazareth,' they repeated. 'I have told you that I am he,' Jesus answered. 'If I am the man you want, let these others go.' (This was to make good his words, 'I have not lost one of those you gave me.') Thereupon Simon Peter drew the sword he was wearing and struck at the high priest's servant, cutting off his right ear. The servant's name was Malchus. Jesus said to Peter, 'Put away your sword. This is the cup the Father has given me; shall I not drink it?'*

In this scene Jesus stands with his own men around him. Some, like Peter, wear swords. (The times called for men to be armed.) The soldiers are ready to attack, yet Jesus' quiet authority must be quickly recognized in this hazardous situation. Even the severing of Malchus' ear does not precipitate the slaughter that could follow if soldiers and police rush forward to overcome them.

According to Luke's Gospel Jesus heals Malchus' ear.

To Peter, the impetuous, Jesus orders, "Put away your sword." Peter's kind of protection has never been needed by Jesus. He now reminds Peter of his mission. "This is the cup the Father has given me; shall I not drink it?" This cup, considered from the human level, is most bitter; but spiritually seen, is a cup of joyous salvation. Has Jesus not told them he wants them to share his joy "in full measure?" (John 17:13).

The bitterness of his cup is not only the physical pain he will experience, but also the indignity to his majestic person. He knows his followers will be plagued by fears and doubts and will come close to abandoning him.

John 18:12   *The troops with their commander, and the Jewish police, now arrested Jesus and secured him.*

Though the disciples have been prepared by their Master for this very event, they are appalled to see him taken into custody, manacled, and led away. He whom they love and revere is being roughly handled and rudely treated. When he finally disappears with the soldiers, the disciples scatter. Matthew and Mark say they desert him, and run away.

It is Mark who comes, so tradition says, among the other stragglers. He bears witness to the scene. "Among those who had followed Jesus was a young man with nothing on but a linen cloth. They tried to seize him; but he slipped out of the linen cloth and ran away naked" (Mark 14:51).

It is prudent that night that they all disperse.

John 18:13-14   *They took him first to Annas, father-in-law of Caiaphas, the high priest for that year — the same Caiaphas who had advised the Jews that it would be to their interest if one man died for the people.*

---

[2] Raymond E. Brown, S.S., *The Anchor Bible*, Volume 29, page 810, second paragraph, Doubleday & Co., Inc..

Jerusalem at this time is nearing the boiling point of rebellion, though it does not come for some time. In order to preserve their leadership, Jewish authorities, on occasion, work together with the Roman rulers, as in this case, stopping the activities of a troublesome renegade. Both groups are glad for the other's help. Annas and Caiaphas have great influence.

Caiaphas' counsel to the Jews "that it is more to your interest that one man should die for the people" (John 11:50) suggests a political assessment of the Jewish predicament under the Romans. The joyous and curious throng that accepts and cheers Jesus as he rides his ass to Jerusalem's Temple are there, not to acclaim a spiritual leader, but a king like David of old who will fight to rid them of the Roman yoke. Another such scene might bring the Romans with swift reprisal! This is to be avoided at all costs! Jesus is expendable in Caiaphas' eyes.

Simon Peter

John 18:15-16   Jesus was followed by Simon Peter and another disciple. This disciple, who was known to the high priest, went with Jesus into the high priest's courtyard, but Peter stayed outside at the door. So the other disciple, the high priest's acquaintance, went back and spoke to the girl on duty at the door, and brought Peter in.

The arresting party, lighted by torches, returns to Jerusalem. In their midst is Jesus. Behind them, in the darkness, Simon Peter and "another disciple" follow. It is quite likely this man is John. Twice we are told that he is the high priest's acquaintance. This gives him access to the courtyard. He knows the high priest, but apparently not well, for he is an acquaintance not a friend. It is touching to see John's thoughtfulness when he returns to speak to the woman who guards the door and secures Peter's admittance.

John 18:17-18   The girl said to Peter, 'Are you another of this man's disciples?' 'I am not,' he said. As it was cold, the servants and the police had made a charcoal fire, and were standing around it warming themselves. Peter too was standing with them, sharing the warmth.

Peter is most anxious to avoid arrest and probably feels uncomfortable in the high priest's house. By this time his mind is racing with kaleidoscopic thoughts, and bit by bit the seepage of doubt creeps in. Is Jesus really the Messiah? He is cold, bewildered, and deeply hurt by all that is happening to Jesus. What can he do? He is frustrated and helpless. Sharing the warmth of the fire with these men he does not know makes him feel very lonely. His Teacher is somewhere in there. He feels utterly bereft — and instinctive self-defense surges within him.

John 18:19-24   The high priest questioned Jesus about his disciples, and about his teaching. Jesus replied, 'I have spoken openly for all the world to hear; I have always taught in synagogues or in the temple, where all Jews congregate; I have said nothing in secret. Why are you questioning me? Question those who heard me; they know what I said.' When he said this, one of the police standing near him, struck him on the face. 'Is that the way to answer the high priest?' he demanded. Jesus replied, 'If I was wrong to speak what I did, produce evidence to prove it; if I was right, why strike me?'
So Annas sent him bound to Caiaphas the high priest.

Annas is a former high priest and it is thought his title remained as an honor and respect due him.

Because Jesus is first brought to him we know Annas still has both power and influence.

Though his arrest is politically expedient, Jesus is here questioned on religious grounds. Just what has he taught? Who are his disciples? Dangerous questions. To give the names of his followers will jeopardize them and this Jesus does not wish to do. Claiming the openness of his teaching and the openness of his remarks in the environment of synagogue and temple, he truthfully states, "If I was wrong to speak what I did, produce evidence to prove it; if I was right, why strike me?"

Even though Jesus has deliberately put his life in the hands of his captors he boldly remonstrates with them. This is no timid, frightened prisoner; they can feel his inherent authority in the ring of his voice.

John 18:25-27 *Meanwhile, as Simon Peter stood warming himself, he was asked, 'Are you another of his disciples?' But he denied it: 'I am not,' he said. One of the high priest's servants, a relation of the man whose ear Peter had cut off, insisted, 'Did I not see you with him in the garden?' Once again Peter denied it; and at that moment a cock crowed.*

While Jesus is being interrogated, the servants and police, with Simon Peter among them, are huddled as close to the fire as possible, for the night is very cold.

A second time comes the question, "Are you another of his disciples?" Peter denies it. The third time he is questioned by a witness of the scene at the garden, "Did I not see you?" "No!" And the cock crows.

Sickening, heavy guilt sweeps over Peter. All that Jesus has prophesied has come to pass. He can hear himself protesting to his Lord, "I will lay down my life for you!" "Will you really lay down your life for me?" his Lord answers (John 13:36-38). Helpless, shuddering grief overwhelms him.

Jesus has called him Peter — Rock — but at this time the rock is not yet hardened. The catalyst of the Holy Spirit will quicken him for his future work.

Pilate and Jesus

John 18:28-32 *From Caiaphas Jesus was led into the governor's headquarters. It was now early morning, and the Jews themselves stayed outside the headquarters to avoid defilement, so that they could eat the Passover meal. So Pilate came out to them and asked, 'What charge do you bring against this man?' 'If he were not a criminal,' they replied, 'we would not have brought him before you.' Pilate said, 'Take him yourselves and try him by your own law.' The Jews answered, 'We are not allowed to put anyone to death.' Thus they ensured the fulfillment of the words by which*

Jesus had indicated the kind of death he was to die.

It is early morning when Jesus is taken by Caiaphas to the Governor's headquarters. The time sequence is interesting.

Presumably it is around midnight when Jesus is arrested. It is dark at the time of the arrest and there is a full moon.

Raymond Brown[3] writes that " 'at daybreak' is the 'early hour,' the last Roman division of the night, (coming after cockcrow), from 3-6 A.M. One can interpret John to mean that the interrogation by Annas, and the simultaneous denials by Peter, come to an end about 3:00 A.M., that during the next three-hour period Jesus is with Caiaphas, and that finally towards 6:00 A.M. Jesus is led to Pilate where the trial lasts until about noon, when he is sentenced. Sherwin-White, 'Trial,' page 114, points out that the working day of a Roman official began at the earliest hour of daylight..."

Though not mentioned in John's text, Brown continues (though this is not a quote) that one assumes that the high priest and priests accompany Jesus to Pilate. They alone are the ones who will be in danger of defilement, as during that afternoon it will be their duty to kill the Paschal lamb. (This coincides with the time Jesus dies). It is controversial whether the cause of defilement would be association with Gentiles, or entering a house in which there is yeast, for only unleavened bread is prescribed for the Holy Days.[4]

Pilate asks them for the formal charge brought against Jesus. "He is a criminal or we should not have brought him to you!" they state. Unwilling to be the judge of such a controversial figure, Pilate tells them to try Jesus under their own law. They protest "We are not allowed to put any man to death!"

Rome has supplied soldiers for Jesus' arrest; so Pilate most likely is well aware of the trumped-up political nature of this charge. The Jews accuse Jesus of misleading the people, forbidding taxes to the Emperor, and aspiring to be a king like David of old. It is this latter charge the Jews emphasize, for Rome will tolerate no undermining of its authority. This

3 Raymond E. Brown, S. S., *The Anchor Bible*, Volume 29, page 844 "at daybreak", Doubleday & Co., Inc.
4 Raymond E. Brown, S. S., *The Anchor Bible*, Volume 29, page 845, fourth paragraph, Doubleday & Co., Inc.

crime is a capital offense and death by crucifixion is the Roman method of execution for those not citizens of Rome.

John 18:33-36 *Pilate then went back into his headquarters and summoned Jesus. 'So you are the king of the Jews?' he said. Jesus replied, 'Is that your own question, or have others suggested it to you?' 'Am I a Jew?' said Pilate. 'Your own nation and their chief priests have brought you before me. What have you done?' Jesus replied, 'My kingdom does not belong to this world. If it did, my followers would be fighting to save me from the clutches of the Jews. My kingdom belongs elsewhere.'*

Reading the above passage one has the strong feeling that Pilate intuitively sees in Jesus a man of authority and position. Jesus can give his human life, but he can never separate himself from his divine nature to such a degree that those around him cannot see it. Pilate knows he has before him an exceptional individual, but Pilate's lack of integrity and vacillating courage obscure his insight. He is a coward. He really wants no part in deciding this man's fate, but it is forced upon him by the strong political currents and the intrigue that always lie just below the surface.

Jesus answers him not servilely but as an equal: "Is that your own question, or have others suggested it to you?" Pilate jumps to his own defense. "Am I a Jew?" He is inferring that for the Jews to make suggestions to him is preposterous. "Your own nation and their chief priests have brought you before me. What have you done?" What has Jesus done to bring such wrath upon himself?

Jesus answers simply "My Kingdom does not belong to this world." He is accused of wanting to be king — and now he admits to a kingdom — but his kingdom is not of this world! Chills run over the superstitious Roman governor at such an assertion from this unknown man. "If it [my kingdom] did [belong to this world]," continues Jesus, "my followers would be fighting to save me from the clutches of the Jews." In this statement Jesus clearly says he is not aspiring to be king of the Jews!

Then Jesus adds, "My kingdom belongs elsewhere."

Jesus does not elaborate. He knows that Pilate knows that he speaks truly.

John 18:37 *'You are a king, them?' said Pilate. Jesus answered, ' "King" is your word. My task is to bear witness to the truth. For this was I born; for this I came into the world, and all who are not deaf to truth listen to my voice.'*

A king, to Pilate, holds authority over the people and territory of his kingdom. This definition is not adequate to describe Jesus' position, his authority, nor his "territory." Jesus answers Pilate, " 'King' is your word. My task is to bear witness to the truth."

In bearing witness to the truth, Jesus possesses the power and authority to reveal the truth, or true state or condition, of whatever he is dealing with at the time.

"For this I was born; for this I came into the world," he has said from the beginning.

It is to reveal the Father in himself; to manifest the man in His image; to show God's control entering the minutia of creation; "for this I was born." It is to deny chance and luck, and reveal God's pattern of events affording His own creation security and peace. This is not kingship in the earthly sense. This kingship accepts only the human will yielding to divine revelation, and the authoritative power of revelation then operating to support and preserve all that manifests God and glorifies Him. Jesus comes to reveal God's kingdom and rule, on earth, and in the lives of men "as it is in heaven."

And Jesus emphasizes, "All who are not deaf to truth listen to my voice!"

John 18:38 *Pilate said, 'What is truth?'*

Pilate, a man of curious reputation in view of the great excesses of his rule, has little knowledge or interest in truth, as Jesus knows truth. Robbery, murder, and inhumanity are attributed to him by Philo. Josephus writes vividly of his blunders and atrocities. Luke 13:1 tells us of the slaughter of the Galileans, yet the Christian tradition seems to ignore these sources and paints a more favorable character. Pilate's post at Jerusalem is difficult and not glamorous — a sort of "back water" — and he is always in danger of his past failures catching up with him. Self-preservation motivates him, and in this instance he hopes to keep a low profile and thus evade taking any decisive stand on the issue of Jesus' fate. There are always those reports that he and others must send to Rome. He does not want local unrest added to his record!

John 18:38-40 *With those words he went out again to the Jews and said, 'For my part I find no case against him. But you have a custom that I release one prisoner for you at Passover. Would you like me to release the king of the Jews?' At this they shouted back: 'Not him; we want Barabbas!' Barabbas was a bandit.*

Pilate has learned from his questioning of Jesus that the political charge is invalid. Appealing to the crowd he offers to release the "King of the Jews." But the manipulators of this event have their prompters scattered through the mob to lead them in asking for Barabbas, and the clamor for Barabbas is great!

Chapter Nineteen

John 19:1-3 *Pilate now took Jesus and had him flogged; and the soldiers plaited a crown of thorns and placed it on his head, and robed him in a purple cloak. Then one after another they came up to him, crying, 'Hail, king of the Jews!' and struck him on the face.*

It is customary at this time to flog, or beat, after an arrest, even though the case may later be dismissed. It is a type of warning, or threat, to the populace.

Beating with sticks or whips is corrective punishment. Beating, flogging, and scourging are practiced in that "ascending gradation." Brown[1] says "the severer punishment was part of the capital sentence."

It is interesting that the various Bible translations use different words in this passage:

King James Bible — took Jesus and scourged him.

Modern Language Bible — took Jesus and had him flogged.[2]

Living Bible — then Pilate laid open Jesus' back with a leaded whip.[2]

New Revised Standard Bible — took Jesus and had him flogged.[2]

Revised English Bible — took Jesus and had him flogged.

Mark and Matthew speak of the whole "band" or "cohort" (600 soldiers) participating in the mockery after he is crowned and robed.

Most readers have not considered this mocking and slapping very seriously. "One after another" is the *Revised English Bible* wording, and it emphasizes repetition. If only one third of the cohort participates — or a tenth, or less, the repetitious slapping (or striking with the fist, as some translations read) will leave his face in dreadful condition! Such treatment not only shows Pilate's inhumanity, but an insen-

sitivity and cruelty inherent in mortals; and it is still with us today.

John 19:4-5 *Once more Pilate came out and said to the Jews, 'Here he is; I am bringing him out to let you know that I find no case against him'; and Jesus came out, wearing the crown of thorns and the purple cloak. 'Here is the man,' said Pilate.*

Under Pilate's orders the soldiers have flogged, slapped, and humiliated Jesus. Humiliation, to the culture at that time, is as devastating as the corporal punishment. The treatment seems very severe since Pilate states "I find no case against him." One questions if Jesus can stand without help. Since he is "brought out" he undoubtedly has soldiers on either side, perhaps supporting him.

Cruelty has reinforced Pilate's courage somewhat. He begins to feel his dominion over Jesus and in a stentorian voice announces "Here is the man" — and his sarcasm is readily understood by all his hearers. For Jesus stands there a pitiful figure, bruised and battered, wearing a mock crown and royal robe. Pilate is saying: "This man is no king — you are crazy to think so — just look at him!"

John 19:6-7 *At the sight of him the chief priests and the temple police shouted, 'Crucify! Crucify!' 'Take him yourselves and crucify him,' said Pilate; 'for my part I find no case against him.' The Jews answered, 'We have a law; and according to that law he ought to die, because he has claimed to be God's son.'*

"Crucify! Crucify!" is the frenzied shout of a mob stirred by religious fanaticism and zeal, thirsting for blood — a "lynch mob." No one is truly safe from

[1] Raymond E. Brown, S.S., *The Anchor Bible*, Volume 29, page 874, notes third and fourth paragraphs.
[2] *The Laymen's Parallel Bible*, Zondervan Bible Publishers, Grand Rapids, Michigan.

their fury. They have not revealed to Pilate their real reason for wanting Jesus' death until now: "He claims to be God's Son." This terrible blasphemy shocks the zealous into action and plays into the hands of conspirators in the Jewish hierarchy. When the cries become too violent Jesus is returned to the safety of the building by the soldiers guarding him.

John 19:8-9 *When Pilate heard that, he was more afraid than ever, and going back into his headquarters he asked Jesus, 'Where have you come from?' But Jesus gave him no answer.*

Pilate is "more afraid than ever!" The possibility that this man is the Son of a god is terrifying to him. No one should provoke the gods!

Pagan Rome accepts the belief that gods visit earth for either good or evil purposes, so the thought that this strange man can be a god, or son of a god, shakes him profoundly. He knows of him and has heard of his "mighty works." This knowledge increases his fears, and superstition colors all his thoughts with sickening dread.

"Where have you come from?" Pilate desperately longs to have this question answered, but Jesus is silent.

John 19:10 *'Do you refuse to speak to me?' said Pilate. 'Surely you know that I have authority to release you, and authority to crucify you?'*

Almost beside himself in frustration and apprehension, Pilate, the whole power of his office in his sneering voice, threatens Jesus: 'Surely you know that I have authority to release you, and have authority to crucify you!'

Jesus can speak to this question without jeopardizing his followers.

John 19:11 *'You would have no authority at all over me,' Jesus replied, 'if it had not been granted you from above; and therefore the deeper guilt lies with the one who handed me over to you.'*

Perhaps Pilate thinks: "There he goes again speaking of authority 'from above' giving me power over him. He must be a god, and I am helpless!" But what is he now saying? "...and therefore the deeper guilt lies with the man who handed me over to you."

A faint glimmer of hope must flash in Pilate's consciousness. There is a way out!

Who is this man who has given Jesus to Pilate? Judas is not mentioned. He is a mere tool of greater forces. Is it Caiaphas, the high priest, who says it is better that one die rather than all of Israel? Or is it Lucifer, who falls from heaven because he wants the power of God as his own. After all it is he who wants to kill the Son that he may have the inheritance for himself.

Jesus is fighting his battle in his own way. He is obedient to his Father in maintaining, throughout this terrible ordeal, that the only power over him comes from above. All he has stood for as he lived among men, all he has taught them, all the love he has shown them, is being laid on the line. The test is upon him. The validity of his teaching and his actions will be shown in his bodily resurrection. He has raised the son of the widow of Nain to life, and Lazarus as well, though he had been in the tomb four days.

The forces and persuasions that flout the prophets of old, when they speak the Word of the Lord, are now joined in conspiracy to destroy God's son, God's Chosen One, who has come that all who hear might have the inheritance of life and be called the children of God.

Jesus is sent to destroy death. This destruction has to take place at the very point where it will seem that life cannot come. At that very meeting place the threshold of death has to be crossed by the Son of Life itself, and the son of Mary has to have faith that the Selfhood of the Son of God will uplift him. Jesus has confidently demonstrated in his life experience that he is not two personalities, son of Mary and Son of God, but that his human self is the human view of his divine Sonship, at all times. The fact that this humanity is the visible manifestation of his divine self enables him to carry out his Father's will and reveal his Father to men.

In the crucifixion experience, his spiritual nature, as divine Son, cannot loose his human self from the Christ protection, but it can let his mortal life be placed in the power of those who will try to destroy all he stands for. Allowing himself to be at death's mercy in its full finality is the only way in which he can penetrate the process and refute utterly evil's claim that it can hold the children of God forever in its grasp.

Lucifer's sin that brings his expulsion from heaven, and entices the children of men to follow him, is the desire for power and control. Jesus refutes this lust in his utter yielding to God and His will. This is the revelation that brings salvation.

John 19:12-13   *From that moment Pilate tried hard to release him; but the Jews kept shouting, 'If you let this man go, you are no friend to Caesar; anyone who claims to be a king is opposing Caesar.' When Pilate heard what they were saying, he brought Jesus out and took his seat on the tribunal at the place known as The Pavement (in Hebrew, 'Gabbatha').*

If you let this man go you are no friend to Caesar! Horrified by this turn of events, Pilate tries to stop them from shouting this accusation. Spies of Rome are everywhere. His mind races! If only he can appease them — if only they will stop shouting that he is no friend of Caesar's!

Spies! He cannot allow such a report to be carried to Rome. He would be ruined!

He orders Jesus brought out and seats himself where capital judgments are pronounced.

John 19:14-16   *It was the day of preparation for the Passover, about noon. Pilate said to the Jews, 'Here is your king.' They shouted, 'Away with him! Away with him! Crucify him!' 'Am I to crucify your king?' said Pilate. 'We have no king but Caesar,' replied the chief priests. Then at last, to satisfy them, he handed Jesus over to be crucified.*

Time is growing short. The high priest and others have the killing of the Paschal lamb scheduled for the afternoon. They have done their work well — "We have no king but Caesar!" is the cry that turns the tide in Pilate's mind. Only feebly does he resist them though he knows Jesus is not seeking kingship —

and finally he gives up. Better Jesus should die than to have his own career destroyed! Even his own life might be forfeit if news of this clamor reaches his superiors.

Jesus is handed over for crucifixion about noon.

John 19:16-18   *Jesus was taken away, and went out, carrying the cross himself, to the place called The Skull, (in Hebrew 'Golgotha'); there they crucified him, and with him two others, one on either side, with Jesus in between.*

The simple words of John makes one feel the aching loneliness of Jesus' position. Soldiers, crowds — some of them his followers and relatives — yet at the moment of crucifixion he is alone.

This account says he carries his cross, an awful load for one who has been flogged and slapped repeatedly. Luke tells us that Simon from Cyrene is commandeered by the soldiers to walk behind Jesus carrying his cross. This seems most likely.

It is customary for the prisoner to carry the crossbar to the place of execution. The vertical portion, about nine feet high, remains at the site.

John tells us nothing of the "two others" crucified with him. Matthew and Mark identify them as bandits, and Luke as criminals.

Josephus calls crucifixion "the most wretched of deaths,"[3] and Cicero speaks of it as "a most cruel and terrible penalty."

John 19:19-22   *Pilate had an inscription written and fastened to the cross; it read, 'Jesus of Nazareth, King of the Jews'. This inscription, in Hebrew, Latin, and Greek, was read by many Jews, since the place where Jesus was crucified was not far from the city. So the Jewish chief priests said to Pilate, 'You should not write "King of the Jews", but rather "He claimed to be king of the Jews".' Pilate replied, 'What I have written, I have written.'*

Pilate is apparently still smarting from the threat "if you let this man go you are no friend of Caesar's." Apprehensive of the tales of his unwillingness to

[3] Raymond E. Brown, S.S., The *Anchor Bible*, Volume 29, page 900, Doubleday & Co., Inc.

condemn Jesus getting back to Rome, he makes the inscription for the cross very clear "Jesus of Nazareth, King of the Jews" and has it written in Hebrew, Latin, and Greek. Let there be no mistake — he tolerates no threat to Caesar!

But this does not please the chief priests, for the inscription puts them in the awkward position of appearing to accept him. They prefer "He claimed to be King of the Jews." No one asks Jesus what he prefers to have written.

The location of the crucifixion is not far from the city, on a slight elevation called the Place of the Skull. Evidence as to why it was so called has disappeared over the centuries.

John 19:23-24 *When the soldiers had crucified Jesus they took his clothes and, leaving aside the tunic, divided them into four parts, one for each soldier. The tunic was seamless, woven in one piece throughout; so they said to one another, 'We must not tear this; let us toss for it.' Thus the text of scripture came true: 'They shared my garments among them, and cast lots for my clothing.'* [4] *That is what the soldiers did.*

Four soldiers have the task of placing Jesus on the cross, and having done so they divide his clothing. His seamless tunic greatly appeals to them. We do not know whether these same soldiers crucify the others or not. It is considered likely that four soldiers are assigned to each prisoner.

When they remove Jesus' clothing they may leave him naked, which is customary with Roman executions. However, out of respect to Jewish customs, for the naked body is very offensive to them, they may leave the breech cloth. [5]

John 19:25-27 *Meanwhile near the cross on which Jesus hung, his mother was standing with her sister, Mary wife of Clopas, and Mary of Magdala. Seeing his mother, with the disciple whom he loved standing beside her, Jesus said to her 'Mother, there is your son'; and to the disciple, 'There is your mother'; and from*

that moment the disciple took her into his home.

What courage and inner strength Mary shows by following her son to Golgotha. It had been prophesied that "...you too will be pierced to the heart" (Luke 2:35). Seeing her son, her babe whom she nurtured and loved, nailed to a cross and lifted on high for all to see and ridicule, must strain her faith in God's wisdom to the very utmost!

She is not alone. Relatives and friends stand by her with dread written in their eyes and despair tugging at each heart. The soldiers are there also, and the farmers coming from the fields, as well as the remnants of the mob who have cried "Crucify!"; and of course there are the curious.

The brutal scene is reflected in the eyes of all who watch. John, the disciple whom Jesus loves, stands close to Mary. They all are as close to the cross as they can go. Perhaps Mary from time to time cups her hands across her mouth to stifle the terror and moan that witnesses her grief; seeing her son fastened to a cross, and no one to take him down!

They stand there waiting, for they know that because of the Sabbath, before the setting of the sun, the three figures will be removed from the crosses.

Seeing those whom he loves standing nearby Jesus says, "Mother, there is your son," and to John, "There is your mother." It is not unusual for a dying man to give a loved one into another's care. The times are very difficult for widows and orphans.

John 19:28-30 *After this, Jesus, aware that all had now come to its appointed end, said in fulfillment of scripture, 'I am thirsty.' A jar stood there full of sour wine; so they soaked a sponge with the wine, fixed it on hyssop, and held it up to his lips. Having received the wine, he said, 'It is accomplished!' He bowed his head and gave up his spirit.*

Jesus hangs on the cross for the relatively short period of three hours. This is almost unheard of, for the excruciating aspect is the length of time, some-

---

[4] Psalm 22:18
[5] Raymond E. Brown, S.S., *The Anchor Bible*, Volume 29A, page 902, Doubleday & Co., Inc.

times as long as three or four days, that the victim lasts.

In Matthew and Mark it is written: "My God, my God, why have you forsaken me?" In Luke's account he gives a loud cry and says, "Father into your hands I commit my spirit." Luke perceives Jesus in full faith entrusting himself completely to the care of his Father.

John writes that he says, " 'It is accomplished!' Then he bowed his head and gave up his spirit." John, like Luke, perceives a more gentle yielding to God's care. All statements are fitting and reveal the writers' attitudes toward that moment of fulfillment. Their viewpoints show the difference between that of a man standing at sea level and one standing on a mountain.

Close to the scene the view is of the immediate condition. The long range view serves Luke and John. They behold in Jesus the complete yielding to God and His complete care of His own.

John 19:31-34   *Because it was the eve of the sabbath, the Jews were anxious that the bodies should not remain on the crosses, since that sabbath was a day of great solemnity; so they requested Pilate to have the legs broken and the bodies taken down. The soldiers accordingly came to the men crucified with Jesus and broke the legs of each in turn; but when they came to Jesus and found he was already dead, they did not break his legs. But one of the soldiers thrust a lance into his side and at once there was a flow of blood and water.*

Only John mentions the request to have the legs broken. This gruesome blow actually hastens death, therefore is a merciful act, but it is mainly used to prevent escape when the bodies are brought from the cross to the ground. The fact that Jesus has died so very quickly surprises all. To be certain of his death a soldier stabs his side with a lance.

While hanging on the cross the infinite resources of Jesus' devotion to his purpose do not run dry. The only way he can counteract the intense hatred leveled against him is to love with forgiveness (Luke 23:34). From this limitless supply of love and forgiveness he directs an outpouring that cleanses every heart that accepts him and fills even some of the dead with life.

Matthew 27:51-53 tells us that God's saints rise from the grave and are seen in the streets of Jerusalem by many at the time of resurrection.

The lance that pierces his side gives symbolic proof, in the flow of blood and water, of the measure of the activity of his spiritual energies and forces. The blood speaks of the life-giving Love that he manifests, the water of the immersion in Spirit that brings our salvation. Sacrificial love, the new birth, and baptism of Spirit sum up his human life. His work of revealing the Father to His children has been accomplished. "...God's only Son, he who is nearest to the Father's heart, has made him known" (John 1:18).

John 19:35-37   *This is vouched for by an eyewitness, whose evidence is to be trusted. He knows that he speaks the truth, so that you too may believe; for this happened in fulfillment of the text of scripture: 'No bone of his shall be broken.' And another text says, 'They shall look on him whom they pierced.'*

An eyewitness whose evidence is to be trusted! What has been written is not hearsay but is the account of an observer. Scholars acknowledge that specific details given in John's account of the trial and crucifixion are apparently factual.

He speaks the truth that we, too, may believe, that we may understand that Jesus Christ is the Son of God. In this understanding we yield to him and to the Father and become the children of God.

John's Gospel continues the emphasis on the necessity of fulfilling the scripture.

"No bone of his shall be broken." The Jews believe that those with broken bodies cannot return in resurrection.

"They shall look on him whom they pierced."

Matthew 27:54 writes: "And when the centurion and his men who were keeping watch over Jesus saw the earthquake and all that was happening, they were filled with awe and said, 'This must have been a son of God!' "

Today we look on him whom they pierced and long to tell him of our love and obedience to him. Enduring abuse of every kind in order that his followers may find salvation, Jesus eases his torture by loving those who hate him most. This love is real and stems from the Father Who gives us the revelation of Himself in His Son.

John 19:38-42 *After that, Joseph of Arimathaea, a disciple of Jesus, but a secret disciple for fear of the Jews, asked Pilate for permission to remove the body of Jesus. He consented; so Joseph came and removed the body. He was joined by Nicodemus (the man who had visited Jesus by night), who brought with him a mixture of myrrh and aloes, more than half a hundredweight. They took the body of Jesus and following Jewish burial customs they wrapped it, with the spices, in strips of linen cloth. Near the place where he had been crucified there was a garden, and in the garden a new tomb, not yet used for burial; and there, since it was the eve of the Jewish sabbath and the tomb was near at hand, they laid Jesus.*

Joseph of Arimathaea and Nicodemus are devoted followers of Jesus. Both are influential and wealthy, and their families and the community will be severely tested if their acknowledgment of Jesus and his teachings are recognized. It is probably known, but politics being what they are, official recognition of their position as Jesus' disciples will be taken only at the time that suits the Jews in power.

Pilate gives them permission to take Jesus' body. Has Pilate lost interest in the whole situation, now that Jesus is dead? Or is there a lingering uneasiness that perhaps Jesus may have been a god? To let a prominent business man have the body of Jesus may even help him a bit in this precarious situation. He wishes he could have stayed out of the whole affair.

So Joseph and Nicodemus take the body away. It is likely they only take it away from the immediate vicinity of the crosses. Time is very short. Sundown and the great sabbath are close. Working quickly they perform with love the burial wrapping that good friends through the ages have given those dear to them. Great reverence is evident in this brief account. A half hundred weight of spices is an enormous quantity. Such large amounts are usually reserved for the burial of kings.

The new tomb in the garden is at hand. It is possible one of them may own it, or have quickly made arrangements to use it.

Their work is finished. They do all they can for this most special One. They lay him in his resting place, close the tomb with its great stone, and depart.

It is now just about sundown and the sabbath is at hand.

Interlude

There is no time to wash the body of Jesus, so Joseph of Arimathaea, and Nicodemus take the long winding sheet and gently put it around his body, tucking in the rich spices. Over his head and under his chin they fasten a linen napkin. Their task completed, they roll the stone across the mouth of the tomb, and hurriedly depart to their homes. A tranquility descends over the small garden, for the High Holy Day of the sabbath has begun.

The stone closes out the clamor, the cruelty, the gruesomeness; and within the tomb there is the music of absolute quiet. The body of Jesus lies in its fragrant wrappings. The body of the Son of Man has ceased its mortal life, but Jesus lives on in his complete oneness with his Christ. Filling this retreat is the light of the Father's love. After the hatred, hurt, and cruelty, this tenderness becomes a healing balm that permeates Jesus' body. There is peace, undisturbed peace. The warmth of love dispels the darkness of cold disdain. The angels of the Lord, present with him from before his human birth, watch over this final period as well.

His mission is not yet complete. His Father has not asked him to do the impossible, in searching out His lost children to bring them home. He is to search, not only among the living, but also among the dead, for those who have never heard the voice of God.

Because he has experienced the death of his mortal body, Jesus' spiritual identity is able to move in that sphere closed to those called "alive." Only as a mortal man can Jesus Christ follow the path a mortal takes through death. The dead Jesus is the vehicle that takes his Christ nature to the very place where death boasts full power. But it is only in this evanescent boast that death can claim to hold those who belong to the Son of God. This is the work Jesus Christ has been given to do: to enter the "unspiritual" realm and seek his own, and to go even where Life cannot go — to death and the grave — there to rescue the children of God, awakening them to immortality.

Though the body of Jesus lies still upon the slab of stone, the immortality of his very being, as the Word and Christ, operates as a force of Life to resurrect his human body, not again as a wholly mortal body, but a body translated to respond to divine laws of the spiritual realm in which he moves. Though transformed to conformity with the substance of Spirit, his body remains the humanly visible means of recognition for his disciples and others.

Roused from his experience of the cross by angels singing hallelujahs of praise, Jesus sits up, no longer restrained by earthly bindings. He removes the face cloth and folds the napkin neatly, placing it by itself.

There is a rumbling sound as the stone rolls away. Cool fresh air blows into the tomb and lifts a strand of his long brown hair. He breathes deeply, for his body functions naturally. The great wound in his side is there, ugly, although causing him no inconvenience. His body's usefulness is not over for it is still needed to prove his death and resurrection. The marks of the thorns show, and his wrists and insteps bear marks of the nails, but no longer give pain.

A gardener has left some clothing in the back of the tomb. He puts it on, for his own clothing has been taken by the Roman soldiers.

Jesus now steps forth into the crisp air of the first Easter morning; birds sing, a donkey brays in the distance, and somewhere a cock crows. He savors the simplicity of the place he is in, and the beauty of the early day. The sun has not yet broken the horizon. Dew dampens the shrubbery and the leaves of the olive trees. He walks to another part of the garden to commune with his Father.

This is his triumphant hour!

Chapter Twenty

John 20:1-2   *Early on the first day of the week, while it was still dark, Mary of Magdala came to the tomb. She saw that the stone had been moved away from the entrance, and ran to Simon Peter and the other disciple, the one whom Jesus loved. 'They have taken the Lord out of the tomb,' she said, 'and we do not know where they have laid him.'*

Anguish and dismay, bordering on hysteria, best describe Mary's condition when she tells them this terrible news. The site of the tomb is not a great distance from the city and these friends are probably staying fairly near. After embracing the frightened girl to quiet her, they dash off quickly to verify what she has told them!

John 20:3-6   *So Peter and the other disciple set out and made their way to the tomb. They ran together, but the other disciple ran faster than Peter and reached the tomb first. He peered in and saw the linen wrappings lying there, but he did not enter. Then Simon Peter caught up with him and went into the tomb.*

After the heaviness and sadness they have all endured since that terrible Friday — now this! What can have happened? Who can have done this? And then there comes to John's thought faint recollections that gain in grandeur. A wonderfully familiar voice speaks in his memory saying, "...for the moment you are sad; but I shall see you again,..." (John 16:22). Reaching the tomb he pauses at the entrance and looks in. Yes, the stone has been moved, as Mary has told them. And there are the wrappings. It is as though they have been removed by someone who no longer needs them. Dare he believe that? He still hesitates at the entrance; and along comes Peter, breathless from running, and barges into the tomb. Peter is consumed with anxious thoughts about his Master; "Where is he?"

John 20:6-9   *He saw the linen wrappings lying there, and the napkin which had been round his head, not with the wrappings but rolled up in a place by itself. Then the disciple who had reached the tomb first also went in, and he saw and believed; until then they had not understood the scriptures, which showed that he must rise from the dead.*

Peter's eyes dart everywhere seeing all of that confined area with a judgment that carefully assesses the evidence which lies before him. The strong sweet smell of the spices pervade the atmosphere; there is no smell of death. The napkin is not tossed aside but neatly rolled and "in a place by itself."

John follows quickly after Peter. His glance in the tomb before Peter's arrival has been sufficient to open his mind. No longer does he fear that his Lord's body has been stolen. He too interprets the evidence before him according to the intuitive understanding beginning to flow again in his consciousness. "He saw, and believed." Their Lord has risen. This they accept. For the moment this is enough. Floodtides of gratitude and love fill their being; bits of scripture that have been obscure take on new and glorious meaning.

John 20:10-13   *So the disciples went home again; but Mary stood outside the tomb weeping. And as she wept, she peered into the tomb, and saw two angels in white sitting there, one at the head, and one at the feet, where the body of Jesus had lain. The asked her, 'Why are you weeping?' She answered, 'They have taken my Lord away, and I do not know where they have laid him.'*

Following their great discovery of the empty tomb and its meaningful evidence, with their faith again soaring, Peter and the other disciple return to their friends. Mary comes back to the tomb after delivering her news, but does not attempt to keep up with

Peter and John. When they leave she sits down at the mouth of the tomb in quiet despair and weeps. She misses her Lord desperately and weeping comes easily. She looks in the tomb. Now seated at the head and feet where Jesus has lain are two angelic messengers clothed in white. Peter and the other disciple do not need such assurance. Their interpretation of the evidence before them speaks volumes in their hearts and minds, but Mary needs comfort and reassurance. The divine messengers ask "Why are you weeping?" This should have roused her, but her mind is closed to all but the great emptiness she feels. She answers, "They have taken my Lord away, and I do not know where they have laid him."

John 20:14-16   *With these words she turned round and saw Jesus standing there, but she did not recognize him. Jesus asked her, 'Why are you weeping? Who are you looking for?' Thinking it was the gardener, she said, 'If it is you, sir, who removed him, tell me where you have laid him, and I will take him away.' Jesus said, 'Mary!' She turned and said to him, 'Rabbuni!' (which is Hebrew for 'Teacher').*

This marvelously touching scene, when Mary is startled from her melancholy by Jesus' insistence that she see him right there at her side, has, through the centuries, comforted and strengthened many. Preoccupied with her own thoughts, she does not open her mind to the angelic messengers. But her Teacher, whom she seeks, rouses her.

Imagine her relief and joy, her mingled laughter and tears, as she seeks to embrace, to really touch, the one whom she has thought lost forever. Ecstasy of happiness fills her!

John 20:17-18   *'Do not cling to me,' said Jesus, 'for I have not yet ascended to the Father. But go to my brothers, and tell them that I am ascending to my Father and your Father, to my God and your God.' Mary of Magdala went to tell the disciples. 'I have seen the Lord!' she said, and gave them his message.*

Jesus knows Mary well. His insight appreciates the turmoil of emotions she is experiencing now that she has found him. Gently pushing her from him he says, "Do not cling to me." Their reunion is natural,

warm, and human. He is whole and recognizable to her. The death she has watched claim him has been overcome and he has come from entombment to be among the living.

Mary is quiet now, and she is able to comprehend his words: "I have not yet ascended to the Father." He will not be staying with her in the flesh, he will go to the Father. But the joy in her heart is unshaken by this news for now she knows her Lord is alive.

The encounter with her Lord transforms Mary from a grief-crushed girl to a shining-eyed, joyous woman capable of bearing important news to the disciples. With close attention she listens to Jesus' instructions. "Go to my brothers," Jesus says, "and tell them that I am now ascending to my Father and your Father, my God and your God."

Her journey is swift and eager. Entering the room where the disciples have gathered, she announces, 'I have seen the Lord!' and gives them his message.

How do those assembled receive her news? There is no account of this meeting in John's gospel. Some will want to believe her, but in view of the fact that she is saying that Jesus has returned from the dead, and that she has seen him — this is something to question. When one thinks about it, however, it is true that he delivered the son of the widow of Nain alive, and Lazarus had been dead four days, yet when Jesus called him he came forth from his tomb alive and well, and he joined with them all at dinner in Bethany. Jesus, their Lord, has said he will rise in resurrection — is this really so? Some probably rejoice with Mary that she has found comfort from whatever source, but it is unlikely that the disciples of Jesus, even though he has prepared them for his resurrection, greet this glorious news with either enthusiasm or understanding. The past few days have caused each one to reexamine his position and ask himself "What do I now believe?" The very foundations of their thinking show cracks of doubt from the impact of the events they have experienced.

The message Jesus sends his disciples, whom he now calls "brothers," speaks of his ascension to "my Father and to your Father, and to my God and your God."

Because they have accepted him, they have become children of God, the offspring of God Himself (John 1:13). As they mature in spiritual understanding they will realize their sonship with their Father, even as Jesus knows his sonship; and as Jesus has done, they too will declare the saving news of God the Father for all to hear. This is their mission.

John 20:19-21 *Late that same day, the first day of the week, when the disciples were together behind locked doors for fear of the Jews, Jesus came and stood among them. 'Peace be with you!' he said; then showed them his hands and his side. On seeing the Lord the disciples were overjoyed. Jesus said again, 'Peace be with you! As the Father sent me, so I send you.'*

The possibility of arrest still plagues the disciples and their friends. They know Jesus' body is gone from the tomb. Will they be held responsible by the authorities once this becomes generally known? Peter and John seem to be assured that Jesus has indeed risen from the dead, and Mary's experience has reinforced this conclusion. But how can they explain the empty tomb to the unbelieving authorities? The Pharisees believe in resurrection, but the Sadduces do not! Political advantage can be wrested from this strange situation. The disciples are not comfortable under these conditions. In fact they are very uneasy. So they sit behind locked doors to converse in quiet and guarded tones about all that has befallen them in the past three days.

Suddenly Jesus stands before them saying, "Peace be with you!"

Silence and astonishment greet him. The doors are locked yet here is what appears to be a man of flesh, bone, and blood, like themselves — yet not like them! How does he get into the room? It is the Master, our Lord! He is showing his hands and side!

Credulence comes slowly at first. Timidly they begin to accept him — then the conviction that "the Lord is here, now!" is overwhelming. Tender, exquisite joy fills their being, and flows in loving recognition to their Lord.

"Peace be unto you," he repeats. Full recognition brings relief and the gift of peace to each one.

John does not permit us to share the conversation they have with their newly returned Lord, but he does tell us the instructions he gives his new "brothers." "As the Father sent me, so I send you."

He is reiterating his earlier charge to them. This must be further proof to all present that he is, indeed, their Lord.

John 20:22-23 *Then he breathed on them, saying, 'Receive the Holy Spirit! If you forgive anyone's sins, they are forgiven; if you pronounce them unforgiven, unforgiven they remain.'*

Luke tells us: "Then he opened their minds to understand the scriptures" (Luke 24:45). Jesus' action of breathing on his disciples follows his designation of their mission. They are to make him known in the world, just as he reveals the Father in himself. By their revelation of Jesus Christ in their own lives, they will also show the Father's presence in the world.

When Jesus receives the Holy Spirit at the beginning of his ministry it is obvious his years of tutelage have ended. He has been taught by the Holy Spirit, but when John baptizes him in water, the heavens open, and through the Spirit he is empowered to carry out his ministry.

John the Baptist says: "...He who sent me to baptize in water had told me, 'the man on whom you see the Spirit come down and rest is the one who is to baptize in Holy Spirit' " (John 1:33). And further he says of Jesus: "...He whom God sent utters the words of God, so measureless is God's gift of the Spirit" (John 3:34).

The disciples have been taught by Jesus. Now he is commissioning them to go into the world to carry on his work. They will not be acting alone. The Holy Spirit, his Holy Spirit, will be with them.

With this breathing of the Holy Spirit comes the demand for judgment. This responsibility will be guided by the continuing presence of the Spirit with them.

John 20:24-25 *One of the Twelve, Thomas the Twin, was not with the rest when Jesus came. So the others kept telling him, 'We have seen the Lord.' But he said, 'Unless I see the mark of the nails on his hands, unless I put my finger into the place where the nails were, and my hand into his side, I will never believe it.'*

Poor Thomas! It is very hard for him to accept the fact of Jesus' resurrected body. The great point of importance is not so much the resurrection of flesh and blood, but the resurrection of individual identity in an appreciable form. The Flesh that Thomas sees identifies Jesus to him, for Thomas cannot yet discern the substance of Spirit, nor can the other disciples. Jesus, in his earthly life, moves in Spirit always, walking on water as well as land. He recognizes no law of earth as taking precedence over the laws of Spirit that give the children of God their freedom.

Thomas cannot believe his friend's words. He must see for himself, and feel the flesh. That is very important to him.

John 20:26-29   *A week later his disciples were once again in the room, and Thomas was with them. Although the doors were locked, Jesus came and stood among them, saying, 'Peace be with you!' Then he said to Thomas, 'Reach your finger here; look at my hands. Reach your hand here and put it into my side. Be unbelieving no longer, but believe. Thomas said, 'My Lord and my God!' Jesus said to him, 'Because you have seen me you have found faith. Happy are they who find faith without seeing me.'*

The doors are locked. Fear still grips them. And perhaps that is what is needed. It makes them cautious and keeps them from flaunting this most marvelous happening of all time. A birth requires a quiet time of gestation before the new arrival is strong enough to stand the buffeting of human life. The church has been conceived; now it must be nurtured by those to whom it is entrusted that it may gather strength and grow.

Thomas is with the disciples. Suddenly he is aware that Jesus is there — right beside him! He is speaking; "Peace be with you!" A marvelous calm possesses his being. All doubts flee before the presence of the man he knows so well. He does not have to touch his hand or side — not now. He is filled with an irrepressible sense of joy and well-being. "My Lord and my God!" he acknowledges.

Jesus knows full well the struggle Thomas has, the doubts that surge. "Because you have seen me you

have found faith." Yes, he believes when he sees Jesus. Thomas has not grown enough spiritually to see beyond the limits of material conditions, but Jesus expects him to do this. In healing he is expected to spiritually discern a man controlled by God, not by disease; he is to see wind and wave responding to divine will, not chaos; he is to see, as Jesus has taught him to see, and by perceiving spiritually, he is expected to believe.

John 20:30-31   *There were indeed many other signs that Jesus performed in the presence of his disciples, which are not recorded in this book. Those written here have been recorded in order that you may believe that Jesus is the Christ, the Son of God, and that through this faith you may have life by his name.*

John explains why he has written this book. But first he says he has omitted many of the other signs that Jesus performed in the presence of his disciples.

What these other signs are we shall never know, but their purpose, no doubt, is to strengthen — to reinforce those teachings already given. The disciples' weakness of character, or incomplete understanding, are probably corrected during this period for our Lord has committed his life-work to these close friends. He is about to leave them, but he will not leave them alone. His own Holy Spirit will be their guiding presence.

John also tells us he has written his book so that we later Christians may understand. He has not given just a record of words and acts of Jesus Christ. He has gone deeper and presented in guarded, yet perfectly clear, language a complete teaching.

At the beginning he lays the foundation — our Lord's preexistence with God. Then he writes of Jesus' ministry and the significant events surrounding it. Everything he records has meaning and value. As we grow in comprehension of his presentation we are transformed by this spiritual study.

The central theme of John's book is that Jesus is the Word made flesh, the Christ, the Son of God. Through this faith we come to possess life through his name. His nature becomes revealed in us.

Chapter Twenty-One

John 21:1-3 *Some time later, Jesus showed himself to his disciples once again, by the sea of Tiberias. This is how it happened. Simon Peter was with Thomas the Twin, Nathanael from Cana-in-Galilee, the sons of Zebedee, and two other disciples. 'I am going out fishing,' said Simon Peter. 'We will go with you,' said the others. So they set off and got into the boat; but that night they caught nothing.*

It is a calm, beautiful night, a night with a dark velvet sky and myriads of stars twinkling in space. Simon Peter, a fisherman before meeting Jesus, lolls on the beach with his close friends. They have talked with Jesus at least twice. They know he is alive, and well, also. He is the same Teacher, yet not quite the same, for he lives by laws still beyond their ken and can appear and disappear as he wills. They have not yet learned how to do this, but they accept their Lord's appearings as legitimate and divinely authentic. The Jewish teaching is strict in forbidding the exploration of the occult, witchcraft, or black magic. Jesus' resurrection appearances partake in no way whatsoever of these practices. His resurrection reveals the omnipresence of Life, God, with men to restore them, to save them, and give them immortality. The teachings of Jesus which are seen as "miracles" of healing, transformation, and multiplication are visible proofs of his application of laws divine. These laws that he teaches are available to men when petitioned through his name.

So while the disciples of Jesus have much to talk about, there is also the quiet moment to say, "I am going out fishing." Night is the fishing time for the commercial fisherman for the catch can be sold in the morning while still fresh. With enthusiasm the others join Peter. Their ship floats gently on the calm sea and they throw the net frequently this way and that. But that night they catch nothing.

John 21:4-6 *Morning came, and Jesus was standing on the beach, but the disciples did not know that it was Jesus. He called out to them, 'Friends, have you caught anything?' 'No,' they answered. He said, 'Throw out the net to starboard, and you will make a catch.'*

The darkness passes and the first gleams of light show on the horizon. On shore a figure can be discerned. The man calls, "Friends, have you caught anything?" Fishermen all over the world thus call, inquiring about the catch; learning nothing has been caught they usually are generous in advising where you may find a better fishing hole. The man on the shore calls his advice, adding — "and you will make a catch." The whole scene is normal and natural.

John 21:6-8 *They did so, and found they could not haul the net on board, there were so many fish in it. Then the disciple whom Jesus loved said to Peter, 'It is the Lord!' As soon as Simon Peter heard him say, 'It is the Lord,' he fastened his coat about him (for he had stripped) and plunged into the sea. The rest of them came on in the boat, towing the net full of fish. They were only about a hundred yards from land.*

Throwing the net where they have been directed, they suddenly find they cannot pull it aboard because it is so full of fish. Instantly John knows! He says to Peter, "It is the Lord!" Peter becomes all action — fastening his coat about him to cover his nakedness he plunges into the sea and soon is on the shore. He can see Jesus clearly now! "Yes! It is the Lord!" John remains in the boat in order to keep private Peter's reunion with the Lord. He knows he needs to talk. Those in the boat leap to the oars, and straining prodigiously they quickly beach the boat with its huge catch floating in the net behind. All the men disembark quickly and rush towards Jesus. How glad and how relieved they are to see him!

John 21:9-12   *When they came ashore, they saw a charcoal fire there with fish laid on it, and some bread. Jesus said, 'Bring some of the fish you have caught.' Simon Peter went on-board and hauled the net to land; it was full of big fish, a hundred and fifty-three in all; and yet, many as they were, the net was not torn. Jesus said, 'Come and have breakfast.' None of the disciples dared to ask 'Who are you?' They knew it was the Lord.*

They all know it is the Lord. A new hesitancy to question Jesus comes to the disciples. He no longer is called Master or Teacher, rather is recognized to be — the Lord. The Presence of his Father in him has become so visible to the disciples that the old familiarity is replaced by a deeper love and reverence.

Peter and the others, when they come ashore, see the charcoal fire. A fish laid upon it is cooking nicely. Some bread is nearby. Almost like shy children the men stand around him, waiting for him to speak. Each is filled with inner joy and happiness, for they are with him again.

Jesus says, "Bring some of your catch." Peter, big and strong, springs into the boat and maneuvers the net from the stern area onto the beach. The others help him drag it on shore. Although the net is greatly overloaded, it is not broken.

Here is a lesson for them all. Like the net, they, too, have been greatly overtaxed during the period of Jesus' crucifixion and entombment — but they, like the net, are unbroken and hold the precious cargo they are to deliver to the world.

Extending both his hands to them, Jesus says, "Come and have breakfast." His smile encourages them and welcomes each one.

John 21:13   *Jesus came, took the bread and gave it to them, and the fish in the same way.*

Jesus serves the breakfast and eats with them. Luke gives the following "They offered him a piece of fish they had cooked, which he took and ate before their eyes" (Luke 24:42).

It is very important that Jesus convince his followers that he is not a ghost or apparition. His coming and going must try their understanding on this score; however, we do not know what private instruction he gives them, during this period, concerning this phenomenon.

This is a moment of Eucharist, for Jesus himself serves the bread and fish as he did for the five thousand. His self-offering, symbolized by this food, meets the disciples needs humanly and spiritually. He gives them food to eat, and, having fished all night, they are probably very hungry. Spiritually it symbolizes the Christ feeding and nurturing them in their spiritual growth. He will watch over them always through the Holy Spirit.

John 21:14   *This makes the third time that Jesus appeared to his disciples after his resurrection from the dead.*

This may not be the last time Jesus appears to his disciples; he may appear many more times. However, this is the last record we have. He needs to establish the fact that he is alive and has overcome death and entombment. Ascension will follow.

At this time Jesus is able to live in a life beyond his disciples' knowledge, yet he still is able to walk the earth and appear to his friends in a form like theirs. He does nothing in a spectacular way, other than the spectacular fact of his sudden appearances. He does not appear in bright light, with choirs of angels singing, in the midst of crowds of people. This would not attract the type of thought he seeks for his new church. Such an appearance would savor of witchcraft or sorcery. Those that believe in such are not ready for the sacrifices of worldly notions necessary to become part of the body and blood of Christ.

John 21:15-17   *After breakfast Jesus said to Simon Peter, 'Simon son of John, do you love me more than these others?' 'Yes, Lord,' he answered, 'you know that I love you.' 'Then feed my lambs,' he said. A second time he asked, 'Simon son of John, do you love me?' 'Yes, Lord, you know I love you.' 'Then tend my sheep.' A third time he said, 'Simon son of John, do you love me?' Peter was hurt that he asked him a third time, 'Do you love me?' 'Lord,' he said, 'you know everything; you know I love you.' Jesus said, 'Then feed my sheep.'*

These men have been up all night. They have eaten well and now relax together with One who means so much to them.

John records two bits of conversation to enhance this early morning scene.

After breakfast Jesus says to Simon Peter "Do you love me more than these others?" In this sentence the Greek word for love is *agape*, a noble or self-offering love. Peter does not respond in kind, but says, "You know that I love you," using the Greek *philein* meaning the love of friendship. Jesus then says, "Feed my lambs," — feed the young thought emerging into this spiritual concept.

A second time Jesus asks, "Do you love me?" and again uses the *agape*, meaning noble or spiritual love with self-offering. Again Peter answers with the love of friendship.

The third time Jesus lessens his demand by using the same word — the love of friends — that Peter has consistently used — with no self-offering in the meaning. Peter is hurt by this and reluctantly answers, "Lord, you know everything. You know I love you." and he still persists in using *philein*.

What have Jesus and Peter been saying in these repeated phrases? Jesus' demand, that Peter acknowledge his own capacity for spiritual love, has been ignored. Jesus is seeking to rouse Peter from self-recrimination, for Peter feels unfit to further serve his Lord. Finally the third time he hurts Peter by using the term for the love of friendship. He has come to Peter's level of thought. Peter now wakens and says, "Lord, you know everything. You know I love you."

Peter remembers Jesus' prediction that he would deny him, and he did just that. Now his Lord wants him to move to new heights of spiritual capacity and he feels most unworthy. The hurt he feels is the stab of bittersweet pain when Jesus comes to his level of misery and accepts him as he is. He not only accepts him but commissions him shepherd of his flock. He is to feed the lambs — those new in faith; to tend and guide his sheep, the mature followers, and to feed them. This blunt, impetuous man will do it well. His love for his Lord is deep and sincere, and Jesus is well aware of this. Does he not name him Peter, the Rock?

John 21:18-19   *'In very truth I tell you: when you were young you fastened your belt about you and walked where you chose; but when you are old you will stretch out your arms, and a stranger will bind you fast, and carry you where you have no wish to go.' He said this to indicate the manner of death by which Peter was to glorify God. Then he added, 'Follow me.'*

These prophetic statements are attributed to Jesus concerning the martyrdom of Peter for his Lord's sake, for earlier Peter has expressed a fervent wish to die for him (John 13:36-38).

Then Jesus adds "Follow me." This can mean "Follow my teaching" and it can also mean: "We have been sitting here long enough. Let us go; follow me."

John 21:20-21   *Peter looked round, and saw the disciple whom Jesus loved following — the one who at supper had leaned back close to him to ask the question, 'Lord, who is it that will betray you?' When he saw him, Peter asked, 'Lord what about him?'*

Jesus and Peter walk together talking, with John just a bit behind. Seeing John behind, Peter's curiosity arises immediately — what will become of John?

John 21:22-23   *Jesus said, 'If it should be my will that he stay until I come, what is it to you? Follow me.'
That saying of Jesus became current among his followers, and was taken to mean that the disciple would not die. But in fact Jesus did not say that he would not die; he only said, 'If it should be my will that he stay until I come, what is it to you?'*

Peter, who has been in the depths of gloomy despair about himself, now accepts himself and the work assigned him. Seeing John following them, in a very childlike way he asks, "What about him?"

Jesus could say, "I will not tell you about him" — but instead he gives an ambigous answer, smiling broadly as he says it. It is the same kind of answer given by a parent to a child who questions and questions about things they cannot be told.

This seems to be a light touch John shares with us.

The dispute among the brethren as to the meaning of the phrase shows how Jesus' words have been studied over the years to sift every slight shade of meaning from them.

John 21:24 *It is this same disciple who vouches for what has been written here. He it is who wrote it, and we know that his testimony is true.*

Controversy is great as to the exact meaning of "He it is who wrote it."

Presumably the writings which have been compiled as "The Gospel According to John" have been either written or dictated by the beloved disciple. If this is not the case, then they have been collected by the disciples of John as the recollections of his teachings. Because of their inspired content the guidance of the Holy Spirit is implicit.

Let us take the message these writings offer and use it to the glory of God.

John 21:25 *There is much else that Jesus did. If it were all to be recorded in detail, I suppose the world could not hold the books that would be written.*

John's account covers a short time, the time of Jesus' ministry and the resurrection period. Jesus' early life can only be inferred from the evidence of his adulthood. His teaching sessions with his disciples are private except for brief references here and there.

But even with all the omissions the strong light of the spiritual demand to "Come, follow me!" shines on in individual lives. It is a beacon to guide us and a promise of safety and peace.

Amen

Study Pages
For
God's Gift

Divisions One through Nine

Preface

The Gospel According to John stands apart as quite different from Matthew, Mark, and Luke.

In each account of the four Gospels there are similar events, though details may be different. John, however, introduces new events and omits many prominent occurrences recorded by the other writers.

Only seven "signs" are given by John, while Matthew, Mark, and Luke give accounts of many "works," and of the healing of many who are sick, by Jesus' word or touch. John makes his point, not for healing, but as the Word-made-flesh.

There are three Passovers mentioned by John, instead of one in the others. He places the cleansing of the Temple, when Jesus overthrows the tables of money changers, early in his ministry.

Many scholars are beginning to think that John's account is more historically accurate — but this still does not account for the differences. What is the reason behind these differences? Why did he write it this way?

This question nagged me until I finally came to the conclusion that something about the order of the events, and above all, the choice of events, was significant. Therefore, I commenced a verse by verse analysis which resulted in *God's Gift*.

Early in the writing I began to discern an underlying message emerging. As the writing progressed a great eagerness possessed me to learn the extent of this hitherto unnoticed communication. This was mystery at its very best!

The Study Pages give my findings and conclusions. In them you may find and verify this discovery.

Ruth E. Dodge
August 1990

Study Pages for God's Gift

and

How to Use Them

First, an agreed upon portion of *God's Gift* should be studied.

These Study Pages may then be used by a group, or an individual. Participation by each one will be helpful, for discussion of the ideas presented should be the means of study. Experiences that illustrate points in the text should be shared.

To facilitate study, the Gospel's twenty-one chapters have been separated into Nine Divisions, each conveying a special message.

Study Pages
Table of Contents

DIVISION ONE

The Standard and Our Standard

Chapter One

John 1:1-5   *These opening verses are basic to the entire Gospel.*
They tell us:

1. of the eternality of God and His Word.

2. that They were before the beginning, preexistent.

3. that the Word is of the substance of God.

4. that the Word expresses the creative force of God.

5. that the Word is the avenue through which all things come to be.

This is where we begin — in Spirit.
This is how we were made — of Spirit.
This is our essence — Spirit.

God is our very Life, for we are His creation, sustained perpetually by Him.

Our capacity to spiritually understand comes right from God, because Christ illumines our thought.

DIVISION TWO

Becoming A Christian

Chapter One

PREPARATION

John the Baptist proclaims the coming of Jesus.

John 1:6-18	1. Through God's provision we are prepared.
John 1:19-34	2. Through humility we are cleansed.
John 1:35-50	3. Jesus chooses his disciples.
John 1:51	4. He begins his ministry.

Chapter Two

COMMITMENT

John 2:1-11 *The Marriage Feast at Cana*

On examination we discover each portion of this story is one of commitment.

1. The bride and groom are celebrating their commitment.

2. Mary commits herself and Jesus by asking him to use power hitherto hidden from all but her.

3. Jesus, through his act, makes his open commitment to his ministry.

4. The disciples, seeing this first sign, are impressed and more deeply committed to Jesus.

5. When we drink the wine of inspiration provided by Jesus we are able to make our commitment to him.

RESPONSIBILITY

John 2:12-25 *Jesus drives commerce out of the Temple*

Having made our commitment we must cleanse the temple of our being of its worldly commerce.

Chapter Three

TRANSFORMATION

John 3:1-21   *Nicodemus visits Jesus*

1. To enter the kingdom of God, to comprehend the universe of Spirit, we must be born again of water and of Spirit.

John 3:21-36

2. We must yield ourselves to the transforming power of the Holy Spirit.
3. "As he grows greater, I must grow less."
4. Levels of thought.

John 3:34

5. John writes: "He whom God sent utters the words of God..."

DIVISION THREE

Measureless Grace

Chapter Four

John 4:1-42 *Jesus and the Samaritans*

    1. The water of life that Christ gives becomes in us our perpetual renewal and enrichment.

    2. Jesus and the Samaritan woman talk on two levels, he on the level of Spirit and she from her earthly standpoint.

    3. Introduction of a new standard of worship.

    4. Do we hear "I am He...speaking to you..."?

John 4:43-54   5. The healing of the officer's son.

Chapter Five

John 5:1-15 *Jesus heals the man paralyzed thirty-eight years, who waited by the pool of Bethesda. This act sets the stage for the whole chapter. It is a chapter defining Jesus' likeness to God, his Father.*

John 5:16-18   1. He could heal because he is the Son of God.

John 5:19-20   2. He works as the expression of God.

    3. It is the Father's love that empowers the work.

John 5:21-22   4. As the Father raises the dead, so the Son gives life as well.

    5. The Son is given full jurisdiction by the Father.

John 5:23   6. The honor due the Father is due the Son as well.

John 5:24-26   7. Trust, faith, and obedience to Jesus Christ gives eternal life.

John 5:27-30   8. The physically dead, and those dead in sin, will hear the voice of Jesus Christ.

John 5:31-40	9. Jesus has two witnesses to testify for him.
John 5:41-42	10. Jesus is accredited by the Father.
John 5:43-47	11. Those who deny Jesus shall be accused by Moses at their judgment.

DIVISION FOUR

The Word Made Flesh

Chapter Six

Jesus Christ, the Bread of Life

John 6:1-15	1. Jesus feeds the five thousand.
John 6:16-21	2. He walks on the water.
John 6:21-37	3. We must seek and eat the Bread of Life.
John 6:38-51	4. We must let the Christ be manifest in our lives as Jesus manifested the Father in his life.
John 6:52-71	5. What does it mean? Eat his flesh, drink his blood.

Chapter Seven

Jesus Christ, the Fountain of Life

John 7:1-36	1. Jesus exposes the tension between the spiritual and material level of thought.
John 7:37-52	2. As the Fountain of Life he illustrates the powerful surging action of Life overcoming materialism and death.

Chapter Eight

Jesus Christ, the Light of the World

John 8:1-11	1. The woman taken in adultery.
John 8:12-32	2. As the Light he exposes the false, the ungodly, and the imperfect.
John 8:33-59	3. As the Light he reveals the man of God created in perfection and pure.

Chapter Nine

Jesus Christ, the Light of the World, continued.

John 9:1-41
   4. Jesus Christ the healer of blindness, physical and mental.
   5. The Pharisees doubt:
      that the man is healed.
      that Jesus comes from God.
      that the man is changed.
      that they, the Pharisees, are blind.

Chapter Ten

Jesus Christ, the Good Shepherd and Door of the Sheepfold.

John 10:1-16   The Shepherd and Door

John 10:17-42   The credentials of Jesus

Chapter Eleven

Jesus Christ, the Resurrection and the Life

John 11:1-44   1. The raising of Lazarus.

John 11:45-57   2. Consternation among the chief priests and Pharisees.

DIVISION FIVE

Victory and Last Supper

Chapter Twelve

Victory

John 12:1-11	1. Thanksgiving dinner celebrating Lazarus' return from the tomb.
John 12:12-19	2. Jesus' triumphant entry to Jerusalem.
John 12:20-36	3. Jesus' victory over the dread of his coming ordeal.
John 12:37-50	4. The summary of Jesus' teachings.

Chapter Thirteen

Last Supper

John 13:1-17	1. Victory through Love enables Jesus to be the servant who washes the disciples' feet.
John 13:18-30	2. Jesus gives the bread to Judas.
John 13:31-35	3. Jesus announces the glorification of the Son of Man.
John 13:36-38	4. Jesus warns Peter.

DIVISION SIX

Our Path, Position and Advocate

Chapter Fourteen

Jesus Christ, the Way, the Truth, and the Life

John 14:1-14   1. Jesus Christ, the Way we must follow;

the Truth we must know;

the Life we must live.

John 14:15-26   2. The Advocate (Spirit of Truth) will instruct us.

John 14:27-31   3. With the Gift of Peace we will feel secure.

Chapter Fifteen

Jesus Christ, the Vine, Oneness with Jesus

John 15:1-27   1. As branches we are given his joy.

2. His friendship.

3. We are his choice.

4. We are lifted above the earth.

5. We have the Spirit of Truth (Advocate) that issues from God.

Chapter Sixteen

Jesus leaves to send the Advocate.

John 16:1-33   1. We are given into the charge of the Spirit of Truth.

2. Through the Spirit we will win our victory.

DIVISION SEVEN

Prayer

Chapter Seventeen

Jesus Christ prays.

John 17:1-26

1. Jesus Christ prays for himself, for his disciples, and for those who believe through them.

2. He prays that they perceive and understand his relationship with God before the world began.

3. He prays for his consecration as a priest of God, and for the disciples' consecration as well.

4. He prays that they be one with him and the Father.

This prayer is of such importance that it should be thoroughly studied and discussed.

DIVISION EIGHT

Arrest, Trial, and Death

Chapter Eighteen

Arrest and Trial
John 18:1-40

1. Jesus is arrested and interrogated.
2. Peter denies him.
3. Pilate offers to release Jesus.

Chapter Nineteen

Crucifixion
John 19:1-42

1. Jesus is flogged.
2. Jesus is crucified.
3. Jesus gives his mother into John's care.
4. Jesus gives up the spirit.
5. Jesus' body is placed in a new tomb.

DIVISION NINE

Resurrection

Interlude

Peace   *The period of entombment. The resurrection.*

Chapter Twenty

Gift of Holy Spirit
John 20:1-31

1. Jesus appears to the disciples and Mary, alive and well.
2. They are given the Holy Spirit.

Chapter Twenty-One

Breakfast and Healing
John 21:1-25

1. Fishing and breakfast with the Lord.
2. Peter is healed.
3. Peter's manner of death is foretold. This gives him the assurance that he will not again deny Jesus.
4. Peter is teased by Jesus when he questions about John's death.